9 PROS

W. W. NORTON & COMPANY
NEW YORK · LONDON

BRONX

LONG ISLAND
SOUND

QUEENS

MANHATTAN

EAST RIVER

BROOKLYN

NEW
JERSEY

HUDSON RIVER

UPPER
NEW YORK
BAY

Miles
0   1/2   1

N

URBAN LANDSCAPES

Map by John H

MAP LEGEND

ALONG THE WATER'S EDGE

1. Historic Battery Park
2. Battery Park City
3. (a) East River Waterfront Esplanade
   (b) East River Park
   (c) Stuyvesant Cove Park
4. (a) Hudson River Park
   (b) Riverside Park South
5. Riverside Park
6. Riverbank State Park
7. West Harlem Piers Park
8. Brooklyn Bridge Park
9. Williamsburg Waterfront
10. Erie Basin Park
11. Newtown Creek Nature Walk
12. Gantry Plaza State Park
13. Concrete Plant Park
14. North Shore Waterfront Esplanade, St. George
15. Freshkills Park
16. Franklin D. Roosevelt Four Freedoms Park and Southpoint Park, Roosevelt Island
17. Governors Island
18. Randall's Island

INLAND

19. High Line
20. Green-Wood Cemetery
21. Woodlawn Cemetery
22. (a) Ocean Parkway and (b) Eastern Parkway
23. Broadway: (a) Madison Square
    (b) Herald and Greeley Squares
    (c) Times Square
24. Columbus Circle
25. Grand Army Plaza, Brooklyn
26. Gansevoort Plaza
27. Midtown Atriums:
    (a) Citigroup Center
    (b) Trump Tower
    (c) Former IBM Building
28. Urban Garden Room, Bank of America Tower
29. Lincoln Center for the Performing Arts
30. Brooklyn Grange, Queens
31. Washington Square Park
32. Union Square
33. Bryant Park
34. Paley Park
35. Conservatory Garden in Central Park
36. Liz Christy Garden
37. Zuccotti Park
38. National September 11 Memorial

FRONT COVER The small, freeform pond known as Dell Water is one of the many appealing features of Brooklyn's 478-acre Green-Wood Cemetery. Situated between Crescent and Vale Avenues, close to the cemetery's western edge, it is the smallest of four ponds at Green-Wood and boasts a grand weeping willow on its edge. *Edward A. Toran*

BACK COVER Pedestrians stroll along the East River on a pathway at the northern end of Brooklyn Bridge Park beside the "Cove Between the Bridges." Other visitors sit on stone steps leading to the pebble-strewn beach, one of the few places in the city with direct access to the water. *Edward A. Toran*

TITLE PAGE The mile-long, two-way bike lane on Prospect Park West, installed by the New York City Department of Transportation in 2010. *Edward A. Toran*

Copyright © 2013 by Robin Lynn and Francis Morrone
Photographs copyright © 2013 by Edward A. Toran

All rights reserved
Printed in China
First Edition

For information about permission to reproduce selections from this book, write to Permissions, W. W. Norton & Company, Inc., 500 Fifth Avenue, New York, NY 10110

For information about special discounts for bulk purchases, please contact W. W. Norton Special Sales at specialsales@wwnorton.com or 800-233-4830

Manufacturing by Everbest
Book design by Abigail Sturges
Production manager: Leeann Graham

Library of Congress Cataloging-in-Publication Data

Lynn, Robin.
Guide to New York City urban landscapes / Robin Lynn and Francis Morrone ; photography by Edward A. Toran ; foreword by Pete Hamill ; introduction by Richard J. Moylan. — First edition.
    pages cm
Includes index.
ISBN 978-0-393-73357-0 (paperback)
1. New York (N.Y.)—Tours. 2. Public spaces—New York (State)—New York—Guidebooks. 3. Landscapes—New York (State)—New York—Guidebooks. 4. Urban landscape architecture—New York—Guidebooks. 5. New York (N.Y.)—Buildings, structures, etc.—Guidebooks. I. Morrone, Francis, 1958– II. Toran, Edward A. III. Title.
F128.18.L96 2013
974.7'1—dc23

                                        2012042388

ISBN: 978-0-393-73357-0 (pbk.)

W. W. Norton & Company, Inc., 500 Fifth Avenue, New York, N.Y. 10110
www.wwnorton.com

W. W. Norton & Company Ltd., Castle House,
75/76 Wells Street, London W1T 3QT

1 2 3 4 5 6 7 8 9 0

CONTENTS

FOREWORD

PETE HAMILL

Almost all New Yorkers, of every generation and origin, long for another time and place. They live vividly in the present. They try to imagine the future. But the past never leaves them. That emotion of memory is called nostalgia.

If they are from other parts of the American republic, they might long for the distant, perhaps rural simplicities of childhood or adolescence. If they are native New Yorkers, nostalgia might focus, in its blurry way, on old neighborhoods, alive with vanished saloons, cherished friends, old songs, first loves, street games no longer played, or baseball teams that left them forever. If they are immigrants, they still long for the Old Country, the places whose poverty or bigotry hurt them into exile, but also the places where they were once five years old, running barefoot in the grass. Usually this sometimes treacherous New York nostalgia is for the time of youth. With all pain, grief, defeat, disappointment edited out.

But this superb book reminds me that for many of us born in this dense, right-angled city of concrete, brick, and steel, the longing can be about beauty. The beauty of nature. Of space at ground level. Of lovely vistas carved from ugliness by human beings. For those of us who were children in crowded tenements or high-rise apartment houses the longing is always for the simplest pleasures. The immense skies, in all seasons, over the outer boroughs, unblocked by buildings that scrape the skies, as finely graded as a painting by Vermeer. The great white paralyzed world after a major snowstorm, where the parks could be part of an Alaskan wilderness, and streets themselves dazzling planes of brilliance, where all noise is smothered.

If you lived near a park when you were young, as I did growing up in Brooklyn, the natural world was always encoded in the larger cityscape. Where I lived, there was no backyard, but that didn't matter. I had more than one park. The great one was Prospect Park, of course, a few short blocks away, full of meadows, hills, lakes, streams, and even, during World War II, anti-aircraft batteries. But we also had Green-Wood Cemetery, where we would climb a fence on darkening evenings and play tag among the trees and tombstones. The Green-Wood was a true theater for our youthful imaginations. And there was Sunset Park on long, broiling summer weekends, plunging into the immense swimming pool across endless days. In memory, the small park was also a stage for spectacular views of the sun descending each evening into Staten Island and New Jersey, just beyond

Bush Terminal, where my father worked nights making bombsights during the war. As darkness came, we then walked to Fifth Avenue to take the trolley car home. On some parts of that avenue you can see the old steel trolley tracks rising slightly through the asphalt, silvery and strong, and perhaps even hear the ding-dong of its bells.

And there were two other parks, as this book reminds me, that we didn't think about as parks: Eastern Parkway and Ocean Parkway. I don't remember a single automobile that ever passed me as I walked those grand boulevards. But I still see old men sitting on benches, reading books borrowed from the main Brooklyn Public Library at Grand Army Plaza, where Eastern Parkway begins. I see the cherry trees in the Brooklyn Botanic Garden (another beautiful park). I see young men, about to enter the Army, finding time to guide an uncertain old woman across a street. I see bike riders, whispering couples strolling in the evening, a lonely man walking a small dog. And trees.

Each time I return to either boulevard, the trees seem plumper in summer, their trunks thicker. And I remember the house where Rocky Graziano lived after he retired from boxing to become a TV star, or where Mary Tyler Moore was a child on Ocean Parkway. And right down that street, until 1957, was Ebbets Field.

This book reminds me that there are such places all over the city now, and more are coming. In Manhattan, and along parts of the Brooklyn waterfront, it is possible now to amble along many long stretches of the rivers (and the harbor) and never lose sight of the water. This is new, since so much of the waterfront has been lost to New Yorkers since the mid-19th century. Now we have the water back, the same water that Herman Melville once saw, and Walt Whitman. In large part, of course, this is because of the drastic shrinking of the commerce of the Port of New York. But New Yorkers know that every loss also presents an opportunity.

Reading this book, I wanted to cheer the visionaries, designers, architects, and urban landscapers who have given us such wonders as the High Line in Manhattan, the new lushness of Randall's Island, the planning for Roosevelt and Governors Island, plazas, circles, and atriums that have added the presence of nature and beauty to the most crowded city in the United States. That is, the people who have given us places for assembly, silence, and views of the sky. I've also made a list of new places I must visit while there is time. With any luck at all, I'll see all of them. I hope you, the reader, can find the time too. They are part of this splendid metropolis. At some point, all of them might become part of your nostalgias too.

INTRODUCTION

RICHARD J. MOYLAN
President, Green-Wood

There are many places in our vast metropolis where New Yorkers go to find refuge. One of the most unique is Brooklyn's historic Green-Wood Cemetery, where I am privileged to serve as president. For us, the idea—and the importance—of green space within the bustling city is at the very core of our existence.

The book you're now holding is a guide to these open spaces. Each of these landscapes is a reflection of the time in which it was created. Green-Wood, established in 1838, is the oldest open space presented in the book. Inspired by the rural cemetery movement of the 19th century, it was designed as a picturesque setting and place for tranquil reflection. Every one of these landscapes has its own interesting story to tell, and I urge you to discover them all.

We New Yorkers need our breathing room. Luckily for me, the search for green space is not quite as elusive as it is for most New Yorkers. I come to work every day at Green-Wood amid 478 acres of lush parkland, glacial lakes, and stunning art and architecture. Founded at a time when the concept of public parks was not yet established in the United States, Green-Wood is one of America's first rural cemeteries and the progenitor of municipal parks, including Manhattan's Central Park and nearby Prospect Park, here in Brooklyn.

As a welcome and much-needed green space for the burgeoning city, Green-Wood was a destination for city dwellers who traveled by ferry and then carriage to enjoy its open vistas and fresh air. In an 1849 essay, renowned landscape designer Andrew Jackson Downing wrote that of America's rural cemeteries, Green-Wood was "the largest and unquestionably the finest ... grand, dignified and park-like."

By the 1850s, Green-Wood was attracting tourists from all over the United States—500,000 visitors a year, rivaling Niagara Falls as the country's greatest tourist attraction. Crowds flocked here to enjoy family outings, carriage rides, and sculpture viewing in the finest of American landscapes.

Similarly today, hundreds of thousands of visitors a year meander through the grounds, taking in panoramic views of the Manhattan skyline, New York Harbor, the Statue of Liberty, the hills of New Jersey, and sculptures and monuments created by the leading artists and architects of their time. Visitors also take advantage of the public programs we offer, including walking and trolley tours, book talks, concerts, scholarly lectures, theatrical

The grand arches of the great Gothic gate (1861–63) at the main entrance to Green-Wood Cemetery.

productions, dance recitals, and special events. Green-Wood is a treasure that we are proud to share. In fact, it's an imperative that we do so.

Designated as a National Historic Landmark, Green-Wood is steeped in a rich history that tells the story of an emerging nation and city. Our commitment to preserving this legacy for future generations is strong. Our nonprofit Green-Wood Historic Fund works to maintain our monuments and buildings of historical, cultural, and architectural significance; to increase public knowledge and appreciation of all our resources; and to preserve our natural beauty. As a result, Green-Wood today has become a living history book, a vibrant classroom, an active community center, and a beautiful, open green space in the city.

We are stewards of this magnificent open space, and it is a responsibility we welcome. We invite you to share our passion and commitment to the city's urban oases. Now get outside and renew your spirit!

ACKNOWLEDGMENTS

ROBIN LYNN AND FRANCIS MORRONE

The *Guide to New York City Urban Landscapes*, like any guidebook, could become dated shortly after publication. The physical city changes that rapidly. The benefit of this guide, which we believe will keep it fresh, is its focus on historic landscapes as well as newer ones. Understanding the evolution of open space in the city provides the context to appreciating more recent projects.

Our gratitude goes to the stewards of Green-Wood Cemetery for sponsoring the *Guide to New York City Urban Landscapes*. Thanks in particular to Richard J. Moylan, President, Green-Wood, and Lisa W. Alpert, Director of Development and Marketing, The Green-Wood Historic Fund, for their support. Green-Wood Cemetery, which opened in 1838, preceded Central Park and is the forerunner of all the great landscapes in the city. Our thanks to Art Presson, Superintendent of Grounds at Green-Wood, for guiding photographer Edward Toran around the vast property on one of the last beautiful fall days of the year.

To Edward Toran, who traveled to every site in the city to find the best angle and right light to present each landscape, our profound appreciation. Edward is a consummate professional, and we are grateful to him for his talent and dedication. His photographs should inspire readers to visit the variety of green and open spaces throughout the five boroughs.

We are grateful to Pete Hamill, the celebrated novelist and journalist, who has spent more than five decades writing about New York and its citizens, for writing the lyrical and moving Foreword. Our thanks to the multitalented Elizabeth Christian, who provided the directions and information about each site, and wrote about the Liz Christy Garden too. Tamara Coombs, formerly of Staten Island, now of Albuquerque, New Mexico, shared her extensive knowledge of the borough by writing the Freshkills Park entry and finding intriguing images. Tamara has a keen insider's and outsider's view of the cityscape.

A special thanks to John Hill, contributor to and founder of the blog *A Daily Dose of Architecture* (archidose.org), an up-to-date look at contemporary work in New York. John is the author, photographer, and mapmaker of his own impressive *Guide to Contemporary New York City Architecture* (W W Norton, 2011). He generously contributed his time and expertise to create our handsome maps. Our thanks to Mark K. Morrison Landscape Architects for providing their site map of Southpoint Park on Roosevelt Island and to Michael Van Valkenburgh Associates for the Brooklyn Bridge Park map.

Our appreciation to Jacqueline Decter for her superb copy editing and to Abigail Sturges for her beautiful design.

We reserve our greatest thanks for Nancy Green, our editor at Norton, who so graciously guided the book toward publication and answered all our queries with assurance and speed. Her interest in and support of the *Guide to New York City Urban Landscapes* allowed us to explore the changing landscape.

GUIDE TO NEW YORK CITY URBAN LANDSCAPES BLOG

New York City is one of the world's leading showcases—perhaps the number one showcase—of contemporary landscape architecture and urban design, or of that intersection of the two that we now call "urban landscape design." Indeed, it is very likely that urban landscape designers soon will have public recognition equal to that of the "starchitects" of today. Today the city boasts major works by Michael Van Valkenburgh, James Corner, Piet Oudolf, Ken Smith, Mathews Nielsen, Thomas Balsley, Lee Weintraub, Lynden B. Miller, Laurie Olin, Oehme van Sweden, Abel Bainnson Butz, Donna Walcavage, George Vellonakis, Diana Balmori, Innocenti-Webel, and others, as well as of public artists who have especially contributed to urban landscapes, including Siah Armajani, Scott Burton, and Mary Miss, and like-minded architects like Machado & Silvetti, SHoP, and Diller Scofidio + Renfro; the Dutch firm West 8 is in the pipeline with their park for Governor's Island. These designers are the heirs of Andrew Jackson Downing, Frederick Law Olmsted, and Calvert Vaux in the 19th century, as well as the many (and often surprisingly innovative) contributions of the city's 20th-century "master builder" Robert Moses (and his gifted landscape architect Gilmore D. Clarke), and such modernists as Zion & Breen, Dan Kiley, and M. Paul Friedberg. This book is the first wide-ranging survey of New York urban landscapes from the first half of the 19th century to, well, tomorrow. And that's why a book alone is not enough.

This book won't be very old by the time a host of new landscapes emerges. The most significant projects of our time are works in progress. New sections of Brooklyn Bridge Park, Hudson River Park, the High Line, and Freshkills Park will open in a year or two—or ten or twenty. The *New York Urban Landscapes* blog will follow the development of these works in progress, as well as changes and reactions to them.

The blog will allow us to comment on vastly more urban landscapes than we can fit between the covers of a book. Not least, one of the pleasures for writers in producing a blog to accompany a book is to be able to update the information. Follow us at www.newyorkcityurbanlandscapes.com.

NOTE TO THE READER:

The initials following each entry indicate who wrote it.

R.L. = Robin Lynn

F.M. = Francis Morrone

E.C. = Elizabeth Christian

T.C. = Tamara Coombs

THE LUNGS

The Lungs," by critic and writer James Huneker (1857–1921), was published in the New York Times on August 2, 1914. The piece next appeared in his book New Cosmopolis (1915) about the great modern cities of the world.

His essay—an appreciation of the character and diversity of Manhattan's parks—is almost a hundred years old, yet it is still remarkably forward-looking. Our parks, he argues, are our "lungs"; they are "both vigorous and varied" and there are "more than some people think."

If Huneker were here today, he would need to expand the scope of his vision; Manhattan is just a starting point. Yet his essay remains a call to walk, then and now. The Guide to New York City Urban Landscapes is written in the Huneker tradition of showing the variety and diversity of open spaces in the urban landscape.

—ROBIN LYNN

A broad chest usually means healthy lungs. Now, Manhattan Island is notoriously narrow-chested. Her scanty space across is not redeemed by greater length. Crowded with humans and their houses, there is consequently little space for the expansion of her normal breathing powers. Her lungs, i.e., her parks, are contracted and not enough of them; there never will be. But more than some people think.

New Yorkers, even the most convinced cockneys, know little of their city, or of its lungs. Not only provincial, but parochial, they are only acquainted with the square or little park that adorns—it's a poor park that doesn't bring a sense of adornment—their native ward. Imagine my amazement when I learned after nearly thirty years' residence here that there were one hundred and eighty-two parks in the five boroughs. I read it in a newspaper and couldn't understand why I hadn't discovered the fact, for I've always been a rambler and my happy hunting-ground usually has been the East Side.

However, seeing is believing, and last summer, with my eyes made innocent by several years' residence in Germany, Austria, Holland, Belgium, France, and England, I determined to verify certain vague suspicions that had been assailing my consciousness: that perhaps New York was not inferior in attractiveness to London, Paris, Vienna, Berlin, or Brussels. Perhaps many who go down to the sea in steamers, their pockets filled with letters of credit, might be equally shocked when confronted by the sights and sounds of Manhattan. Perhaps—but let us start on a little tour into intimate New York, without a megaphone or a ready-made enthusiasm; above all, let us be meek and avoid boastful rhetoric; also dodge statistics. Go to the guide-books, thou sluggard, for the latter!

When a writer tackles such a big theme as New York he as a rule fetches a deep breath in the lower bay, steams as far as Staten Island, and then lets loose the flood-gate of adjectives. How the city looks as you enter it is the conventional point of attack. I am sorry to say that whenever I have returned from Europe, the first peep of lower Manhattan, with its craggy battlements, its spires splintering the very firmament, and the horrid Statue of Liberty, all these do so work on my spirit that I feel like repining. Not because I am home again—not, my friend, because the spectacle is an uplifting one, but, shame that I must confess the truth, because my return means back to toil, back to the newspaper forge, there to resume my old job of wordsmith. Why, the very symbol of liberty, that stupid giant female, with her illuminating torch, becomes a monster of hated mien, her torch a club that ominously threatens us: Get to work! Get to work!

Therefore I'll begin at Battery Park, leaving the waterways, the arteries and veins of the city, for a future disquisition, The image stamped on my memory is the reverse of the immobile. A plastic picture. The elevated roads debouching here are ugly, but characteristic. I'm afraid I can't see in our city anything downright ugly—it is never an absolute for me; as Dostoievsky said, there are no ugly women. The elevated road structure is hideous if aesthetically considered, and that is precisely the way it should not be considered. It rolls thousands daily to this end of the town; they usually take the ferries or subways, a few stroll under the scanty trees, or visit the Aquarium, so we must be critically charitable, too.

Oh, how tired I am of being told that Jenny Lind made her debut in this same Castle Garden, "presented" by the late Phineas T. Barnum! Wasn't it a historical fort before it became a hall of immigrants and the abode of the fishes? This much may be said for the latter—it is a real aquarium, and, excepting the absence of an octopus or two, the collection rivals those at Brighton, England (where there are octopi); Naples, Hamburg, and elsewhere. More exciting than the fish, the seal, or the porpoises are the people. Thousands elbow through the rather narrow aisles and stare as solemnly at the finny inhabitants as they are stared at in return. The sightseeing coaches give their passengers a quarter of an hour's grace to "do" the show, while

Finding shade in historic Battery Park with the former fort, Castle Clinton, in the background.

ragged boys dance about them, obsequiously pilot them, mock them, quite after the manner of the ragged boy on the Marina at Naples.

A veritable boon is this open Battery Park when the gang of wage-earners have fled the lower reaches of the city, when the dishes have been washed, when the janitors and caretakers of the tall buildings bring their wives and children to catch the breeze from the bay. On moonlit nights there are few situations more romantic. Here is freedom for the eye, for the lungs. There are not enough benches, but the walking is good, and to stand on the edge of the "wharf" and watch the bright eyes of ferries, the blazing eyes of the Jersey and Brooklyn shores, and the eyes of Staten Island as the unstable floor of the water mirrors (a cracked mirror) the moonlight and distorts the tiny flames about it, is to enjoy a spectacle fit for men and women who are not afraid to love their birthplace. I like it better when the weather has a nipping freshness and the day is grey-coloured and full of the noises of broken waters, and the cry of birds.

The seamy side of Battery Park is the poor castaway who has sought its coolness after a hot day of panhandling. But—given a certain amount of leeway—he is harmless. When a woman, the case assumes the pathetic. Begging is semisecretly indulged in. You drop your nickel and escape. If it be daytime you make for South Street to pay that long-deferred visit to Coenties Slip and Jeannette Park.

Sunbathers on the grass of the upper level of Pier 15, part of the East River Waterfront Esplanade, with views of skyscrapers and schooners.

Perhaps you have seen C. F. W. Mielatz's coloured etching of the slip; if you have, the optical repercussion will be all the stronger when looking at the place itself. The fine old musty flavour of the slip, the canal-boats near the little Jeannette Park—a backwater with its stranded humanity stolidly waiting for something to turn up—and the lofty, lowering warehouses bring memories of London docks; docks where slunk Rogue Riderhood in search of rum after he had landed his dead cargo; docks from which sailed, still sail, wooden ships with real wooden masts, canvas sails, and sailors of flesh and blood, bound on some secret errand to southern seas where under the large few stars they may mutiny and cut the captain's throat; or else return to live immortally in fascinating legends of Joseph Conrad. I almost became sentimental over Coenties Slip, probably because Mielatz had etched it, and also because I had been reading Conrad. Art always reacts on nature, and the reactions may be perfectly sincere.

However, I thought it time to ask a policeman the direction of Corlears Park. He didn't know. No one knew, until an old chap who smelt of fish and whisky said: "It's Cor-*lears*, you want?" I had misplaced the accent, and the ear of the average longshoreman in South Street for quantity would please a college professor of Greek.

I went my winding way, finally enlightened. I like the London bobby, for he is obliging and instructive, but I also like our policeman. He is gruffer than his English contemporary—a shy sort of gruffness. I found myself at Canal Street and the Bowery—I don't know why—and was told to continue eastward. If I had taken a Grand Street car to the ferry my journey would have been simplified, but then I should have missed East Broadway and a lot of sights, of which more anon.

I dived into the east. It was a noisy, narrow lane rather than a street, and the inhabitants, mostly babies, were sprawling over the sidewalks. Often I followed the line of the gutter. Then I reached an open space and was disappointed. It was Corlears Park, and the absence of shade was painful. This lack of trees is a fault to be found in the majority of municipal parks and playgrounds. Night, if you don't feel too scared or lonely, is the proper time to enjoy the Hook. The view of the East River is unimpeded. The water is crowded with craft. A breeze always fans one. Women and children, principally Italians and Jews, sit or walk. Cats are friendly. So is the small boy who knocks off your straw tile with his stick. A venerable steamboat, rotting and dismal, the relic of a once proud excursion career, is warped to the wharf. It has flowers on its upper deck, and pale, sick people sit on the lower. You are informed by the inevitable busybody who traipses after strangers that the old boat is now for tuberculosis patients, living or dying, in the neighbourhood. What an ending for man and machine! Hecker's huge structure dominates the upper end of the park, as does Hoe's building over in Grand Street. The chief thing is the cleanliness and spaciousness. The same may be found at Rutgers Park, but without a water-front, always an added attraction.

Tompkins Square stirred memories. It lies between Seventh and Tenth Streets and Avenues A and B. When I first remember it, it was also called the Weisse-Garten, and no foreign nationality but German lived on its arid fringes.

The anarchists of those days gathered at Justus Schwab's, whose saloon was on First Street. There I first became acquainted with Johann Most, an intelligent and stubborn man, if ever there was one, and other "reds," the majority of them now dead. I remember, in 1887, the funeral parade in commemoration of the anarchists executed in Chicago because of the Haymarket affair. A sombre procession of proletarians with muffled drums, black flags, and dense masses of humans. I didn't go home that night. To my

A wintry day in Central Park.

surprise I found the old-fashioned bird store—where they once sold fold-
ing bird-cages (collapsible)—in the same place, on Avenue A, near Seventh
Street. The park is mightily improved. There are more trees, and also playgrounds for boys and girls, a band-stand, and refreshment pavilions.

I entered. On the benches I found "lobbies" of old men, Germans,
Israelites for the most part. They were very old, very active, contented, and
loquacious. They settled at a "sitzung" the affairs of the nation, keeping all
the while a sharp lookout on the antics of their grandchildren, curly-haired,
bright-eyed kiddies who rolled on the grass. The boys and girls literally
made the welkin ring with their games, in the enclosures. They seemed
healthy and happy. There are vice and poverty on the East Side—and the
West—but there are also youth and decency and pride. I should say that
optimism was the rule. Naturally, in summer, even poverty wears its rue with
a difference. I saw little save cheerfulness, and heard much music-making by
talented children.

The Tenth Street side of Tompkins Square reminds me of upper
Stuyvesant Square. It is positively well-to-do, many doctors and dentists
hanging out their shingles on the quaint, pleasant-looking brick houses. A
very old German Lutheran meeting-house is at the corner of Ninth Street
and Avenue B, and one block lower is St. Bridget's Church. Not afar is a
synagogue or "Shool," as they call it, and you may catch a glimpse of the
stately Church of the Holy Redeemer on Third Street near Avenue A, with

its cartridge-shaped spire (easily seen from Brooklyn Bridge), that suggests shooting the soul to heaven if you are willing.

Time was when the Felsenkeller, at the foot of Fifty-seventh Street, East River, was an agreeable spot of summer nights. It was an open-air cafe, and while sipping your beverage you could watch the wheels of passing steam boats. It exists no longer. You must go up to East River Park, at Eighty-sixth Street and the river, or to Jefferson Park, opposite Ward's Island, to enjoy the water. There are little grassy hills, with rocks, at the former park that give you the illusion of nature.

I can't say much in favor of Union Square—now hopelessly encumbered with debris—or of Gramercy Park, locked to the public (you are permitted the barren enjoyment of gazing at the bleak enclosure), or of Madison Square, with its wonderful surroundings. These be places familiar. Nor do I care to drag you over to Hudson Park, on the West Side, to Abingdon Square, to Chelsea, De Witt Clinton, Seward, to other parks of another kind duplicated everywhere, even to the scarcity of foliage and benches. Mount Morris Park, at One Hundred and Twenty-fourth Street and Madison Avenue, was, a few decades ago, not so crowded as it is to-day. The hegira up-town has made it as populous as Tompkins Square. And not so pleasant. A little café, with a back garden on the west side of the square, was once a favourite resort years ago. Schmierkäse and pumpernickel, and—Tempus fugit!

II

I positively refuse to sing the praises of Central Park—which was laid out in 1857 (avaunt, statistics!)—simply because that once haughty and always artificial dame is fast becoming an old lady in plain decadence. Who has not sung her praises! Hardly a park, rather a cluster of graceful arboreal arabesques, which surprise and charm, Central Park is, nevertheless, moribund, and all the king's horses and all the king's men can never set her up again in her former estate. The city itself has assassinated her, not by official neglect, but by the proximity of stone, steel, and brick, which is slowly robbing her of her sustenance of earth, air, and moisture.

In the first flush of spring or a few early summer days she wears her old smile of brightness. How welcome the leafy arch of the Mall, how impressive, how "European" the vista of the Bethesda fountain, the terrace, and the lake; how pleasing it is to sit under the arbour of the Casino piazza and watch the golden girls and slim gilt lads arrive in motor-cars!

Then the Ramble, or the numerous bypaths that lead to the reservoir, or that give on the bridle-paths, wherein joyous youth with grooms flit by,

The concrete plant, in the aptly named Concrete Plant Park along the river in the South Bronx, operated from 1945 until 1987. The machinery was deliberately left in place to remind visitors of the area's industrial heritage, but the remains were painted a startling color to show off their new life as part of a community park.

or prosperous cits showing lean, crooked shanks painfully bump on horses too wide for them. Ah, yes! Central Park will continue for years to furnish amusement (if that wretched Zoo were only banished to the Bronx!) and deep breathing for the lucky rider who lives on its borders. Also furnish fun for May parties, June walks, and July depredations. It is a miracle of landscape-gardening, notwithstanding its absence of monotony—it abounds in too many twists and turns; it is seldom reposeful, because broad meadows are absent. You can't do much in decoration without flat surfaces. But what mortal could accomplish what Frederick Law Olmsted and Calvert Vaux accomplished; the impending ruin is the result of pitiless natural causes.

I once said that one can't be a flâneur in a city without trees. New York is almost treeless, and Central Park soon will be. When not so long ago I saluted the Obelisk on the Thames embankment, that antique and morose stylite sent its regards to its brother in our Park. Some day when the last Yankee (the breed is rapidly running out) will look at the plans of what was once Central Park, hanging in the Metropolitan Museum, his eye will caress the Obelisk across the way. That strange shaft will endure when New York is become an abomination and a desolation.

Arthur Brisbane's notion that the nasty little lakes and water pools be drained and refilled with salt water for bathing purposes is a capital one. Gone at a swoop malaria and evil odours; gone, too, the mosquitoes which make life miserable for nigh dwellers. But the park is doomed; let us enjoy its ancient bravery while we may.

I never skated at Van Cortlandt Park, because I can't skate; but I love the spot, love the old mansion and its relics, love the open feeling about it. Atop of the highest part of the island is Isham Park. To reach it get off at the Two Hundred and Seventh Street Subway station and walk westwardly up the hill, or through Isham Street. On the brow is the little park, looking up and down the Hudson and across Spuyten Duyvil. A rare spot to watch aeroplane races. Not far away is the Billings castle, and across the Fort Washington Road the studio and Gothic cloisters of the sculptor George Grey Barnard.

Often have I enjoyed the Zoological Garden in the Bronx, the Botanical Garden, and the Bronx Park. Our Zoo is easily the largest and most complete in the world. I've visited all the European Zoos, from Amsterdam and Hamburg to Vienna and Budapest. As for the Botanical Garden, I have the famous botanist Hugo de Vries of Amsterdam as a witness, who told me he would be happy to live near it always. The Bronx River is an "intimate" creek and malodorous, but do you remember what cunning little French restaurants were in vogue up there two or three decades ago? F. Hopkinson Smith celebrated one of them in a short story. To-day they charge you more for wine and cookery that are inferior to the old-time establishments. Or has Time intervened with its soft pedal on the gustatory sense? I don't believe it. The enjoyment of the table is the longest surviving of the sociable peccadilloes, and nothing can prove to me that either my Burgundy or my Bordeaux palate has deteriorated. But if I get on the subject of food we shall never see Pelham Parkway.

I didn't drive the devil wagon, else I should never have seen what I did—at least not in such brief time and in such a pleasant way. For ten hours my friend wheeled me up Tremont Avenue, the Southern Boulevard—and such boulevards!—to Pelham Parkway, with the park of one thousand seven hundred acres and more (I read this in a guide-book) up from the Harlem River, through magnificent shore and country, the Sound in sight, and a general sense of being in a primeval forest that had been cultivated by super-apes. On grey days the mist along the sedge grass of the water evokes delightful melancholy. We whizzed through towns I had heard of but never visited. Oh, shame! Think of Mount Vernon, Yonkers, Irvington, and Tarrytown! All new to this desperate cockney.

However, it was Pelham Bay that set me shouting. There's a park for you! The entire cityful could go out there, hold a cyclopean picnic, and have plenty of room to turn around in. It is not Fairmount Park, for that is the largest in the East, but it's the nearest thing to it. It is the combination of water and woods that is attractive. The Philadelphia park has the same, but on a vaster scale. Of European parks I can recall none that approaches Pelham—the Boboli Gardens and Cascine at Florence, Hyde, Regent, St. James's, and other London Parks, the Bois, Tuileries, and the Jardin d'Acclimatation, Paris, the Prater, Vienna (a lovely spot), Charlottenburg Chaussée, Berlin—none of these matches Pelham Parkway. The automobiles seem to eat space on the smooth roadbeds. When the projected Bronx Parkway is an accomplished fact, the motorists ought to be forever satisfied.

We crossed from the Sound over to the Hudson on excellent roads. I began to wonder why any one could abide living in Gotham when such a delectable land of milk and honey is so near. I have noticed that when I ride in another man's motor-car I feel optimistic and inclined to see the "slaves of toil" in a rosy mood. And this mood was not banished by our arrival at the Sleepy Hollow Club. From its terraced lawns the Hudson may be viewed in all its majesty. This former home of Elliott F. Shepard is a palace, and, forgetting the joys and woes of Corlears Hook and Tompkins Square, I trained my eyes on the prospect. There is justice in the boast that nowhere may be seen such an extraordinary collocation of the grandiose and the familiar in landscape and waterscape. The Rhine is domestic, colloquial by comparison. Down the Danube at the Iron Gates there is some hint of the dazzling perspectives of Palisades and Hudson, but there again the barbaric note sounds too loud in the symphony of rugged rocks and vegetation. And great Highland Park, Bear's Nose, the new State Park, gift of Mrs. Harriman—what a wealth of natural park lands! When the wicked blasters blast no more, restrained from sinful destruction by the law courts (when?), and there are better travelling facilities, the Palisades side of the river will entertain thousands where to-day it hardly counts its hundreds.

We flew along the riverside. I had renounced all hope of seeing Jerome Park, St. Mary's, Claremont, and Crotona Parks, or even the little Poe Park at Fordham—we had passed High Bridge, Fort Washington, and Macomb's Dam Parks earlier—and farther down I had often visited Morris Heights and Audubon Park, but I was consoled by the sharp contrasts of the shifting landscape. Of course, there was a "panne" on upper Broadway, a burst tire, and the ensuing boredom, but nothing lasts, even impatience, and soon we were through Yonkers, and then across the city line past Palisades Park, with its lights, and, finally, on Riverside Drive, surely vantage-ground from which the ravishing spectacle of down-river may be enjoyed.

It would be unjust to pass City Hall and its park, not because it allures—it does not—but because City Hall is the priceless gem in our architectural tiara. Buried as it is by the patronising bulk and height of its neighbours, it more than holds its own in dignity, simplicity, and pure linear beauty—qualities conspicuous by their absence in the adjacent parvenu structures.

Nor must I miss Prospect Park, Brooklyn, near enough to reach in a half-hour, and from the grassy knolls of which the turrets and pinnacles of Manhattan may be seen. It is far more captivating than Central Park, and the Flatbush Avenue entrance reminds one of some vast plaza in a European capital, upper Brussels, for example. It is imposing with its MacMonnies monument, its spaciousness, and general decorative effect—an effect enhanced by the Italianate water-tower and the Museum farther down, whose vast galleries house so little original art, with the exception of the Sargent watercolours and former Chapman pictures. It is only fair to add that Prospect Park began with natural advantages superior to Central Park, advantages made the most of. This park really makes Brooklyn habitable and not merely an interlude of bricks and mortar before achieving the seashore.

Well, we are not far from Battery Park, whence we started. It is only a swallow's flight this—for I could have dwelt on the special characteristics of each park, on the elevated playgrounds at Williamsburg Bridge, on the various recreation piers—but celerity was my aim, the impression as we skimmed; all the rest is guide-book literature—as Paul Verlaine did not say. I didn't start out to prove anything, yet I think I have suggested that, despite its contracted chest and waist, the lungs of Manhattan are both vigorous and varied.

A view of a portion of the linear Hudson River Park, looking downtown from Pier 45, the park's 850-foot-long pier in the West Village.

Along the Water's Edge

- NELSON A. ROCKEFELLER PARK

Chambers St

Warren St

West Broadway

Greenwich St

Murray St

Church St

City Hall
Park

TEARDROP PARK •

West St

Broadway

North End Av

Park Pl

River Terrace

Barclay St

• Irish Hunger Memorial

Vesey St

WINTER GARDEN,
WORLD FINANCIAL
CENTER •

Fulton St

World Financial Center Plaza •

• NATIONAL SEPTEMBER 11 MEMORIAL

Maiden Ln

Liberty St

• ZUCCOTTI PARK

Albany St

Washington St

Greenwich St

Trinity Pl

Broadway

Wall St

South End Av

West St

Rector St

• Rector Park

W Thames St

THE ESPLANADE •

Battery Pl

Little West St

Museum of Jewish Heritage •

1st Pl

• The Skyscraper Museum

Pearl St

Water St

ROBERT F. WAGNER, Jr. PARK •

HISTORIC BATTERY PARK •

State St

Peter Minuit Plaza/
Whitehall Ferry Terminal •

N

Miles 0   1/8   1/4

BATTERY PARK CITY AND LOWER MANHATTAN

Map by John Hil

MANHATTAN

HISTORIC BATTERY PARK

Accessible from State Street and Battery Place in lower Manhattan

When P. T. Barnum presented the Swedish soprano Jenny Lind at Castle Garden in 1850, the structure that New Yorkers once called (and that we again call) Castle Clinton stood on an island some 200 feet from the Manhattan shore. That shore was the Battery, for many years the only centrally located bit of Manhattan waterfront given to recreation rather than shipping and industry. The Battery was the epicenter of fashionable New York life in the 18th and early 19th centuries—"the small but promising capital which clustered about the Battery and over-looked the Bay," as Henry James described it in *Washington Square*. As the rich and fashionable migrated uptown, and before Central Park was built, the Battery served a great cross section of the population as a place of relaxation and passive recreation. The journalist Nathaniel Parker Willis described it thus in 1845:

> The Battery on Sunday is the Champs-Elysées of foreigners. I heard nothing spoken around me but French and German. . . . They are not the better class of foreigners who frequent the Battery on Sunday. They are the newly arrived, the artisans, the German toymakers and the French bootmakers— people who still wear the spacious-hipped trowsers and scant coats, the gold rings in the ears, and the ruffled shirts of the lands of undandyfied poverty. . . . They sit and smoke on the long benches. They run hither and thither with their children, and behave as they would in their own garden, using it and enjoying it just as if it were their own. And an enviable power they have of it!

Many old prints attest to the charm and diversity of users of the Battery shoreline in the 19th century.

The city used landfill to extend Battery Park several times from the late 18th to the late 19th centuries. By 1855, when Castle Garden became the immigrant processing center (replaced in the 1890s by Ellis Island), it no longer stood on an island. Castle Clinton, where today one goes to purchase tickets for the Statue of Liberty and Ellis Island, was a fort, built in the years leading up to the War of 1812, when New York feared British attack. In 1896, the structure became the New York Aquarium, for many years the single biggest tourist attraction in New York City. In 1941, however, the city's parks

LEFT AND FACING PAGE The 23-acre Historic Battery Park at Manhattan's southern tip is one of the oldest public open spaces in the city in continuous use.

commissioner, Robert Moses, relocated the aquarium to Coney Island and closed Battery Park for twelve years while the Brooklyn-Battery Tunnel was being built. When the park reopened, it bore the stamp of Moses, with a clean, formal layout and a waterfront esplanade. The 23-acre park has a kind of oozy, amoeba-like shape as it follows the contours of the shoreline and, on the east, State Street. The "head" is near the intersection of Broadway (just across from Bowling Green), Battery Place, and State Street. From this point Moses placed a long, straight mall, with a planted median and flanked by ovoid lawns, on axis with and leading to Castle Clinton (which Moses had unsuccessfully tried to demolish). In the "tail" to the east was a large, amoeboid lawn, replicating the shape of the park as a whole. Over the years the park filled with memorials and monuments. The most notable is the East Coast Memorial, a little to the east of Castle Clinton and right off the esplanade. Dedicated by President John F. Kennedy on May 23, 1963 (his last public address in New York City), the memorial, by the sculptor Albino Manca and the architects Gehron & Seltzer, commemorates the 4,601 Americans who perished in the Atlantic in World War II. Eight tall, polished-granite slabs set in parallel rows bear inscriptions of the names, ranks, organizations, and home states of the deceased servicemen. Facing down the center between the rows is a large bronze eagle, its talons clutching a funeral wreath, oriented toward the Statue of Liberty. Except for the eagle, it's hard not to think that this served as a model for Maya Lin when she designed the Vietnam Veterans Memorial in Washington, D.C.

Just a tad inland from the East Coast Memorial is the affecting Wireless Operators Memorial (1915). Designed by the architects Edward S. Hewitt and William Lawrence Bottomley, this should be a model for all kinds of memorials. It's given a full setting, with benches in a semicircle around a simple, elegant granite fountain basin facing a granite cenotaph bearing the names of wireless operators lost at sea, beginning with Jack Phillips of *Titanic* fame. The novelist Willa Cather, who was one of her generation's most insightful art critics, wrote: "This monument is one of the most attractive and most friendly commemorative works in New York ... These men died in storm and terror, but their names are brought together here and abide in a pleasant place with cheerful companionship."

Over the years, Battery Park decayed, as did all of New York's parks. The lawns and malls became scruffy, the pavements cracked, benches splintered, esplanade railings dangerously buckled. Then, as with so many parks in the city, a public-private partnership, in this case the Battery Conservancy, rode to the rescue. Warrie Price founded the Battery Conservancy in 1994 to implement a master plan for the rejuvenation of Battery Park that had been presented in 1986 by architects Ehrenkrantz & Eckstut and landscape architect Philip Winslow. Work began immediately on reconstructing the esplanade, where a new seawall railing by the artist Wopo Holup bears plaques relating the natural and human history of the Battery (with texts by Tony Hiss). In 2003 the Conservancy installed, parallel to the water to the west of Castle Clinton, the 10,000-square-foot

Gardens of Remembrance, commemorating September 11, 2001, by the renowned Dutch garden designer Piet Oudolf. Of Oudolf, James Gardner wrote in the *New York Sun*,

> Like some nouvelle cook relentlessly seeking out new flavors through unheard of ingredients or unheard of combinations of known ingredients, Mr. Oudolf creates a rare environment that repudiates roses, lilacs, and the like in favor of herbaceous plants with character and, above all, grasses with attitude. His postmodern aesthetic falls somewhere between the abstract patterns of French gardens and the counterfeit naturalism of English gardens.

A Dutch journalist said that Oudolf, in his native country, enjoyed the status of a rock star. The Gardens of Remembrance was his debut performance in America. Oudolf next gave us the Battery Bosque, in a 53,000-square-foot band parallel to the river east of Castle Clinton encompassing the East Coast Memorial. Mature London plane trees—140 of them—combine with 34,000 perennials, old-fashioned (yes, from an avant-gardist!) lamp standards and "world's fair"–type benches, winding paths, a sleek circular fountain of polished granite (park visitors encouraged to plash), and two food kiosks (bow to urbanist William H. Whyte) to form one of the most ambitious additions to an existing New York City park in recent decades. The trees, wild grasses, and perennials have the Olmstedian-Vauxian aim of putting the park user into intimate contact with nature (believed now by cognitive scientists to be more important to our mental health than was previously known)—without sacrificing the kinds of amenities William H. Whyte felt open spaces needed to possess. One may perhaps view the Battery Bosque as an attempt at a kind of combination of Teardrop Park and Bryant Park (see pp. 40 and 234).

At the time of writing, Oudolf was at work on the plantings along the Battery Garden Bikeway, which provides the link between the Hudson River Park bike path and that of the East River Waterfront.

At the far eastern end of Battery Park—the southeastern tip of the island—lies Peter Minuit Plaza, a forecourt to the Staten Island Ferry Terminal. Here another avant-garde Dutchman, architect Ben van Berkel of UNStudio, created the "futuristic" (as some people like to say) New Amsterdam Plein and Pavilion in 2011. This is an information and food kiosk meant to make the lives of the tens of thousands of commuters who pass daily through this plaza easier and the plaza a bit livelier during non-rush hours. The glowing (at night) structure of concrete and fritted glass has a form impossible not to see as a slightly more angular variation on Eero Saarinen's classic TWA Terminal (1962) at Kennedy Airport, and reminds us that a lot of what passes for avant-garde today is really a kind of modernist pastiche—which need not be a put down. —F. M.

REGULATIONS: Dogs must remain on leashes, may not drink from fountains, and are not permitted in gardens, lawns, or playground

Smoking is prohibited

MAP & DETAILS AVAILABLE AT: www.thebattery.org/battery/directions.php

BY SUBWAY: 4, 5 to Bowling Green

R to Whitehall Street

1 to South Ferry

BY FERRY: Staten Island Ferry to Whitehall Terminal Manhattan (South Ferry)

BY BUS: M15 Select Bus Service, M20 to South Ferry

BATTERY PARK CITY 2

Teardrop Park is located between Warren and Murray Streets, east of River Terrace

Nelson A. Rockefeller Park is located at the north end of Battery Park City, west of River Terrace

Robert F. Wagner, Jr. Park is located just north of Historic Battery Park, off Battery Place

Winter Garden is located on West Street between Vesey and Liberty Streets, between World Financial Center 2 and 3, across from the World Trade Center site; the garden is at the back (river) side of the building

Battery Park City occupies a 92-acre landfill that was completed in 1976. The 1.5-mile esplanade at the water's edge affords spectacular views across the Hudson River.

B attery Park City occupies a 92-acre landfill that was completed in 1976. About twenty of those acres came from the excavations for the World Trade Center. (As about half of the World Trade Center was itself built on landfill, some of Battery Park City's landfill includes earlier landfill.) Public officials and business investors envisioned Battery Park City as a whole new mixed-use neighborhood in lower Manhattan, adjacent to the Financial District. In 1976, however, New York City could scarcely bear the costs of such a project. Neither the government resources nor the private demand existed to make Battery Park City a reality, and for several years the landfill lay barren, a ghostly expanse occasionally enlivened by temporary "Art on the Beach" installations organized by the nonprofit group Creative Time. Had Battery Park City been built according to schedule, it would have been very different from what we see today. Early plans worked out by Governor Nelson A. Rockefeller, an amateur architect, with his friend the architect Wallace K. Harrison envisioned "towers in a park"— the standard form of "superblock" planning in the urban-renewal decades of the 1950s through the 1970s. By the time the Battery Park City Authority (which had been created as far back as 1968) got the show on the road, a transformation in attitudes toward urban planning and urban design had taken place. A new generation, fired by new enthusiasms, had come on the scene. In 1979 two young architects—thirty-six-year-old Stanton Eckstut and forty-one-year-old Alexander Cooper—devised a new master plan for Battery Park City. Eckstut and Cooper had come of age in the 1960s, when the writings of Jane Jacobs and others unceremoniously upended the inherited ways of urban planning.

The new master plan contained no Corbusian superblocks. It looked nothing like the adjoining World Trade Center. Cooper and Eckstut instead took their cues from old New York neighborhoods. Focusing on the successful ones, they noted the building features that gave them their distinctive character. In places like Gramercy Park and West End Avenue, the buildings seemed to follow certain rules, or patterns. For instance, all the buildings had cornices—a nicety the superblock planners had long discarded. On West End Avenue, stone, not brick, faced exterior walls at pedestrian level. And so on. Equipped with these patterns, Cooper and Eckstut created design guidelines that ensured coherence. As each building lot was to have a different architect who could do as he pleased so long as he did not violate the basic guidelines, the coherence, the planners hoped, would not become uniformity—just as at Gramercy Park all the buildings seem to hang together even though each retains its individuality. It seems a simple idea, to study the best of the past for the lessons it may yield, but such an idea marked a radical departure from modernist orthodoxy. It had much in

The 3.5-acre plaza of the World Financial Center's four office towers, opened in 1989.

common with the postmodernism of the time, when young (and some old) architects stopped being afraid of embracing traditional forms or designing ornamental and symbolically rich buildings (or at least buildings that were something other than glass boxes). At the same time, Berkeley, California, architect Christopher Alexander was promoting his concept of "pattern languages," based on the study and cataloguing of successful patterns found throughout global vernacular architecture. From this ferment emerged the New Urbanism, a movement—led by the husband-and-wife team of Andrés Duany and Elizabeth Plater-Zyberk, who had been partners in the

Miami-based architectural firm Arquitectonica—that seeks to create walk-able, environmentally responsible towns and places by drawing lessons from urban design of the pre-automotive age.

The plan for Battery Park City called for high-rise residential sections north of Vesey Street and south of Liberty Street, with a large office com-plex—the World Financial Center—in the middle. Significantly, the archi-tects left 30 percent of the site—the narrow strip of land bordering the Hudson River from Battery Place on the south to Chambers Street on the north—as open space. A 1.5-mile-long esplanade at water's edge would afford spectacular views across the river and out into the harbor.

More than thirty years after Cooper and Eckstut's master plan, New Yorkers have become used to Battery Park City. Some love it, others hate it. What cannot be denied is that nothing else like it has ever been attempted, let alone accomplished, in New York. The scale is vast. But the scale of Stuyvesant Town and Peter Cooper Village is even vaster. The really impres-sive thing about Battery Park City is the complexity of the undertaking, especially in the relationship between buildings and open spaces. What makes it a kind of New Urbanist model for central-city redevelopment is that it achieves a remarkably high population density (slightly greater than that of Manhattan, by far the densest place in America, as a whole) without feeling crowded or overbuilt. And that is a testament to the extraordinary emphasis placed on the design of the open spaces. Here we have not "tow-ers in a park" but parks among the towers—and the distinction is crucial.

Let's begin at the north and work our way down.

Nelson A. Rockefeller Park

All the way west, at water's edge, Governor Nelson A. Rockefeller Park extends south from Chambers Street to Vesey Street. The 8-acre park, opened in 1992, serves active recreation. Some parks are meant for con-templation, or what is nowadays called "passive recreation." Calvert Vaux and Frederick Law Olmsted conceived of Central Park largely in terms of an environment for contemplation and communing with nature. Most water-front esplanades exist for the soothing experience of staring at water. But other parks—always in as short supply in cities, as are spaces for contempla-tion—are for sports, exercise, running around. An example from the early 20th century is 35-acre McCarren Park at the border of Greenpoint and Williamsburg in Brooklyn. Robert Moses, who became parks commissioner in 1934, strongly advocated parks for active recreation. To Central Park he added playgrounds, ball fields, skating rinks, a swimming pool, and such, forever altering the way the park was used and valued by the people of

Open space along the water's edge next to high-rise residential towers.

New York. Moses transformed Hudson Park, on St. Luke's Place in the West Village, from one of the city's very few classical formal gardens (designed by Carrère & Hastings) into a place of basketball courts, playgrounds, and a swimming pool. In McCarren Park he built one of the most stupendous swimming pools in the world—and added several others to parks around the city.

Rockefeller Park belongs to this tradition. Early critics who said the park had a too-busy appearance completely missed the point. Along the park's inner edge we find basketball, volleyball, and handball courts. There are also lawns for throwing footballs or Frisbees or for sunbathing. In the southeastern part of the park is a dense and elaborate children's playground designed by Sonja Johansson and Donna Walcavage and opened in 1992. Writing in the *New Yorker* in the following year, Tony Hiss called it "everyone's favorite new playground" and continued:

> which daily draws strollers from at least as far away as Greenwich Village, a forty-five-minute walk to the north. For once, no corners were cut to save money. There's a rubberized safety surface, for instance, covering almost the entire playground; you could probably have put some fine Oriental rugs over the area for the same money.

We take playgrounds for granted these days. But, like everything else, they have a history. Indeed, early-20th-century Progressivism spawned a playground movement, exemplified by Lillian Wald and Charles Stover's Outdoor Recreation League, which advocated for the city's first municipally built playground, opened in 1903 in Seward Park on East Broadway. Since then, and especially thanks to Robert Moses, playgrounds have become a common feature throughout the city—even though parents may claim that there are never enough of them. The playground in Rockefeller Park ranks among the best.

In the northeastern corner of the park, just south of Chambers Street, is a seating area with game tables that features sculptural adornments by Tom Otterness. Born in 1952 in Wichita, Kansas, Otterness has been a figure on the New York art scene since the late 1970s, when, with Jenny Holzer, Kiki Smith, and others he founded the artists' collective Collaborative Projects, or Colab, which was notable for, among other things, organizing the Times Square Show in 1980 in an empty massage parlor on 41st Street and Seventh Avenue in a pre-reformed Times Square that had reached its seedy nadir. There's nothing seedy about Rockefeller Park (well, except for the grass), and today Otterness specializes in whimsical bronze figures of people and animals that delight children (and grown-ups) while also slyly expressing anticapitalist messages (*New York Times* architecture critic Herbert Muschamp called them "sugar-coated Marxism"). The Rockefeller Park installation bears the title *The Real World*. So delightful, in fact, do children find *The Real World* that it is a de facto playground—minus any playground equipment. Otterness is also famous for *Life Underground* (2001), a Metropolitan Transportation Authority Arts for Transit installation in the Eighth Avenue and 14th Street subway station, made up of figures similar to those in Rockefeller Park. The temporary installation *Tom Otterness on Broadway* (2005) featured twenty-five of his sculptures, positioned all along the Broadway median from Columbus Circle at 59th Street to 168th Street. And in 2009 he created a real playground on 42nd Street between Eleventh and Twelfth Avenues.

Art installations such as *The Real World* represent another important design element of Battery Park City—the view that strategically placed works of art serve as critical place-making devices in landscape design. Thus many notable contemporary artists—including Martin Puryear, Scott Burton, Siah Armajani, Richard Artschwager, Mary Miss, Louise Bourgeois, and Jim Dine—have contributed to the outdoor spaces of Battery Park City.

The Pavilion

A little to the south of *The Real World* stands the Pavilion, a wood and brick peristyle designed by Demetri Porphyrios in an exacting classical style. It dates from 1991. One strand of the 1980s postmodernism from which much of the earlier phase of Battery Park City sprang involved the attempt to revive the classicism that the architecture schools had long ceased teaching. On their own or through classes offered by the New York–based Classical America (and later the Institute of Classical Architecture), some architects mastered the painstaking techniques of classical design. (Alas, those painstaking techniques daunted many other architects who then turned violently against classicism.) Porphyrios, born in Greece in 1949, has designed some of the notable works of traditional architecture of recent decades, including Grove Quadrangle at Oxford University and Whitman College at Princeton University (he holds a Ph.D. in architectural history from Princeton). The Pavilion features a perimeter of twelve extremely slender cedar columns topped by voluted metal capitals. The columns support a roof with wood-bracketed eaves. From this perimeter, stone steps rise up to an atrium described by four brick columns with Doric capitals. The original plans called for a tree to grow out of the center, but that idea got dropped somewhere along the way. Notwithstanding, its proportions and details make this garden folly a perfect object—the most pleasing thing of its kind in New York since Stanford White's 1904 peristyle in Brooklyn's Prospect Park. (Many of the follies on the large country estates of Britain took a classical temple form.) It is instructive to compare the unapologetic classicism of Porphyrios' Pavilion with the postmodernist whimsy of Kohn Pedersen Fox's similarly scaled "tempietto" in the plaza of 135 East 57th Street, at Lexington Avenue, completed in 1988.

Two long-established and prestigious firms designed Rockefeller Park: the Cambridge, Massachusetts–based Carr, Lynch, Hack & Sandell and the Washington, D.C.–based Oehme, van Sweden & Associates. The former firm was founded in 1977, and its partners have included Kevin Lynch (1918–1984) and Gary Hack, two longtime Massachusetts Institute of Technology professors whose book *Site Planning*, the first edition of which came out in 1962, remains a required text in graduate schools of urban planning throughout the country. Formerly dean of the School of Design, Hack today is professor emeritus of City & Regional Planning at the University of Pennsylvania, one of the country's most influential centers of landscape architecture education. The firm of Wolfgang Oehme and James van Sweden also dates from 1977 and pioneered in what has been called the New American Garden style, emphasizing native grasses and the blanketing use of perennials to achieve a naturalistic meadow effect. Carr, Lynch is credited with the park's hardscape elements, which include the rustic field house, with its eyebrow dormer, located just to the south of the playground, and, south of the field house, a balustraded waterfall and lily pool. Among the park's most felicitous features are structures with rough stone walls, classical balustrades, and stairs that recall the remarkable curving stairs leading up to the East River esplanade of Carl Schurz Park on the Upper East Side.

Teardrop Park

Just to the east of the Pavilion, in the block bounded by Warren Street on the north, North End Avenue on the east, Murray Street on the south, and River Terrace on the west, we find Teardrop Park, which ranks high among the ambitious park projects of recent years. Credit goes to landscape architects Michael Van Valkenburgh, Matthew Urbanski, and Laura Solano of Michael Van Valkenburgh Associates, and the artists Ann Hamilton and Michael Mercil. (For more on Michael Van Valkenburgh Associates, see Brooklyn Bridge Park, p. 97.) Though Teardrop Park, opened in 2004, covers only a couple of acres, it packs a punch, with carefully designed, dramatically shifting sightlines (reminiscent of some of Vaux's and Olmsted's visual effects in Central Park and Prospect Park), a great deal of lush vegetation, and a dramatic wall of stacked sheets of Albany County bluestone that appears to be collapsing and becomes an ice wall in winter. A doorway cut into the bluestone wall entices the walker—a Vauxian device—into the half of the park that is otherwise made invisible by the great bisecting structure. Native New York State plantings dominate, and the park feels, overall, like a Catskill retreat.

Not everyone admires Teardrop Park. The watchdog and advocacy group Project for Public Spaces (PPS), for instance, places Teardrop Park in its "Hall of Shame." The group says Teardrop Park "serves primarily as a private courtyard arboretum to the surrounding high-rise development." Indeed, four large apartment towers conceal Teardrop Park—it can't be seen from surrounding streets. This seclusion gives rise to the concern that "Landscape Urbanism" (see High Line, p. 156, and Brooklyn Bridge Park,

Teardrop Park, nestled between four apartment buildings, may provide a greater concentration of naturalistic landscape effects than any other 2-acre space in the city.

p. 97), with which Van Valkenburgh is associated, seeks to overturn the kind of open-space design championed by William H. Whyte (see Bryant Park, p. 234) and by PPS, design marked by openness, amenity, activity, and choice (exemplified, says PPS, by Rockefeller Park). According to PPS, Teardrop Park:

> is not inviting because its spaces feel threatening—many parts are obscured from view as you experience it, and at every turn you might run into something unexpected. There is little to reward the few brave souls who do

explore the park: Most turns reveal nothing more than shrubs and another mysterious turn. Other than the [children's] slide, the only thing you can do here is sit on an isolated patch of grass, or on some of the lonely benches that face the confined pathways and passive building walls. The real mystery is how the landscape architect expected humans to participate in this space—or perhaps they hoped to deter any use. If that is the case, they were certainly successful.

Of course, not everyone agrees. In 2004, after the first part of Teardrop Park opened, David Dunlap wrote in the *New York Times*:

> By the time you have found a perch on the storybook hill, stumbled through the boggy marsh, ascended the glistening wall of craggy bluestone, scuttled through a notch in the limestone boulders and—attention, first graders!—slid into the sand pit, you will be amazed that you have covered only 1.9 acres.

"There is," Van Valkenburgh told Anne Raver of the *New York Times* in 2005, "a voracious appetite for parks that are vigorous, robust places, that provide the kind of complexity that only nature gives you." In a 2004 letter to the editor of the *New York Times*, Ellen F. Crain, a professor of pediatrics at the Albert Einstein College of Medicine, wrote:

> The significant amount and variety of vegetation in the new Teardrop Park at Battery Park City is good news for children and their families. Research indicates that green places captivate children and reduce the attention problems that are so widespread today.
>
> There is also some evidence that play in natural settings becomes more creative and that aggressive behavior diminishes. I hope that parks throughout the city will follow the Teardrop Park model.

In 2008, Helene Stapinsky wrote in the *Times*,

> A favorite spot for my children is Teardrop Park, tucked inside a shady cavern between apartment buildings on Warren and Murray Streets. Teardrop is only four years old, as old as my daughter, Paulina, but it is already a hot spot because of its two-story tubular slide that lands in a giant sand pit. There are no swings. No jungle gym. Just that awesome slide, which recently caused my 8-year-old son, Dean, to exclaim, "Now this is what sliding is all about!"

Indeed, Robin Moore, professor of landscape architecture and director of the Natural Learning Initiative, a program devoted to children's play and learning environments at North Carolina State University, served as a consultant to Michael Van Valkenburgh Associates in the design of Teardrop Park. The designers paid great attention to the child-friendliness of the space and to the maximal exposure to nature that is increasingly considered vital to cognitive development.

In 2009 science writer Jonah Lehrer wrote in the *Boston Globe*:

> Now scientists have begun to examine how the city affects the brain, and the results are chastening. Just being in an urban environment, they have found, impairs our basic mental processes. After spending a few minutes on a crowded city street, the brain is less able to hold things in memory, and suffers from reduced self-control, While it's long been recognized that city life is exhausting ... This new research suggests that cities actually dull our thinking, sometimes dramatically so.

The antidote? Nature, in the form of parks. And not just any parks, but parks that take you out of the city—just as Frederick Law Olmsted and Calvert Vaux, and Andrew Jackson Downing before them, believed. And so, after years in which open-space planners have tried to reintegrate parks and plazas into their surrounding streets, to make of such spaces places that are of and not just in the city, now, it seems, the old idea—the very anti–Jane Jacobsian idea—of parks as secluded retreats from the city is back. With a vengeance.

Irish Hunger Memorial

To the south of Teardrop Park, right at the axis of Vesey Street, stands the Irish Hunger Memorial. Teardrop Park dropped an Adirondack preserve onto Battery Park City; the Hunger Memorial brings us a slice of the Irish countryside. Dedicated in 2002 in a ceremony at which Irish president Mary McAleese was present, Brian Tolle's competition-winning design features, on its inland-facing side, an actual fieldstone cottage imported from County Mayo. The house stands upon a hill sown with 62 species of Irish plants and grasses, as well as stones from each of Ireland's 32 counties. One may clamber up the hill and enter the cottage. The memorial evokes the ruined countryside of the famine years of the late 1840s and early 1850s, when some third of the nation's people migrated to other countries, especially the United States. On the side of the memorial facing the river, an installation features walls banded with quotations from period letters, diaries, songs, poems, and recipes, as well as with statistics relating to the famines and migrations. Brian Tolle's work represents a popular strand of contemporary public art, one that favors extreme literalness—here is an actual Irish cottage, actual Irish grasses, quotations from primary sources, and so on. This trend comes out of 1970s Conceptual Art and Environmental Art, in which the record of research became integral to the artwork. This approach has strongly influenced Landscape Urbanism.

Dining next to the World Financial Center Plaza and nearby North Cove, a marina for large yachts.

World Financial Center Plaza

To the south, the towers of the World Financial Center enfold a broad plaza that provides lunchtime seating for the thousands of office workers in the complex, as well as a place of passive recreation day and night for myriad visitors to the center. Opened in 1989, the 3.5-acre plaza was planned by M. Paul Friedberg & Partners, an important landscape architecture firm founded in 1958, and Cesar Pelli & Associates, the architects of the World Financial Center. The firms worked with the artists Siah Armajani and Scott Burton. The utterly relaxed quality of the plaza's design may reflect the ease with which the two artists (who were close friends) were able to work together and with the architects. As Calvin Tomkins wrote in a 1990 *New Yorker* profile of Armajani:

> [he] and a number of other, like-minded artists—the list includes Robert Irwin, Mary Miss [see below], Nancy Holt, Richard Fleischner, George Trakas, Jackie Ferrara, Athena Tacha, Elyn Zimmerman, and the late Scott Burton— have devoted themselves almost exclusively to working on projects in puh-

lic spaces, usually in collaboration with architects, city planners, real-estate developers, landscape architects, engineers, and city officials. These artists have had a hand in the designing or the redesigning of parks, playgrounds, gardens, indoor and outdoor plazas, traffic interchanges, sidewalks, bus stops, drainage basins, and other spaces that are in the public domain.

In other words, Armajani and Burton belong to a loose group, or movement, of contemporary artists who have submerged their egos and engaged the public. The World Financial Center Plaza opened the same year that the General Services Administration removed Richard Serra's 120-foot-long, 12-foot-high COR-TEN steel wall, entitled *Tilted Arc*, from 26 Federal Plaza, facing Foley Square, only eight years after installing the controversial sculpture. For the office workers and others who clamored for the brutal sculpture's removal, Serra's work exemplified the imperiousness of the modern artist—as did the painter Jennifer Bartlett's South Gardens design (see below) for Battery Park City, from around the same time. Armajani and Burton represented a movement, in the words of New York Times art critic John Russell in 1983, "away from the hectoring monumentality of 'public sculpture' and toward a kind of art that gets down off the pedestal and works with everyday life as an equal partner."

Scott Burton, who was born in Alabama in 1939 and died in New York in 1989 (the year the plaza opened), began making his signature chair sculptures in the 1970s and started receiving public commissions in the 1980s. In New York, in addition to his work at Battery Park City, he created the two installations—Urban Plaza South and Urban Plaza North—that are part of the Equitable Center on 51st and 52nd Streets between Sixth and Seventh Avenues; completed in 1986 and 1987, these installations comprise stone tables, benches, chairs, and planters. At the World Financial Center, an inner plaza gives onto an outer plaza via broad stairs (which serve as seating). Along the inner rim of the outer plaza, at the foot of the stairs, Burton created low granite chairs in a stepped form and low, circular granite tables. "A granite chair by Burton," wrote John Russell in 1983, "has an unforced, almost nonchalant majesty, but it is also very comfortable to sit in. A table by Burton is a poetic object, but it also tempts us to settle in for a long evening of eating, drinking and talking." At the outer rim, near the iron fence where you stand to look out at the water, Burton created elegant, almost Art Moderne granite benches with curving contours. A nearby metal fence, designed by Armajani, bears quotations from the poems of Walt Whitman and Frank O'Hara, poets whose works—Whitman's in the mid-19th century, O'Hara's in the mid-20th—celebrated New York. From Whitman's "City of Ships" (1867):

City of the sea, city of wharves and stores—city of tall facades,
  of marble and iron!
Proud and passionate city—mettlesome, mad, extravagant city!

From O'Hara's "Meditations in an Emergency" (1957):

One need never leave the confines of New York to get all the greenery one wishes—I can't even enjoy a blade of grass unless I know there's a subway handy, or a record store or some other sign that people do not totally regret life.

(It's an Armajani trademark to incorporate into his works the words of poets he admires. See North Shore Waterfront Esplanade, p. 127, for more on this.)

The outer plaza curves into the water of North Cove, which serves as a marina for very large private yachts. Within the semicircle of this curve, in a place where the Central Park Obelisk would not be out of place, Armajani and Burton instead gave us a kind of stylized, Egyptianized version of an old-fashioned streetlight—tubular shaft and urnlike luminaire by Armajani, stepped granite base by Burton. The design derives from the Central Park–style lamp standards all along the Esplanade (see below). Where other artists might have gone monumental, Armajani and Burton struck an almost defiantly homey note.

To the north, a long, double row of plane trees shades café tables beside a reflecting pool. To the south, the plaza takes the form of a mazelike garden, punctuated with birches; then, about in line with Liberty Street, there's a small oval garden set with flowering Yoshino cherry trees and benches. In the southeast corner of the plaza stands the New York City Police Memorial, designed by Stuart B. Crawford and dedicated in 1997. It is well worth a visit.

Winter Garden

The vast Winter Garden, the centerpiece of the World Financial Center, fronts the plaza. Its volume roughly equals that of the Main Concourse of Grand Central Terminal. Part Crystal Palace, part Galleria Vittorio Emanuele II, the great glass shell allows light to rain down on sixteen 45-foot-high Washingtonia *robusta* palm trees from Florida—our most hardy remnant of the 1980s mania in which developers vied to see who could get the least likely thing to grow in a Manhattan skyscraper atrium. Comprising 45,000 square feet of floor area, the space is 200 feet long, 120 feet wide, and crests at 125 feet high. It was designed by Cesar Pelli & Associates with landscape architect Diana Balmori. The paper-thin masonry veneers

The Winter Garden is the centerpiece of the World Financial Center, and comparable in scale to the Main Concourse of Grand Central Terminal.

may seem, in a characteristically 1980s way, brittle, but the mellow color scheme (the brown, beige, and gray of the stone walls and the green of the steel framework supporting the great glass vault recall Grand Central's Main Concourse) soothes. This is meant to be a tranquil place, and it is. The grand staircase at the east end originally led to an aerial walkway across West Street to the World Trade Center. The attacks of September 11, 2001, crushed the Winter Garden. Two thousand glass panes shattered, the grand staircase crumbled, and the palm trees were destroyed. The structure was rebuilt, however, and—it seemed miraculous at the time—reopened in September 2002. The grand staircase now leads not to a bridge but to a viewing platform from which one can look directly down on the World Trade Center site. Before the 2011 opening of the World Trade Center Memorial, this viewing platform served New Yorkers and visitors as a place where one could come to remember and to mourn—and to monitor the progress of the rebuilding of the devastated site across West Street. At this writing, however, Brookfield Properties, owner of the World Financial Center, has announced its intention to remove the staircase and create a grand entrance on West Street to a comprehensively reimagined retail and dining destination. Stay tuned.

The Winter Garden, off of which radiate corridors filled with shops and places to eat (and public restrooms), contains seating among the palm trees, with spectacular views of the Hudson River through the vast glass wall to the west. Concerts, exhibitions, and film screenings also take place in the space.

Rector Park

To the south of the World Financial Center is the earliest-built portion of Battery Park City. Three of its "side streets"—Liberty, Albany, and Rector— are continuous of their namesakes on the other side of West Street. Turn left off the Esplanade (see below) onto Rector Place. At first you encounter what can only be called a gaudy sci-fi "triumphal arch" of metal with lighting elements. Called Rector Gate, it is by the artist R. M. Fischer and was installed in 1988. Occupying the median of Rector Place is Rector Park, a two-block-long oblong park (bisected by South End Avenue) inspired by such residential squares as Gramercy Park. Completed in 1985, Rector Park is an anomaly in New York, where romantic, naturalistic gardens, following the path laid down by Olmsted and Vaux, predominate. Rector Park, in contrast, is a formal garden, one of only a few in the city: Bryant Park (p. 234) and the Conservatory Garden in Central Park (p. 242) rank as the most notable examples of classical principles applied to garden or park design in New York. The closest match to Rector Park, however, is the Osborne Garden in the Brooklyn Botanic Garden, designed by Harold ap Rhys Caparn in the 1930s. The designer of Rector Park, the German-born Richard K. Webel (1900–2000) began his practice with Umberto Innocenti in 1931. Rector Park was his last major work. It was, wrote Paul Goldberger in the New York Times in 1986, "the best thing of its kind in New York since Gramercy Park."

Rector Park exudes elegant simplicity, with rectangular lawns and neatly clipped hedges outlining the curved ends of the tapering oblong site. "Here is where Webel," wrote Gary R. Hilderbrand in his 1997 book, *Making a Landscape of Continuity: The Practice of Innocenti and Webel*, "shows the seasoned hand: refined shape, careful detailing, and the controlled layering of an enclosing landscape—lawn, ground cover, hedge, small tree, canopy tree and street tree, fence, wall, and curb. It is ordered and lush—like the forecourt of the Evelyn Marshall Field Residence, some fifty years earlier," a reference to a work of Innocenti and Webel in Syosset, Long Island from 1932–34. Some critics may be appalled that a firm's work should change so little in more than fifty years. Others, however, find inspiration in the quiet precision of Webel's work. Rector Park is one of the things in Battery Park City that might not have been built in later years. Webel's highly refined classicism (like that of a later generation's Demetri Porphyrios) became briefly fashionable in the post-modernist 1980s, only to ebb again in the next decade. And that's too bad, because such balance and rigor can do the heart good, like superbly performed chamber music.

Battery Park City Esplanade

Along the river edge of Battery Park City runs a 1.5-mile-long pedestrian esplanade, designed by Cooper, Eckstut Associates with Hanna/Olin. It opened in stages between 1983 and 1990. The model derives from such Robert Moses projects as the John Finley Walk and Carl Schurz Park Esplanade on the East River of 1941, and the Brooklyn Heights Promenade of 1950–51. These were, in their day, thrilling. New Yorkers were only just being introduced to the use of the city's waterfronts for passive recreation, with Moses leading the way. On these esplanades, park benches faced the river, and one could stand at a secure metal railing and gaze down upon the water.

The Battery Park City Esplanade follows suit with its old-fashioned railings and lamp standards (the latter similar to those in Central Park, with their slender stems and graceful, urn-shaped luminaires), wooden benches with the looping iron armrests made popular by the 1939 World's Fair, and hexagonal paving stones. In the section south of the World Financial Center, the viewer looking out at the mighty Hudson is backed by an allée of shade trees and behind that by a line of apartment towers. The northern section rims Rockefeller Park and thus lacks the comforting sense of enclosure that the southern part provides. It is much closer in feeling to the esplanade at Riverside Park (p. 81).

Pedestrians, bicyclists, and roller skaters share the Battery Park City Esplanade. Most of the time, everyone gets along. Regulations require cyclists to go slowly. Unfortunately, some of the time—enough to matter—New York cyclists, no matter where they are, speed or otherwise ride recklessly. On this esplanade, as elsewhere in the city, cyclists can frighten pedestrians—elderly pedestrians especially. What should be one of the most relaxing places in the city becomes anything but. One hopes that in time cyclists and pedestrians in New York will learn to coexist as amicably as they do in many European cities.

For many years, no one thought to question the railing-at-water's-edge approach. In the last couple of decades, however, a combination of factors, not least among them the increased cleanliness of the area's waterways, has encouraged designers to bring people, as much as is practical, right down to the water. The designers of Finley Walk and the Battery Park City Esplanade simply presumed that no sane person would wish to dip his or her toes in the acid waters of the East River or the Hudson River. Today, it's different. Many new waterfront-park designs—Hudson River Park (p. 67), Brooklyn Bridge Park (p. 97), Grand Ferry Park (p. 106)—are all about toe dipping. They're also about wild grasses and boulders cascading into the water, part of the trick bag of Landscape Urbanism, and the next bit of Battery Park City waterfront pointed the way.

South Cove Park

The 3-acre South Cove Park, designed by architect Stanton Eckstut, landscape architect Susan Child, and environmental artist Mary Miss, opened in 1988. "South Cove ... overflows," wrote Tony Hiss, one of our most sensitive observers of urban places, in the New York Times in 1990, "with a quiet power so potent that first-time visitors can take the taste and feel of it home with them, and run it over in their minds, like a vivid childhood memory." Here the inspiration is much less the traditional New York esplanade than an evocation of the 17th- and 18th-century waterfront of wooden piers, wooden railings, wooden pilings, and wooden lampposts juxtaposed to jagged rock outcrops, wild grasses, and densely spaced trees and shrubs. South Cove continues the line of the esplanade and features an elevated viewing platform (shaped to evoke Liberty's crown), from which one may gaze out into the harbor. Extending under and outward from the viewing platform is a looping wooden jetty edged with tufts of beach grasses. The river plashes the boards of the jetty underfoot, making this the only spot in Battery Park City where the park user may come into contact with the water.

The park also includes secluded seating areas, and cobalt blue deck lamps that cast an ethereal nighttime glow. Boulders cascade down a hill planted with wild grasses and wild roses, and though the boulders don't touch water, as is the fashion today, they suggest as much, and may be seen as a forerunner. No other park quite like this one existed in New York in 1988. Some of its elements—particularly the concern with native ecology—find precedent in Alan Sonfist's *Time Landscape* (1978) at Houston Street and La Guardia Place, an artist's remarkable recreation, within the compass of a small garden, of the primeval forest of Manhattan Island. Since South Cove Park, the idea of mixing native ecology with industrial archaeology has been wholly embraced by the Landscape Urbanists and those whom we may loosely group under that rubric. A lot of what we see in the High Line (p. 156) and Brooklyn Bridge Park (p. 97) comes out of the Environmental Art of the 1960s and 1970s, so it should not surprise us that the artist Mary Miss played a major role in the creation of South Cove Park. Indeed, rather than terming South Cove a landscape, *New York Times* art critic Roberta Smith called it "one of the best works of public art in town." (Smith also called it "a Japanese-style garden" and referred to the jetty's "pagodalike arbor.") Miss was born in New York City in 1944, and found inspiration in the works of such artists and musicians as Robert Rauschenberg and John Cage. She has made a name for herself as one of the group of artists, including Siah Armajani and Scott Burton (see above), who have dedicated their careers to creating public places. As much as any Landscape Urbanist, she has "mapped the plumes" (see High Line, pp. 156–64) of the sites on which she has worked. South Cove is one example. So is her Arts for Transit "installation" (the word seems inadequate, as what she created is more like an environment), entitled *Framing Union Square*, in the Union Square subway station. In this 1998 work, she uncovered buried decorative and structural elements and placed bright red frames of different shapes around them. (These always remind me of the red frames around the second-story windows of the buildings surrounding World Financial Center Plaza, which Miss must have seen while working on South Cove.) This created a sort of archaeological cross section of the station, a recontextualization of found elements. South Cove does not dredge up any actual part of what was once on its site—which was, after all, until recently under water. Rather, it imagines what this shoreline would have been like had it existed—and provides what Brendan Gill, writing in the *New Yorker,* called "an irresistibly romantic stage set of New York Harbor as they [Eckstut, Child, and Miss] wish us to believe it may have looked in the seventeenth century." It's easy to see the line connecting at least one strand of Environmental Art to Landscape Urbanism—and to see that those plumes are sometimes imaginary. As Brendan Gill wrote, "If we sniff in the air not only the delicious odor of Atlantic brine but of Disneyland as well, no matter: a fictional seascape of considerable beauty is surely better than no seascape at all."

Robert F. Wagner, Jr. Park

Altogether different from South Cove is Wagner Park. Originally, this section of Battery Park City was supposed to be South Gardens, the creation of the well-known painter Jennifer Bartlett. Bartlett, who frankly acknowledged that she knew nothing about gardens, sought to upset people's expectations of what a public space—in particular, a public space at the tip of Manhattan, with panoramic views of river and harbor—should be. By this conceit the modern artist wishes to confront us and get us to reassess our expectations, habits, and values. If we like to be surrounded by flowers and stare out at large bodies of water, an artist such as Bartlett would ask us why. Bartlett posed her question by designing a claustrophobic warren of twenty-four "rooms" so crammed with plants that when the design was made public, horticulturists and garden experts, led by *Wall Street Journal* gardening columnist Patti Hagan, sounded the alarm: nothing could thrive in this "garden." Not only were the plants too close together to survive, but the rooms could barely accommodate human visitors. To further upset expectations, Bartlett planned a concrete wall to block views of the water! What seemed not to occur to the artist in all this is that New York routinely confronts and upsets people's expectations. (We might view Rector Park's Richard K. Webel as Jennifer Bartlett's opposite.) Thankfully, the critics prevailed. Bartlett's rooms were shelved. And a triumphant new park took shape.

Wagner Park, completed in 1996, is a collaboration between the Philadelphia-based landscape architects Hanna/Olin (who had worked with Stanton Eckstut on the design of the esplanade), the Boston-based architects Machado and Silvetti Associates (both Rodolfo Machado and Jorge Silvetti were, like Cesar Pelli, born in Argentina), and the New York–based "public gardener" (as she calls herself) Lynden B. Miller. Miller rose to prominence in the 1980s with her very first public commission: the restoration of the Conservatory Garden in Central Park. (See Conservatory Garden, p. 242, for more on Lynden B. Miller.) She has been the gardener-in-charge on some other high-profile reclamation projects, such as Bryant Park and Madison Square. She stands in sharp contrast not only to artists such as Jennifer Bartlett (Miller is also a painter, by the way) but also to many proponents of the current trends in Landscape Urbanism. The same may be said of Hanna/Olin. (For more on Hanna/Olin, see Bryant Park, p. 234.) Whereas Teardrop Park wraps us in a cocoon of nature (as do parts of Central Park), Wagner Park (like Rockefeller Park) is wide open. But whereas Rockefeller Park is made for active recreation, Wagner Park is more for passive recreation. About the most strenuous thing you see people doing in Wagner Park is sunbathing—and on sunny summer days its lawn becomes a sea of sunbathers.

Located at Manhattan's southwesternmost point, Wagner Park is open to the water and serves as lower Manhattan's front lawn.

When Wagner Park opened, Paul Goldberger, architecture critic for the *New York Times*, lavished it with praise:

> The heart of this 3.5-acre public park is a great rectangle of lawn, utterly empty, absolutely flat and tightly enclosed by a brick walkway, low granite walls and gently curved, backless teak benches. Somehow it manages to feel as rich and as sensual—and as tranquil—as a thousand acres in the country, and it is a minor miracle.

The rectangular lawn that Goldberger mentioned is lower Manhattan's front lawn. Set right into the southwesternmost crook of Manhattan Island, it is angled for a perfectly axial view of the Statue of Liberty. Structures surround it on three sides. On the north is the Museum of Jewish Heritage—A Living Memorial to the Holocaust, housed in a distinctive hexagonal granite building designed by Kevin Roche John Dinkeloo & Associates that was completed in 1997, and a larger addition, the Robert M. Morgenthau Wing, that opened in 2003. The Morgenthau Wing includes, on a north-facing second-story terrace, the British environmental artist Andy Goldsworthy's Garden of Stones—18 hollowed-out granite boulders ranging in weight from 3 to 13 tons. Eighteen is the numerical value of the Hebrew word chai, life. From each boulder grows a dwarf oak sapling. Over the decades, the trees will reach a height of about 12 feet. Goldsworthy says he found inspiration when he stayed in a hotel on Broadway. Looking out his upper-floor window, he saw that a tree had seeded itself in and was growing out of the side of a building across the way. Goldsworthy's conceptual and environmental work has much in common with that of Brian Tolle (of the Irish Hunger Memorial) and Mary Miss (of South Cove Park). Garden of Stones cannot be viewed without admission to the museum.

To the south of the lawn is Pier A, jutting out at a 45-degree angle to the lawn. Built in the 1880s for the Harbor Police, it's the last remaining pre-20th-century pier in Manhattan. It has been under renovation to serve as a visitors' center for Battery Park (which is located to the immediate south of Battery Park City) for at least thirty years, and may be the longest-running restoration show in town. To the east of the lawn is a remarkable structure designed by Machado and Silvetti Associates [440]—a brick pavilion divided into halves connected by a bridge. When viewed from the water side, the asymmetrical form comprises three bold arches of varying sizes and heights. It's a strong backdrop to the park, providing just the right note of definition. From the east, the two halves form a perfect frame for the view of the Statue of Liberty. Broad flights of steps ascend to the top of both halves. At the top, a deck provides great views of the harbor and, just as important, of the park elements such as the lawn (and, on summer days, its sea of sunbathers) and some of Lynden B. Miller's garden plots. These beds of flowers, sometimes recalling floral imagery in Impressionist paintings, are set within low granite rims and scattered about the park site, with a particularly heavy concentration in the part of the park that leads down from the Museum of Jewish Heritage to the Machado & Silvetti pavilion. The pavilion—a functional folly—does several things (it also houses a restaurant and restrooms), and does them all well. And even though the brick today shows some signs of deterioration, the structure has splendidly stood the test of time (sixteen years at this writing), and may be said to be one of Manhattan's most successful works of architecture of the 1990s.

Wagner Park also contains works of sculpture by Louise Bourgeois, Jim Dine, and Tony Cragg, though these seem like afterthoughts, not at all integral to the park. On the whole, however, it's hard to argue with Paul Goldberger's 1996 judgment that "Wagner Park is one of the finest public spaces New York has seen in at least a generation." The city was spared Jennifer Bartlett's South Gardens. But one may wonder: Could Wagner Park—no wild grasses, no cascading boulders, no direct access to the water, no industrial salvage, no high-flown rhetoric—be built in New York today?

Overall, Battery Park City presents us with an almost encyclopedic variety of contemporary urban landscapes designed by a number of the leading practitioners in the field and cared for by a first-rate horticultural and maintenance staff that operates with few budgetary constraints. The lavish care that Battery Park City's open spaces receive may make them unsuitable as models for other areas in the city. But the lover of urban landscapes will want to visit over and over. —F.M.

HOURS: 6 am–1 am

Winter Garden: 7 am–11 pm

RESTROOMS: Near Teardrop Park and Rockefeller Park at the northwest corner of the Solaire (on River Terrace between Park Place West and Murray Street); Ferry Terminal; Wagner Park; Winter Garden, near the West Street entrance

REGULATIONS: Smoking is prohibited

MAP & FURTHER INFORMATION AVAILABLE AT:
www.bpcparks.org and www.worldfinancialcenter.com

BY SUBWAY: Teardrop Park: 1, 2, 3 or A, C to Chambers Street, walk west along Chambers Street, cross West Street, and continue for 2 blocks to River Terrace, turn left on River Terrace, and continue south for 1 block to Warren Street

ROCKEFELLER PARK:
1, 2, 3 or A, C to Chambers Street, walk west along Chambers, and cross West Street into the park

WAGNER PARK:
4, 5 to Bowling Green or 1 to Rector Street, walk south on Greenwich Street, and turn right on Battery Place past Historic Battery Park

WINTER GARDEN:
A, C, J, M, Z, 2, 3, 4, 5 to Fulton Street, walk west on Fulton Street, turn right on Church Street, then left on the Vesey Street pedestrian path

E to World Trade Center, walk north on Church Street, turn left on the Vesey Street pedestrian path

R to City Hall, walk south on Broadway, turn right on Vesey Street, continue across Church Street to the Vesey Street pedestrian path

BY PATH: Winter Garden: Newark–WTC or Hoboken–WTC lines to World Trade Center, from the Church Street exit, turn left on Vesey Street

BY BUS: M22 to Battery Park City (Vesey Street and North End Avenue)

M9 to City Hall (Park Row and Beekman Street)

M15 and M20 to South Ferry

BY FERRY: Nelson A. Rockefeller Park: Trans-Hudson ferry from Hoboken and Jersey City

WINTER GARDEN:
NY Waterway to World Financial Center landing, walk east on Vesey Street 1 block, turn right, and follow pathway to the entrance between 2 WFC and 3 WFC

3 EAST RIVER WATERFRONT

East River Waterfront Esplanade

When completed in 2013, the East River Waterfront Esplanade will extend two miles from the Battery Maritime Building to a couple of blocks north of the Manhattan Bridge. The first phase, from Wall Street to Maiden Lane, opened in summer 2011, and Pier 15 opened in fall 2011.

The East River Waterfront Esplanade stretches from Pier 11 (on the line of Gouverneur Lane, just south of Wall Street) to Pier 15 (roughly on the line of Maiden Lane, just south of the South Street Seaport). The FDR Drive viaduct separates the esplanade and piers from the streets of the Financial District.

Pier 11, opened in 2000, serves a ferry terminal designed by Smith-Miller + Hawkinson. Broad eaves of corrugated metal supported on steel girders overhang the low, horizontal, glass-walled structure. When it opened, critics such as Joseph Giovannini in *New York* magazine hailed the terminal for heralding a return to the old themes of Modernist architecture that had briefly yielded to the Postmodernism that, Giovannini said, informed the design of the South Street Seaport (see below).

The first of three planned phases of the esplanade opened in 2011. The design is a collaboration between SHoP Architects and landscape architect Ken Smith. SHoP Architects has in recent years shot to the top of the standings among New York architecture firms. Their well-known projects include Atlantic Yards in Brooklyn, the pedestrian bridges built across West Street in the wake of the September 11, 2001, attacks, the Porter House (2003) on 15th Street between Eighth and Ninth Avenues, the 290 Mulberry Street apartments (2009), the Botswana Innovation Hub in Gabarone, the redevelopment of Pier 17 at the South Street Seaport, and, not least, the East River Waterfront Esplanade. Between the latter two, the downtown-based SHoP (a name derived from the surnames of founding partners Christopher Sharples, Coren Sharples, William Sharples, Kimberly Holden, and Gregg Pasquarelli) has pretty much made lower Manhattan's East River waterfront its own. SHoP's partner-in-charge here is Gregg Pasquarelli, who, like the firm's other four founding partners, earned a Master of Architecture degree from Columbia University in the early 1990s. Pasquarelli helped found SHoP in 1997.

Ken Smith, who was born in Iowa in 1953 and attended Iowa State University and the Harvard Graduate School of Design, established his New York–based firm in 1992. Like SHoP, he has received great acclaim in recent years. His best-known works include the private roof garden at the Museum

The East River Greenway will extend from the Battery to 125th Street when complete. The FDR Drive viaduct separates the East River Waterfront Esplanade (shown here) and piers from the streets of the Financial District.

of Modern Art, the park in front of 7 World Trade Center, the landscape restoration in the plaza of Lever House, Santa Fe Railyard Park in Santa Fe, New Mexico (on which he collaborated with architect Frederic Schwartz and artist Mary Miss), and a 1,300-acre park under construction in Orange County, California (on which he is collaborating with TEN Arquitectos). His collaboration with SHoP on the esplanade is not Smith's only contribution to Manhattan's East River waterfront. He is also the landscape architect of Planters Grove, a new park on the grounds of the New York City Housing Authority's Lillian Wald Houses, a sixteen-building complex across the FDR Drive from East River Park between East Houston and East 6th Streets in

LEFT AND FACING PAGE Views from the upper level of Pier 15, which extends 500 feet into the East River, with the Manhattan Bridge in the background.

the East Village (see below). That park was paid for by Planters Nuts (a division of Kraft Foods), which has also funded parks in New Orleans and Washington, D.C. Smith designed all three Planters parks. At the Lillian Wald Houses, Smith's park, which opened in 2011, features fields of edible herbs (sage, rosemary, thyme) that housing project residents are encouraged to pick and use in their cooking—and that are also said to repel rats.

The FDR Drive (originally the East River Drive) runs from Battery Park up the East Side waterfront to 125th Street (where it becomes the Harlem River Drive). Postwar urban renewal turned the East Side waterfront from the Brooklyn Bridge to 23rd Street into the nearest approximation in New York of Le Corbusier's Ville Radieuse. The city bulldozed whole tenement and factory districts and replaced them with high-rise "towers in a park," with the FDR Drive whizzing past. (This was done largely under the direction of Robert Moses but guided by the vision of the 1929 Regional Plan of New York and Its Environs, with which Moses had not been involved.) South of the Brooklyn Bridge, in the Financial District, the FDR Drive's elevated roadway formed both a physical and a psychological barrier to the waterfront. The South Street Seaport development in the 1980s, however, helped break the barrier by enticing people across South Street and under the viaduct to the Pier 17 pavilion and the historic sailing ships of the South Street Seaport Museum. It then took another thirty years for further park development to happen along this waterfront.

The East River Waterfront Esplanade proves that a viaduct such as that of the FDR Drive need not create what Jane Jacobs called "border vacuums." One of the things she had in mind was the dark, dank, malodorous,

garbage- and glass-strewn pedestrian underpasses of roadway or railway viaducts that people naturally seek to avoid. As a result, an outward-spreading vacuum occurs, where for a block or two (or more) on either side of the underpass one finds at best only marginal uses, at worst barbed-wire-cordoned, weed-filled lots. It does not have to be like that, however. At Forest Hills, in Queens, the underpasses of the viaduct of the Long Island Railroad beautifully negotiate between the bustling sidewalks and white-brick high rises of "greater Forest Hills" and the fairyland of Forest Hills Gardens. Similarly, several years before the High Line's conversion to a park, art galleries migrated to the blocks of the twenties to the west of the elevated structure, and the High Line's underpasses seemed like a formal gateway to the new gallery district. At the East River Waterfront Esplanade, the viaduct enhances the experience of the pedestrian approach by making the prospect of water all the more exciting for being partly veiled at first, and for the delicious sensation, often found in architecture, of moving from a low-ceilinged to a high-ceilinged space. In addition, the viaduct provides shade—a critical element in the new waterfront parks, sorely lacking in long stretches of Hudson River Park (p. 67).

Along the waterfront path, Ken Smith has placed discrete plots of native grasses, shrubs, and flowers. Seating consists of slatted wooden benches—including chaises longues, high chairs (sometimes described as bar stools), and traditional park benches—and low stone walls and steps.

The esplanade's most notable element is the dramatic new structure at Pier 15. SHoP's design is on two levels. A complexly tiered elevated platform planted with grass rests on a glass base. The underside of the platform, painted a vivid red, evokes a ship in dry dock. Stairs lead to the top of the platform, where at the edges one hovers over the shore. This is something different. Neither is it the safely-fenced-off-from-the-water kind of esplanade that Robert Moses built or that we find at Battery Park City (p. 33), nor is it the boulders-cascading-into-the-water style we find at Brooklyn Bridge Park (p. 97). Here the pier suspends one over the water-front—the experience may actually be slightly unnerving for someone with balance issues or acrophobia. One can feel the sway in the wood-floored platform.

On the lower level, the pier extends out into the water under and beyond the upper platform. Hexagonal pavers floor this level, which has slatted wooden benches and peanut-shaped—shades of Planters Grove?—plastic seats. On its north side it pulls up right alongside the Wavertree, the 279-foot-long iron-hulled sailing ship built in England in 1885, part of the South Street Seaport Museum's ship collection. On the south side of the lower level is a rectangular garden of native plants with a perimeter of seating.

One can also see, to the north, the South Street Seaport's Pier 17, which is radically different from Pier 15. In the early 1980s, the Rouse Corporation, which had transformed Boston's and Baltimore's waterfronts with critically lauded and extremely popular "festival marketplaces," came to lower Manhattan to work its magic. Make no mistake, city officials and the public alike regarded Rouse as a deliverer of magic, an urban savior in the years of falling fortunes for old cities. The festival marketplaces would lure suburban fun-seekers back to the city—and point the way toward future uses of an obsolete industrial waterfront. In collaboration with the South Street Seaport Museum (founded 1967), Rouse restored several historic structures, most notably Schermerhorn Row, the early-19th-century counting houses along Fulton Street between Front and South Streets, and added several new structures that, though modern in design, blended in with the preserved old buildings. Among the new structures was the Pier 17 pavilion, designed by the Cambridge, Massachusetts–based Benjamin Thompson & Associates, extending into the river to the east of the FDR Drive and north of the line of Fulton Street. (To its west, operating on both sides of the viaduct, was once the ancient and olfactorily distinctive Fulton Fish Market, which relocated to the Bronx in 2005.) Today, however, sophisticated opinion considers Rouse's festival marketplaces to be passé. The goal of luring shoppers from the suburbs has been superseded by an unexpectedly large turnaround in many inner cities' fortunes as old areas such as the Financial District have become fashionable and often family-oriented places to live—the "Great Inversion," as urbanist Alan Ehrenhalt calls it, upending the old sociological adage of "upward and outward." Many people view the South Street Seaport today as a failed enterprise, and downtown's new residents find it—with its chain stores and fast-food eateries—a vaguely distasteful thing in their backyard.

Yet the Thompson firm designed Pier 17 very carefully and sensitively to be the best possible visual neighbor for the Brooklyn Bridge. Their structure did not ape the forms of the bridge or any other surrounding buildings, yet succeeded—through its scale, colors, materials, jauntily gabled skyline, outdoor decking, and not least its superbly handled nighttime lighting—to be both in itself an emblematic waterfront structure (appearing in countless establishing shots in movies and TV shows), and an almost transcendently successful complement to the Brooklyn Bridge and the ships owned by the South Street Seaport Museum. It shall yield, however, to a new glass pavilion designed by SHoP, with landscaping by James Corner Field Operations (of High Line, p. 156, and Freshkills, p. 131, fame). This continues SHoP's utter domination of this waterfront.

Phase 2 of SHoP's and Smith's esplanade will be to the south, between Pier 11 and Broad Street (where one can get the ferry to Governors Island, p. 145). Phase 3 will take place to the north, in line with Pike Street, just north of the Manhattan Bridge. Both sections are scheduled to open in 2013.

This stretch of the waterfront was, from the city's 17th-century beginnings to the mid-19th century, the location of the docks to which sailing ships arrived from overseas, and from which ships set out on their voyages around the world. In sailing days, the East River offered greater protection to ships in port than the Hudson, which was too open, leaving ships exposed to the damaging elements. By the second half of the 19th century, the new, larger, and less fragile oceangoing steamships required an entirely new port infrastructure, which was built along the Hudson. In the East River's heyday, the docks near South Street were where New York's earliest mercantile fortunes were made (sometimes in piracy and the slave trade, alas), the first Black Ball Line packets were launched, hundreds of thousands of Irish and German immigrants disembarked after horrifying journeys across the ocean, and such merchants as Abiel Low and William Aspinwall commissioned the classic, speedy clipper ships that engaged in the China trade. New Yorkers came in droves to witness the launch of a new clipper and followed its progress in the newspapers to see if it would set a new speed record. It was like a sporting event. Later, when the port shifted to the Hudson, this area remained home to the Fulton Fish Market, immortalized in the heavily fictionalized reporting of Joseph Mitchell in the *New Yorker*.

HOURS: East River Waterfront Esplanade, 6 am to midnight

Pier 15, Upper Deck: 8 am to dusk

Pier 15, Lower Deck: 6 am to midnight

MAPS & FURTHER INFORMATION AVAILABLE AT:
www.nycedc.com/press-image/east-river-waterfront

DIRECTIONS TO PIER 15: Located at John and South Streets, the pier extends 500 feet out into the East River at the end of John Street.

BY FERRY: New York Water Taxi provides hop-on, hop-off service to Pier 17 from Fulton Ferry Landing, DUMBO; Battery Park, Slip 6; Christopher Street, Pier 45; West 44th Street, Pier 84; then walk south to Pier 15

BY SUBWAY: A, C, J, Z, 2, 3, 4, 5 to Fulton Street, walk southeast down Fulton Street toward the water to South Street Seaport, and walk south to Pier 15

BY BUS: M15 to Water Street and Fulton Street, walk toward the water on John Street to South Street Seaport, and walk south to Pier 15

QM11 and QM25 to Water Street and John Street, walk toward the water on John Street to South Street Seaport, and walk south to Pier 15

X8, QM7, QM8 to Water Street and Maiden Lane, walk toward the water on Maiden Lane to the South Street Seaport, and walk south to Pier 15

BM1, BM2, BM3, BM4 to Water Street and Pine Street, walk north to Maiden Lane, turn right on Maiden Lane, walk to the South Street Seaport, and then walk south to Pier 15

East River Park

To the north of Phase 3 of the esplanade is the linear, 57-acre East River Park, which runs from Jackson Street (about six blocks north of Pike Street)

to East 12th Street, to the east of the FDR Drive. The park follows the contour of the FDR Drive and rims four large New York City Housing Authority projects: the Corlears Hook, Baruch, Lillian Wald, and Jacob Riis Houses. Robert Moses conceived of the park in the 1930s. At that time, Moses tried always to integrate parks into his roadway projects. Arguably, his most notable success in this regard was the section of the Belt Parkway in Brooklyn's Bay Ridge and Bath Beach areas, between Owl's Head Park and Bay Parkway. At East River Park, he used a combination of eminent domain to acquire properties along the riverfront and landfill to secure the space for the park, which was intended to serve the needs of the park-deprived, working-class residents of the Lower East Side. East River Park finally opened in 1939.

East River Park once boasted an outdoor theater and in the 1950s, Joseph Papp staged his first Shakespeare-in-the-Park productions there. Since Papp's productions moved to Central Park so many years ago, we may forgive playgoers for forgetting that the "Park" in "Shakespeare in the Park" originally referred to East River Park on the Lower East Side. The outdoor theater later fell into disrepair and abandonment, but was renovated and reopened a few years ago. As is typical of Robert Moses park projects, East River Park contains a great deal of space for active recreation, from handball to soccer. To these may be added biking and running, as the park forms a link in the chain of the East River Greenway, part of the Manhattan Waterfront

FACING PAGE AND BELOW The linear, 57-acre East River Park follows the contours of the FDR Drive.

Greenway, a partially completed 32-mile "foreshoreway," to use the recent coinage that refers to a public right-of-way along the edge of a body of water. Footbridges across the FDR Drive can be found near Jackson Street, at Delancey Street (where the park runs under the Williamsburg Bridge), near East 6th Street at the Lillian Wald Houses, and at East 10th Street in the Jacob Riis Houses complex.

At the southern end of East River Park, and actually on the inland side of the FDR Drive, at South and Jackson Streets, is the 4.5-acre Corlears Hook Park, opened in 1905. Many years before East River Park and the housing projects with their playgrounds and strolling paths, this small park was the only green oasis for the residents of one of the poorest and most densely populated urban neighborhoods in the world. In his 1914 essay "The Lungs" (reprinted in full at the beginning of this book), the great critic James Gibbons Huneker paid a visit to Corlears Hook Park and captured its mood:

> Then I reached an open space and was disappointed. It was Corlears Hook Park, and the absence of shade was painful. This lack of trees is a fault to be found in the majority of municipal parks and playgrounds. Night, if you don't feel too scared or lonely, is the proper time to enjoy the Hook. The view of the East River is unimpeded. The water is crowded with craft. A breeze always fans one. Women and children, principally Italians and Jews, sit or walk. Cats are friendly. So is the small boy who knocks off your straw tile with a stick. A venerable steamboat, rotting and dismal, the relic of a once proud excursion career, is warped to the wharf. It has flowers on its upper deck, and pale, sick people sit on the lower. You are informed by the inevitable busybody who traipses after strangers that the old boat is for tuberculosis patients, living or dying, in the neighborhood.

The site of East River Park, the housing projects, and this stretch of the FDR Drive was the location of New York's biggest shipyards in the 19th century, when shipbuilding and maritime commerce were the mainstays of the city economy. The legendary names included Novelty Iron Works, William Henry Webb, and Jacob Westervelt. As elsewhere along New York City's waterways, the maritime enterprises have faded away, leaving opportunities for new uses, such as parks.

Across 14th Street from East River Park and the Jacob Riis Houses is Stuyvesant Town, which, with its sibling, Peter Cooper Village (20th to 23rd Streets), was, when built in the 1940s, the largest housing development in history. Between First Avenue and Avenue C (along the west side of the FDR Drive), these developments comprise 56 high-rise apartment buildings on 80 acres of land, and house 25,000 middle-income people. The complexes were built as a limited-profit project by the Metropolitan Life Insurance Company using federal slum-clearance funds. Needless to say, Robert Moses orchestrated the whole thing. Stuyvesant Town and Peter Cooper Village represent the ultimate in towers-in-a-park planning. Though the projects drew sharp early criticism for their aesthetic aridity, the passage of years has been kind, as trees have matured and the park portions have grown lush. Many people who live in the developments today truly do feel that they live in a park.

HOURS: Dawn to dusk

RESTROOMS: Located near the park side of the East 10th Street pedestrian bridge

REGULATIONS: Smoking is prohibited

Map & further information available at: www.nycgovparks.org/parks/eastriverpark

BY SUBWAY: J, M, Z to Essex Street, walk east 11 blocks along Delancey Street, cross under the Williamsburg Bridge to Delancey Street South, walk east 1 block, cross the FDR Drive using the Delancey Street South pedestrian bridge

F to Delancey Street, walk east 12 blocks along Delancey, cross under the Williamsburg Bridge to Delancey Street South, walk east 1 block, cross the FDR Drive using the Delancey Street South pedestrian bridge

BY BUS: M14A/D, M21 to East Houston Street and Mangin Street, walk east 2 blocks across the FDR Drive, using the level crossing

M14A/D, M21 to Cherry Street and Jackson Street, walk through Corlears Hook Park to the Corlears Hook Park pedestrian bridge and cross into the park at the amphitheater

M14A/D to Delancey Street and FDR Drive, cross Delancey Street, and use pedestrian bridge to enter the park

M8, M14A/D to East 10th Street and Ave D, walk east 1 block and use the pedestrian bridge to enter the park

Stuyvesant Cove Park

Stuyvesant Cove Park is located between the FDR Drive and the East River from 17th to 23rd Street, adjacent to Stuyvesant Town and Peter Cooper Village.

At about 14th Street, where a Consolidated Edison power plant separates Stuyvesant Town from the FDR Drive, the foreshoreway narrows so considerably that bikers must dismount to pass through. But between 18th and 23rd Streets it widens again, this time in the form of the 2-acre Stuyvesant Cove Park. Opened in 2002, Stuyvesant Cove occupies a "brownfield" site, once the location of a concrete plant and a parking lot. In 1997 the New York Times referred to this waterfront as "a desolate stretch of shore." It is hard for people not of a certain age to believe just how desolate so many of the local shores were not so very long ago. They were the kinds of places where the bad guys went to dispose of the dead bodies in old cop movies and TV dramas (and sometimes

in real life!). In the 1980s developers proposed building a vast mixed-use apartment, office, hotel, and marina complex called Riverwalk on the land. Neighborhood residents opposed Riverwalk, which would have seized a valuable length of waterfront that, they said, was ideally suited to be a park. The residents prevailed. A community group called the Stuyvesant Cove Park Association secured federal, state, and city funds to finance the construction of the park, designed by Donna Walcavage Landscape Architecture + Urban Design. (This firm grew out of Johansson & Walcavage Landscape Architects, and has been absorbed into the global design and consulting firm AECOM.) The Walcavage firm began work on Stuyvesant Cove in 1996. The design process was truly a collaboration between landscape architects and community groups. Walcavage's design features curving walkways along the water's edge with surprising vistas; in spots flowerbeds or shrubbery on the river side of the metal railing foreground views of the water. The seating, designed by Carr Lynch & Sandell as part of their master plan for the East River Greenway, is of wood, and all of it is fixed. The vegetation consists exclusively of native species.

Though Hudson River Park preceded the comparable redevelopment of the East Side waterfront, critics have hailed the East River Waterfront Esplanade and Stuyvesant Cove Park as perhaps the best Manhattan has to offer in the way of new shorefronts. The design talents of Gregg Pasquarelli, Ken Smith, and Donna Walcavage have a lot to do with this, of course. The success of the East River parks, however, also owes a great deal to the edge-defining and shade-making presence of the FDR viaduct, and a generally more intimate relationship to nearby neighborhoods than is found on the West Side. —F.M.

RESTROOMS: None

MAP & DETAILS AVAILABLE AT: www.solar1.org

BY SUBWAY: 6 to Park Avenue South and 23rd Street, walk east approx. 6 blocks, and cross under the FDR Drive to the park

L to 14th Street and 1st Avenue, walk north to 20th Street (approx. 10 minutes), turn right on 20th Street, and cross under the FDR Drive to the park

BY BUS: M16, M23 to 23rd Street and Avenue C, cross under the FDR Drive

M23 to 20th Street and Avenue C, cross under the FDR Drive

M9 to 16th Street and Avenue C, walk north 1 block on Ave C, and cross under the FDR Drive

HUDSON RIVER PARK AND RIVERSIDE PARK SOUTH

4

Hudson River Park

The five-mile Hudson River Park stretches along the waterfront from the Battery to 59th Street on Manhattan's West Side

B etween them, Hudson River Park and Riverside Park South connect or, more accurately, will someday connect Battery Park City to Riverside Park to form a (more or less) continuous ribbon of parkland along the Hudson shoreline. In fact, there are a number of interruptions along the way, some of them rather jolting (the city's tow pound, for example). The *AIA Guide* is right: "Right now the landscape feels more like a series of parks, each serving a different neighborhood, with its own character (and characters). But that's not necessarily a bad thing."

Hudson River Park comprises 550 acres; Riverside Park South, 29. That is 579 acres—only six acres shy of Prospect Park. Together, the two parks (which we here treat together, as park users do not make a distinction between them) represent a remarkable achievement. New Yorkers today live in a city where so many public-works projects seem to languish for decades for want of money and/or will—the Second Avenue subway, the rebuilding of the World Trade Center site, the forthcoming conversion of the former General Post Office into a new Penn Station, even so modest a project as the renovation of Pier A in Battery Park. Costs escalate dizzyingly out of control. Labyrinthine regulations mean that only powerful people employing armies of lawyers can even get in the game. Many a New Yorker who once hated Robert Moses now thinks he may not have been so bad after all.

All of that is true, and depressing. However, it is far from the whole story. What about the High Line? When Robert Hammond and Joshua David first began their campaign to save the viaduct from destruction, who imagined that in a few years it would become what it has become (p. 156)? After the September 11 attacks put Brooklyn Bridge Park on indefinite hold, who could have imagined that it would be where it is today (p. 97)? Once a project trapped in the torpor of the city's fiscal malaise, Battery Park City (p. 33) today ranks as one of New York's historic achievements. And in 1997, when the *New Yorker*'s James Traub stood with Albert Butzel, the founder of the Hudson River Park Alliance, on a service road of the West Side Highway in the West 40s and listened to the crusading lawyer describe how this waterfront would be transformed, not one reader of "Talk of the Town" imagined the reality of just a few years later. Butzel, wrote Traub in April 1997:

> walked out onto Pier 84, a long lick of asphalt that has begun crumbling into the river. "This is what the park is really about," he said. "The piers will be cleaned up and opened up for public recreation." He went on to describe a transformation that would replace rot with tennis and basketball courts, cafés and concert pavilions. Turning his back to the river, he added, "I love it because you can look at the city in a way you can't usually do." It was true: there, in the gray light of morning, was a vision that, in recent years, only the gulls have been lucky enough to enjoy.

The battle to redevelop the West Side waterfront had been going on for decades and was intertwined with the redevelopment of the West Side Highway. In the 1930s, as part of the same West Side Improvement that

Hudson River Park features renovated and new piers for public access. Compare the old pier on the far left, with its rotten wood pilings sticking out of the water, to the new Pier 45.

brought us the High Line, the Miller Elevated Highway went up. (It had to be elevated to avoid blocking access to the docks, warehouses, and factories all along the river.) Yet this vast undertaking yielded an infrastructure that functioned for fewer than fifty years. The last train to run on the High Line was in 1980. The highway did not make it that far: On December 15, 1973, a dump truck fell through the roadbed at Gansevoort Street, marking the end of the Miller Elevated Highway and the beginning of searches for an alternative high-speed automotive thoroughfare for the West Side. The city had pulled down most of the elevated structure by 1989, although a portion of it remains in Riverside Park South (see below). In the early 1970s, the ambitious Westway plan took shape. Planners proposed building a vast concrete platform extending out to the ends of the existing piers along the Hudson waterfront. For a sizable stretch, a new highway would run in a tunnel under the platform. The top of the platform would be parkland. Westway boasted the backing of many very powerful interests, including a succession of governors and mayors and the editorial page of the *New York Times*. At times it appeared to be a "done deal." However, environmental activists and community groups rallied against the project and the opponents finally prevailed in 1983, when a District Court ruling, based on a U.S. Army Corps of Engineers study, halted the project, which, the ruling said, would destroy the habitat of the striped bass that lived in the river. (One could hear many a New Yorker say, "There are striped bass in the Hudson River?") The city gave up on its Westway dreams in 1985. Interestingly, another opponent of Westway was Robert Moses, by then out of power but still commenting from the sidelines. He thought it recklessly complicated and advocated instead for something very close to what was later done. The West Side Highway became a six- to eight-lane surface roadway from the Brooklyn–Battery Tunnel to West 59th Street. (At that point, the roadway rises up onto the surviving portion of the old elevated highway structure. At 72nd Street, the highway becomes the Henry Hudson Parkway.) Work on the new road (officially the Joe DiMaggio Highway) took place between 1996 and 2001.

Meanwhile, to the west of the highway the rotten piers lay languishing. But not for long. On September 8, 1998, shortly after construction of the new highway began, and a year after James Traub stood with Albert Butzel on Pier 84, Governor George E. Pataki stood triumphantly with Mayor Rudolph W. Giuliani on Pier 25, at North Moore Street in TriBeCa. As Douglas Martin reported in the *New York Times*:

> Saying Manhattan's western waterfront has been an embarrassment since his days as a young lawyer on Wall Street, Gov. George E. Pataki signed a law yesterday to create a park nearly five miles long, from Battery Park City to 59th Street.

In fact, work had already begun on sections of the park, including Pier 25. Its 1995 remodeling gave it a children's playground. (Though reconstructed in 2011, the pier still has a children's playground.) The legislation, however, designated the whole waterfront as parkland. Funds from city, state, federal, and private sources, tended by the Hudson River Park Trust, which was created by the legislation, led to the parceling out of the park area to teams of architects and landscape architects. On May 30, 2003, Governor Pataki stood on another pier, the dramatic, newly constructed Pier 45, at Christopher Street, to dedicate the first fully completed segment of the park, between Leroy and Jane Streets. Hudson River Park, he said, is "the Central Park of the 21st century."

Here are the segments, from south to north, as they exist at this writing:

HARRISON STREET TO LEROY STREET

The landscape architects Mathews Nielsen and Weisz + Yoes (WXY) Architecture designed the segment extending north from Battery Park City, between Harrison Street and Leroy Street, opened in 2008. The abundant wild grasses and long wooden walkway feel in parts much like South Cove Park in Battery Park City (p. 33). And, as at Battery Park City, the riverfront esplanade features granite paving and "World's Fair" benches. The Manhattan-based firm of Kim Mathews and Signe Nielsen has designed many notable landscapes, principally in the New York area. Their major works in the city include the renovation (1999) of the ancient Duane Park, at Hudson and Duane Streets, in TriBeCa; the new landscaping (completed 2004) of Stuyvesant Town and Peter Cooper Village; the landscape design (completed 2010) of the renovated Lincoln Center for the Performing Arts; the marvelous Fulton Street Pier (1995, see Brooklyn Bridge Park, p. 97) on the Brooklyn waterfront; new urban design features (completed 2000), including lighting and block paving, that helped revitalize Stone Street in lower Manhattan, and far too many other projects to name.

Much of Hudson River Park is about active recreation. There are regulation-size outdoor basketball courts (illuminated for nighttime play) at Harrison Street and at Canal Street. Pier 25, at North Moore Street, rebuilt in 2011, features, in addition to its children's playground, three beach volleyball courts (illuminated for nighttime play), an 18-hole miniature golf course, a 360-foot floating dock for boat moorings, a "skatepark" (for skateboards and roller skates), and the mooring site of two historic ships: Pegasus, a restored 1907 tugboat, and Lilac, a 173-foot-long steamship built in 1933 for the U.S. Lighthouse Service. There are tennis courts just south of Pier 40, at Houston Street, and Pier 40 has athletic fields.

Washington Market Park

At the northeast corner of Greenwich and Chambers Streets, a block from the southernmost point of this segment, lies the delightful Washington Market Park. Located at the southern end of the superblock that contains the immense Independence Plaza urban renewal project, which replaced a significant portion of the city's old wholesale produce market, the park opened in 1983. On just under 2 acres, the landscape architects Weintraub & di Domenico created a gem of a small neighborhood park. With its playground, community garden plots, and space for community gatherings, it proved a godsend to an old industrial neighborhood that, by the early 1980s, had become a popular place for young families to live. From the design standpoint, Washington Market Park partook of the postmodernist ethos of its time. Its many traditional touches, from a Vauxian undulating lawn and border of trees to the Victorian-style cast-iron gazebo (with its crockets and quatrefoils and pendants) and fence, marked a definitive break from the modernist landscape design of Paley Park (1967) by Zion

& Breen, on 53rd Street just east of Fifth Avenue (p. 240), Greenacre Park (1971) by Sasaki, Dawson, DeMay Associates, on East 51st Street, and the Ford Foundation atrium (1967) by Dan Kiley, on East 42nd Street. It is just as different from the neomodernist designs of Landscape Urbanism, such as we find at the High Line (p. 156) and throughout Hudson River Park. At Washington Market Park there are no wild grasses, no rusting gantries. It is as "artificial" as Central Park. In 1984 Carter Wiseman of *New York* magazine described Washington Market Park as "an urban oasis as precious as any Sahara waterhole." Back then, neither Rockefeller Park nor Hudson River Park yet existed. But in a neighborhood that today possesses a near-surfeit of parkland, Washington Market Park remains as precious as when TriBeCa suffered a dearth of open space. (For more on Lee Weintraub of Weintraub & di Domenico, see Erie Basin Park, p. 110.)

LEROY STREET TO JANE STREET

The section between Leroy Street and Jane Street was designed by the landscape architecture firm Abel Bainnson Butz and dates from 1999 to 2003. The first substantial section of Hudson River Park to open was a portion of this segment, between Christopher and Bank Streets, in 1999. The remainder was completed by 2003. This segment features three new piers, at Christopher, Charles, and Jane Streets, perpendicular to a continuous landscaped esplanade fronting a lawn that rolls back from the riverfront. The new Pier 45, at Christopher Street, ranks as one of Hudson River Park's greatest accomplishments. This dramatic, 860-foot-long pier (longer than the Woolworth Building is high) required 1,200 concrete pilings of up to 110 feet in length. These provide support for, among much else, the soil and irrigation needed by the 25 locust trees found on the pier, along with a great lawn and vast canvas umbrellas that provide much-needed shade for the sun-scorched space. The pier offers movable chairs, an amenity not found in all the new waterfront landscapes. It also offers a stop for the New York Water Taxi. From the water end of the pier, the views up and down and across the Hudson may be as good as you'll find. This section of park is also notable for its views of the sleek glass condominium towers by Richard Meier at 165 Charles Street (2006) and 173 and 176 Perry Street (2002). Other projects by the Manhattan-based firm of Abel Bainnson Butz include the General Motors Building plaza (2006), which surrounds the Apple Store at Fifth Avenue and 59th Street, the renovation (completed 2000) of Ocean Parkway in Brooklyn (p. 177), the private courtyard (2008) of the newly renovated Plaza Hotel, and, with the architects Richard Dattner & Partners, the ambitious Riverbank State Park (1993, p. 88) in Harlem.

JANE STREET TO WEST 26TH STREET

Michael Van Valkenburgh, who is steadily leaving his indelible imprint on the city, designed the segment between Jane Street and West 26th Street, built between 2008 and 2010. This section runs past the Chelsea Piers complex.

Originally, the Chelsea Piers extended from Little West 12th Street to West 22nd Street. Designed by Warren & Wetmore and built in 1902–7, the piers served as a terminal for the great Cunard passenger liners, such as the *Lusitania*. The *Titanic* was to have completed its maiden voyage at Pier 60, at West 20th Street. The *Carpathia* carried *Titanic* survivors to Pier 54, at West 13th Street. When these historic piers underwent modernization in the 1960s, however, all the grandeur of the old Warren & Wetmore structures was erased. The Chelsea Piers of today, occupying the banal sheds of the 1960s, have nothing to do with passenger liners. Instead, they form a vast sports and athletic complex that began opening in phases in 1995, when Roland W. Betts and Tom A. Bernstein, movie producers (*Pretty Woman*) and part owners of the Texas Rangers baseball club, sought a space to handle the overflow from the Sky Rink, an overbooked ice-hockey facility that used to be at the top of the gigantic Westyard Distribution Center on Tenth Avenue between 31st and 33rd Streets. From that modest beginning, Chelsea Piers has expanded over the years to incorporate two ice-hockey rinks, a golf club, batting cages, basketball courts, a bowling alley, a health club, lacrosse and soccer fields, a swimming pool, a sand volleyball court, a rock-climbing wall, and much more. There is also a major television and film production

Sleek glass condominium towers by Richard Meier at Charles and Perry Streets.

studio, where such shows as *Law and Order SVU* are shot. As a reclamation project, the sports complex is truly impressive. It predates Hudson River Park, however, and does not fit in gracefully.

At the western end of West 23rd Street is Chelsea Waterside Park, which was built by the city in 1907 as part of a program to provide poor neighborhoods with sorely needed open space. In 1923 the Parks Department named it for Tammany Hall politician Thomas F. Smith. The park acquired its present name, and was transferred to the jurisdiction of the Hudson River Park Trust in 2000, following a redo by landscape architect Thomas Balsley (see below, on Riverside Park South, for more on Balsley). The park includes a regulation-size outdoor basketball court (illuminated for nighttime play), a dog run, a children's playground, and an all-purpose athletic field.

It is just north of Chelsea Piers that Van Valkenburgh's artistry shines through. Here Hudson River Park, up to this point a ribbon park, becomes improbably expansive—a great rolling meadow reminiscent, in its undulating topography, of the Long Meadow in Brooklyn's Prospect Park. This portion, known as Chelsea Cove, also has densely planted pathways, several piers, and a riverfront esplanade.

Pier 62, at West 22nd Street, features a carousel ($2 a ride) with 33 hand-carved figures of animals found in the Hudson River Valley, from a horseshoe crab to a peregrine falcon to a turkey. The carousel shares Pier 62 with a "California-style skatepark," nestled amid trees and shrubs. Best of all is the year-round entry garden, designed by the redoubtable Lynden B. Miller, the famed "public gardener" (see also Wagner Park at Battery Park City, p. 52, and the Conservatory Garden in Central Park, p. 242). The garden at neighboring Pier 63 was also designed by Lynden B. Miller; its lawn is the setting for Riverflicks, nighttime al fresco movie screenings during the summer (2012 featured such fare as *Moneyball*, *Bridesmaids*, and *Crazy, Stupid Love*). Pier 64, at West 24th Street, is simple and elegant: an ovoid lawn gently swells up in the center, English oaks line its inner rim, and its outer rim is edged with park benches facing the water.

At Pier 66, at West 26th Street, is an old Delaware, Lackawanna & Western Railroad carfloat barge, used to transport railroad cars across the river, and a Baltimore & Ohio Railroad carfloat bridge, used to transfer cars from barges to the freight trains that ran up and down the riverfront. The operation worked like a Rube Goldberg contraption. Alongside the barge is the Frying Pan, a 133-foot-long lightship built in 1929. After her years of service off Cape Fear, North Carolina, had come to an end, her owners abandoned her in Chesapeake Bay, where she eventually sank. Dredged from the bottom of the bay and restored, she moved to New York in 1989. Also moored here is the John J. Harvey, a 130-foot-long fireboat that in her many years of service (1931–94) for the New York City Fire Department could pump 18,000 gallons of water a minute, making her one of the most powerful fireboats ever built. A popular bar and grill operates on the pier. Pier 66 is also home to Hudson River Community Sailing, a non-profit organization that seeks, through classes and excursions, to bring sailing—usually considered a pastime of the rich—within the means of all city dwellers.

WEST 26TH STREET TO WEST 59TH STREET

The section between West 26th Street and West 59th Street, designed by Richard Dattner Architects and the landscape architects Miceli Kulik Williams, came into being between 2000 and 2007. This is the stretch that really fights for breath against big, preexisting waterfront structures, such as the aforementioned tow pound at Pier 76 (West 34th Street). It is a measure of how forlorn the waterfronts once were that a facility such as this, which could have been located anywhere, ended up here, out of the way. At Pier 78 (West 39th Street) is the West Midtown Ferry Terminal of NY Waterway, a company that began operation in 1986 with a route between the Port Imperial Terminal in Weehawken, New Jersey, and here, and that, at this writing, operates to and from twenty locations. The company is strongly associated with the 1980s and 1990s revival of ferry service on area waterways. The Circle Line sightseeing boats have called Pier 83 (West 43rd Street) their home since 1955. Pier 84 (West 44th Street), where the New Yorker's James Traub stood with Albert Butzel in 1997, opened in 2006. It is a large pier, with a boathouse, an outdoor café, bicycle rentals, a dog run, a children's playground, lawns for sunbathing, and a New York Water Taxi station. (The Red Hook, Brooklyn–based New York Water Taxi, like NY Waterway a major provider of ferry service in the area, began operation in 2002.)

Along this stretch, too, is the immense USS Intrepid, at Pier 86 (West 46th Street). The 872-foot-long aircraft carrier dates from 1943. She served in the Pacific in World War II, and later in the Vietnam War; she was also the recovery craft for Mercury and Gemini space missions. In 1982, eight years after her decommissioning, the Intrepid opened at West 46th Street as the Intrepid Sea-Air-Space Museum. The aircraft carrier is large enough to hold many other historic sea- and aircraft, including the USS Growler submarine, a Concorde SST, and, beginning in 2012, the space shuttle Enterprise. The museum underwent a complete refurbishment between 2006 and 2008, and is well worth a visit.

On the inland side of Twelfth Avenue, between 30th and 34th Streets, be sure to note the former New York Central Railroad freight yards. The freight and passenger terminal of the Hudson River Railroad was located here in the mid-19th century. The line became freight-only after it was absorbed into Cornelius Vanderbilt's New York Central system. These yards were the source of the High Line. Today the yards, located directly to the west of Pennsylvania Station (though they belonged to the Pennsylvania Railroad's archrival), serve the trains of the Long Island Railroad. Planners and developers are eager to deck over the yards and create a new mixed-use neighborhood of offices and apartments. To make the neighborhood more accessible and inviting, the Metropolitan Transportation Authority plans a southward extension of the 7 subway line from 42nd Street to provide much-needed service to the area. These yards—now known as Hudson Yards—are also the site where Mayor Michael R. Bloomberg proposed building an Olympic stadium in the city's failed bid for the 2012 games. To the immediate north of the yards, from 34th to 39th Streets, occupying what had once been railroad yards, is the Jacob K. Javits Convention Center, a striking 1986 glass building by James Ingo Freed of I. M. Pei & Partners.

Between 55th and 57th Streets is Richard Dattner's and Miceli Kulik Williams's two-acre Clinton Cove, the northernmost part of Hudson River Park before Riverside Park South begins. Clinton Cove is the best this heavily obstructed segment of the park has to offer. It consists of two sizable lawns and a waterfront esplanade (with "world's fair" benches). Pier 95 is described by the Hudson River Park Trust as a "get-down," a shaded platform with seating below the bulkhead, intended to bring park users closer to the water. Pier 96 has a boathouse for kayaks and other vessels. Pier 97 is under construction as a recreational pier. One of the most popular elements of Clinton Cove is the unusual public sculpture *Private Passage* by Malcolm Cochran (b. 1948). This is an outsize wine bottle, on its side, made of bronze and zinc. It has portholes in its side and bottom, and through those and the bottle opening one can peer inside to a stylized rendition, in sheet metal, of a stateroom in the old *Queen Mary*, which used to dock nearby.

Hudson River Park does not yet give us the dreamed-of continuous swath of waterfront parkland. Challenges remain, not least among them funding in these economically troubled times, but also the removal of nuisances such as the tow pound. That park planners have accomplished so much, however, counts as a great success in our post–Robert Moses world. Some parts of the park as it is—Mathews Nielsen's walkway, Abel Bainnson Butz's Pier 45, and Van Valkenburgh's Chelsea Cove—rank as unqualified triumphs.

HOURS: 6 am–1 am (unless otherwise posted)

Playgrounds and restrooms close at dusk

The bike/walkway west of Rte 9A is open at all times unless otherwise posted

RESTROOMS: Courtyard Fields at West Houston Street; Chelsea Waterside Park; Ferry Terminal; near Piers 45, 51, 62, 84, 95 (Clinton Cove), and 97

REGULATIONS: Dogs must remain on leashes, are not permitted in playgrounds or bathing facilities, and may drink only from fountains designated for animal use

Smoking is prohibited

MAP & DETAILS AVAILABLE AT: www.hudsonriverpark.org

BY SUBWAY: I
Broadway and 59th Street-Columbus Circle, walk west 4 blocks (Northern End/ Clinton Cove)

7th Avenue and Christopher Street-Sheridan Square, walk west 6 blocks (Greenwich Village)

Varick Street and Houston Street, walk west 4 blocks (SoHo)

Varick Street and Canal Street, walk west 4 blocks (TriBeCa)

West Broadway and Chambers Street (also 2, 3), walk west 2 blocks (TriBeCa)

A, C, E
8th Avenue and 50th Street, walk west 4 blocks (Midtown West)

8th Avenue and 42nd Street-Port Authority, walk west 4 blocks (Midtown West)

8th Avenue and 34th Street-Penn Station, walk west 4 blocks (Midtown West)

8th Avenue and 23rd Street, walk west 4 blocks (Chelsea Waterside Park)

8th Avenue and 14th Street-8th Avenue (also L), walk west 3 blocks (Greenwich Village)

BY BUS: MIDTOWN WEST:
M50: 46th Street and 12th Avenue; 42nd Street and 12th Avenue

M42: 42nd Street and 12th Avenue

M11: 10th Avenue and 45th Street, walk west 2 blocks on 45th Street

M34: 34th Street and 12th Avenue

CHELSEA WATERSIDE:
M14: 18th Street and West Street

M23: 23rd Street and 12th Avenue

CHELSEA AND GREENWICH VILLAGE
M8: West Street and Christopher Street

M14: West Street and 15th Street

M11: 10th Avenue and 14th Street, walk west 1 block

SOHO AND TRIBECA
M21: Spring Street and Greenwich Street, walk west 2–3 blocks

X7: West Street Chambers Street,

BY PATH: Newark–33rd Street and Hoboken–33rd Street lines to Christopher Street, walk west 2 blocks (Greenwich Village)

GREENWAY BIKEPATH: entrances spaced one or three blocks apart along the West Side Highway from 59th Street to Battery Place.

Riverside Park South

The park runs along the Hudson River between West 59th and West 72nd Streets

The Pier I recreational area is located at 70th Street

Though it might seem to be the next segment of Hudson River Park, Riverside Park South is an entirely different entity, albeit one designed to serve as a link in the continuous park chain that stretches from Battery Park City, through Hudson River Park and Riverside Park South, to Riverside Park. New York Central Railroad freight yards once occupied the site of Riverside Park South and the new residential neighborhood up the slope from the park. Developer Donald Trump took control of the disused yards—considered one of the most desirable development sites left in Manhattan—in 1983, and initially proposed a mixed-use development that would include a new world's tallest building, designed by Chicago's Helmut Jahn. Predictably, groups formed in opposition to that plan. (Savvy developers often propose plans they know will arouse opposition. Then they can "negotiate" down to what they really wanted all along.) A new plan gained approval in 1992, on the condition that the developer fund construction of a new park between 59th and 72nd Streets to the west of the elevated Joe DiMaggio Highway. Part of that plan also involved relocating the highway to make it less obtrusive, but community opposition led to an indefinite postponement of that large undertaking. In fact, the giant looming presence of the last remaining bit of the old West Side Highway (constructed in the 1930s as part of the West Side Improvement that also gave us the High Line) lends this park much of its particular flavor.

Riverside Park South has emerged in phases. Phase I opened in March 2001 and involved the renovation of a once burned-out 750-foot-long pier at West 70th Street. Long and sinuous, the renovated pier affords dramatic views up and down the river. One of the most amazing sights—until January 2011—was the ruin of the New York Central's old Pier D, at West 64th Street. The pier burned down in 1971 and lay partly submerged as a heap of charred and gnarled steel. Original park plans called for its removal, but through the efforts of Parks Commissioner Adrian Benepe it remained untouched for several years in the hopes that it could be rendered a stabilized ruin and become a permanent attraction in the park. At last the Parks Department determined that stabilzation was not feasible, and after sitting in the river for fully seven decades, it was carted away over a single winter weekend. (Two other piers burned in the same fire: the nearby Pier C, at West 62nd Street, known as the Spaghetti Pier, which was removed along

Above the ball field is the last remaining bit of the old West Side Highway—the southbound exit ramp to West 70th Street, begun in the 1930s but never completed.

with Pier D, and the renovated 70th Street pier.) Though the ruined piers vanished, there are still the remains of a splendid carfloat transfer bridge at West 69th Street. Landscape architect Thomas Balsley chose to keep the transfer bridge in its evocatively ruined state. (Balsley also designed Gantry Plaza State Park, in Long Island City, Queens, p. 119. There he incorporated old carfloat gantries but spiffed them up with new paint and wove them tightly into the fabric of the park.) Another reminder of rail yard days stands at West 62nd Street: a 1946 locomotive that, though it operated on the Brooklyn waterfront, is identical to the locomotives that once operated in the yards on this site.

Phase I involved the swath from 72nd to 68th Streets; Phase 2 extended the park to 65th Street, and opened in 2003; and phase 3, to 62nd Street, opened in 2006. When Phase 4, to 59th Street, opened in 2008, Riverside Park South, though not yet complete, effected the highly anticipated link-up between Hudson River Park and Riverside Park, and Manhattan was a step closer to realizing the improbable dream of transforming the West Side waterfront into a great urban park. By 2008 the riverside portions were in place, leaving the slope of land up to the apartment towers of Riverside

The 750-foot-long pier, off of West 70th Street, opened in March 2001.

Boulevard still awaiting their conversion to parkland. Extell Development Corporation (which took over the project from Trump in 2005) has undertaken to build a tunnel under Riverside Boulevard for the diversion of the West Side Highway. Eventually, the elevated structure will come down. It may, however, take decades.

Park designer Thomas Balsley has been at the forefront of a movement to bring to New York's public spaces new kinds of furniture, and is largely responsible for the proliferation of chaises longues in the city's parks. The idea that someone might recline, or semirecline, and potentially nod off in a New York City park reflects the steep decline in people's fear of crime. It also reflects a change in what people want and expect from their city. Riverside Park South has a remarkable variety of seating, including slatted wooden chaises longues under shady pergolas, wooden park benches under broadly craning slatted wooden shades, and, best of all, sinuous chaises, of a composite material, that are movable.

As at the High Line, nature had claimed a derelict industrial landscape. Thomas Balsley sought to evoke that landscape by using native grasses and wildflowers and industrial archaeology. His park is not yet complete. We await an upland sward—and, eventually, removal of the elevated highway structure. Still, New York has reclaimed the riverfront, and for Balsley the job probably could not have been more demanding, or more deftly executed. —F.M.

RESTROOMS: Seasonal public restrooms are located at the Pier i Café, at Pier 1, West 70th Street. To enter, descend the stairway at West 68th Street and Riverside Drive and pass under the West Side Highway

REGULATIONS: Smoking is prohibited

MAP & ADDITIONAL INFORMATION AVAILABLE AT:
www.riversideparkfund.org/visit/Park-Map/?c=Park-Map or

www.nycgovparks.org/sub_your_park/vt_riverside_park/vt_rs_12_riverside_park_south.html

BY SUBWAY: 1, 2, 3 to Broadway and 72nd Street, walk south 2 blocks to 70th Street, west 3 blocks to Riverside Drive, and south 2 blocks to 68th Street

BY BUS: M5 to West 72nd Street and West End Avenue, walk south 2 blocks to 70th Street, west 3 blocks to Riverside Boulevard, and south 2 blocks to 68th Street

M57 to West End Avenue and 72nd Street, walk south 2 blocks to 70th Street, west 3 blocks to Riverside Blvd, and south 2 blocks to 68th Street

M72 to Riverside Boulevard and 69th Street, walk south 1 block to 68th Street

From 68th Street and Riverside Drive, walk down stairway or ramp, near the playground, and pass under the West Side Highway to the park.

RIVERSIDE PARK 5

The park runs along the Hudson River on Riverside Drive from West 72nd Street to West 155th Street

By comparison, the castled Rhine with its Lorelei is a mere trickle
between vine-clad slopes. I wonder sometimes whether our people,
so obsessed with the seamy interior of Manhattan, deserve the Hudson.

—ROBERT MOSES

"Couldn't this be the most beautiful thing in the world?" asked 25-year-old Robert Moses to his incredulous friend Frances Perkins as they sat in a boat on the Hudson River, and Moses waved his arm toward the utterly unprepossessing waterfront of the Upper West Side. The year was 1914. At that time, Riverside Park was only a little more than half its present size, and its name a misnomer: the park pulled up well short of the river. Between park and river lay the tracks of the New York Central Railroad's freight division, which with its affiliated uses made of the West

The West 79th Street Boat Basin, one of two marinas in Manhattan operated by the NYC Department of Parks & Recreation, Marine Division, has a five- to seven-year wait for seasonal summer dockage.

Side waterfront a noisy, noisome, smoky industrial strip. At that time, Moses was far from being in a position of power. As he described to Frances Perkins just what he thought should be done with the West Side waterfront, it sounded to her like a pipe dream. She recounted this story after Moses had made the West Side Improvement a reality in the 1930s, and had done so pretty much along the lines of what he had described to her in 1914.

The West Side Improvement was a vast Depression-era project, not initiated by Moses but largely carried through by him, that gave us the High Line and the Miller Elevated Highway, the Henry Hudson Parkway (considered by some at the time to be the most beautiful roadway in the world), and, not least, a near doubling of Riverside Park, making its name true by doing what the original developers of the park had been unable to do in the 19th century: extending the park all the way to the riverside.

There are three distinct phases to the history of the development of Riverside Park: the Olmsted phase, the City Beautiful phase, and the Robert Moses phase (as Elizabeth Cromley pointed out in "Riverside Park and Issues of Historic Preservation," *Journal of the Society of Architectural Historians*, October 1984, pp. 238–49).

The Olmsted Phase

Frederick Law Olmsted laid out the original part of Riverside Park in 1873–75 as part of the project that left us the lovely, sinuously curving Riverside Drive, which opened in 1880, though parts remained incomplete until 1902. Olmsted and Calvert Vaux had had to design Central Park to fit inside a perfect rectangle carved from the Manhattan grid. Within the park's borders, they used every trick to dispel straight lines. Given the job of laying out upper Manhattan's westernmost thoroughfare, Olmsted found himself in a unique position. He did not have to make it a straight line! The waterfront was pretty dismal. By placing a long, narrow strip of parkland between the railroad tracks and the houses and apartments on the east side of Riverside Drive, Olmsted could shield the Drive's residents from the soot and clangor. He could also create his curvy thoroughfare. The Drive traverses a deliriously winding path from its beginning, at West 72nd Street, to its end, at West 181st Street. Olmsted's long, narrow, curvy, buffering strip of green comprised 175 acres. But it was not, in any way, shape, or form, a riverside park.

It is also, as historian Elizabeth Collins Cromley pointed out, a bit of a misnomer to think of Riverside Park as an Olmsted park at all. While it is true that he was its original designer, others—including Olmsted's former partner Calvert Vaux and Samuel Parsons, Jr.—added to and tinkered with the park all the way up to 1910. Nonetheless, in its first few decades the park was "Olmstedian," a naturalistic sward punctuated by rock outcrops sloping toward the river.

The City Beautiful Phase

Between 1897 and 1928, several monuments and memorials were built to embellish Riverside Park. This period of civic adornment is known as the City Beautiful movement, which gained great favor with the public after the World's Columbian Exposition in Chicago in 1893. A stately classicism, very different from the picturesque Victorian naturalism of Olmsted and Vaux, now ruled. Strung along the park's inner edge on Riverside Drive, these monuments and memorials appeared along with grand houses on the Drive, such as Charles Schwab's 75-room mansion, at 73rd Street, designed by Maurice Hébert (1902–6; demolished, 1948), and the Isaac Rice mansion, at 89th Street, designed by Herts & Tallant (1901–3; still standing).

The City Beautiful embellishments in the park include the Robert Ray Hamilton Memorial Fountain at 76th Street, designed by Warren & Wetmore and dedicated in 1906. The Tennessee marble fountain was originally a watering trough for horses. At West 89th Street (across the street from the Rice mansion) stands the Soldiers' and Sailors' Monument, a 96-foot-high (tall enough to be a highly visible landmark when viewed from a boat in the Hudson River) version, in marble and granite, of the Choragic Monument of Lysicrates of 4th-century B.C.E. Athens. Designed by Stoughton & Stoughton with the French architect Paul Duboy and dedicated in 1902, the monument deteriorated to such an extent over the decades that in the 1950s modernist architects petitioned Mayor Robert F. Wagner to replace it with a simple illuminated shaft. The city decided, sensibly, to restore it instead. At West 93rd Street, note the equestrian statue of Joan of Arc, dedicated in 1915. Anna Vaughn Hyatt (later Mrs. Archer Huntington), a celebrated animalier, executed the girl and the horse in bronze; John Van Pelt designed the handsome base. At West 100th Street stands the grand and affecting Firemen's Memorial, dedicated in 1913, the work of the sculptor Attilio Piccirilli and the architect H. Van Buren Magonigle. It features a broad flight of steps leading to a balustraded terrace, in the center of which rests a marble sarcophagus that bears a relief of horses pulling a fire engine. At either end sit allegorical figures of Sacrifice and Duty. At West 106th Street is the bronze equestrian statue of Civil War general Franz Sigel (1907) by

Riverside Park extends from West 72nd Street on the south to West 155th Street on the north. In 1910 it was proposed to cover over the railroad tracks that separated the park from the river and extend the park down to the river's edge. Metal grating in the median provides ventilation for the trains passing below.

the sculptor Karl Bitter and the architect Welles Bosworth. Other bronze statues stand at West 112th Street (Samuel J. Tilden by William Ordway Partridge, dedicated 1926) and 113th Street (Lajos Kossuth by János Horvay, dedicated 1928). Finally, and most famously, at West 122nd Street we find the 150-foot-high Grant's Tomb, a design by John H. Duncan, dedicated in 1897. The white granite monument might not have looked as grandiose if its full sculpture program had been executed as originally planned. The additional decoration would have relieved the stone massiveness of America's second largest mausoleum. Nevertheless, this was once one of the most popular monuments in the country, and for decades defined Riverside Park in the popular imagination.

It was during this City Beautiful phase that the city acquired additional land for the park, on the water side of the railroad tracks (including underwater land that would later be filled), and developed initial proposals for covering over the tracks and extending the park down to the river's edge. In 1910 Parks Commissioner Charles B. Stover recommended the enclosure and bridging of the railroad tracks, the westward extension of the shoreline, and the construction of a riverfront esplanade. Administrative wrangling meant that no progress occurred until the 1930s. In fact, from the city's purchase of underwater land in 1894 to the beginning of landfill operations in 1934, a full forty years elapsed. This reminds us that the lengthy delays and lead times we experience in our time are in fact the historical norm in New York City, and periods such as that dominated by Robert Moses are the historical anomaly.

The Robert Moses Phase

More than anyone else in his time, Robert Moses saw the potential for recreational development of the waterfronts of New York City. In 1934–37, as part of the West Side Improvement, he added 148 acres to Riverside Park. The park was now (and remains) 323 acres, extending from West 72nd Street on the south to West 155th Street on the north.

Do bear in mind that Robert Moses did not conceive the majority of the changes he implemented. His extension of Riverside Park followed the ideas of others, such as Charles B. Stover and the architects McKim, Mead & White, brought in (long after the deaths of White and McKim) to serve as consultants on the park. What Moses did was to take the talk of four decades and make it, in a breathtaking three years, a reality.

Moses completed the landfill. He encased the tracks in a gigantic concrete box, 66 feet wide and 30 feet high, with walls two feet thick. The box extends from 72nd to 126th Streets. Atop a portion of the box, Moses built the Serpentine Promenade, which extends from 83rd Street to 91st Street.

Open-air patio of the Boat Basin Café, next to the limestone arches of the covered rotunda in Riverside Park, overlooking the West 79th Street Boat Basin.

Though only eight blocks long, this promenade identifies the park in many people's minds.

From the 1950s to the 1990s, the tracks inside the box lay unused, as the waterfront freight operations the tracks once served disappeared. In the 1980s, a number of homeless people took up residence in the box. Amtrak subsequently reclaimed the tracks for passenger service to and from Pennsylvania Station, and today trains rumble through every forty minutes.

Earlier proposals had suggested encasing the tracks and building a vehicular roadway atop the box. Moses instead built an elevated roadway, the Henry Hudson Parkway, slightly to the west of the box. In the 1920s and 1930s, Moses was a big believer in parkways. As chairman of the Long Island State Park Commission, he built beautiful automotive parkways to allow city dwellers to drive out to his magnificent new parks and beaches in Nassau and Suffolk Counties. Before Moses built the Henry Hudson, all his parkways extended out from the urban peripheries. The Henry Hudson was a Moses parkway right in Manhattan. Not only was it a crucial early means of allowing automobiles to negotiate Manhattan more easily and speedily, but it was also a crucial element in the transformation of the West Side into "the most beautiful thing in the world."

The Henry Hudson Parkway opened in 1937. It begins at West 72nd Street and extends for about eleven miles through upper Manhattan and the

Bronx to the Westchester County line. It sits on a great, arcaded viaduct, permitting pedestrian passage beneath it to the waterfront, where Moses built another promenade. The western promenade was the first of Moses's waterfront esplanades, a long pedestrian path (now continuous with the waterfront paths of Hudson River Park and Riverside Park South, p. 67, and part of the Hudson River Greenway) where one could stand at the railing and gaze dreamily at the mighty Hudson, across to the beautiful Palisades, or north to the majestic man-made wonder known as the George Washington Bridge.

Moses and his designers carefully integrated the Henry Hudson Parkway into the park. They made use of the grade separations pioneered by Olmsted and Vaux almost eighty years before in Central Park. Most remarkably, Moses and company built a traffic rotary for the parkway at 79th Street. Here the traffic flows atop the roof of an arcaded circus that encloses a fountain. Pedestrians move through the arched openings on the circus's west side to a restaurant, and from there to the riverfront esplanade and a marina with 105 slips for boats. Here, many houseboat dwellers live year-round.

In addition, Moses transformed Riverside Park into a place for active recreation, with children's playgrounds, baseball fields, and courts for basketball, tennis, and handball. If we owe the defining weave of the park's eastern edge largely to Frederick Law Olmsted, then we owe most of the rest of Riverside Park to Robert Moses.

Riverside Park's many appearances in the movies are a barometer of the city's fortunes. In the 1974 film *Death Wish*, vigilante Charles Bronson tracks down and shoots muggers in the park. In 1998 in *You've Got Mail*, written and directed by Nora Ephron, who lived on the Upper West Side, the mood of the park is completely different. This movie vividly portrays life on a houseboat at the 79th Street marina, and in its romantic climax, Tom Hanks and Meg Ryan meet on the Serpentine Promenade. —F.M.

RESTROOMS:

Ten Mile River Playground at 148th Street

Riverbank Camel Playground and Skating Rink, both at 142nd Street

Tennis Courts at 138th Street

Claremont Dolphin Playground near Tiemann Place

Tennis Courts at 119th Street

Hudson Beach between 106th and 105th Streets

Dinosaur Playground at 97th Street

Riverside Clay Tennis Courts at 96th Street

Hippo Playground at 91st Street

River Run Playground at 82nd Street

O'Neals Boat Basin Cafe at 79th Street

Henry Neufeld Elephant Playground at 76th Street

Classic Playground between 76th and 75th Streets

REGULATIONS: Smoking is prohibited

MAP & DETAILS AVAILABLE AT: www.nycgovparks.org/parks/riversidepark/

BY SUBWAY: 1 makes regular stops on Broadway between 157th Street and 72nd Street, walk west 2 blocks

2, 3 to 96th Street and Broadway, walk west 2 blocks; 72nd Street and Broadway, walk west 2 blocks

BY BUS: M4 makes regular stops on Broadway between 157th Street and Cathedral Pkwy, walk west 1–2 blocks

M5 makes regular stops on Broadway between 157th Street and 135th Street and continues along and within the park to 72nd Street

M11 makes regular stops along Riverside Drive between 145th Street and 135th Street and continues on Amsterdam and Columbus Avenues between 135th Street and 72nd Street, walk west 3–4 blocks

M7 makes regular stops on Amsterdam and Columbus Avenues between 106th Street and 72nd Street, walk west 3–4 blocks

Bx6 to Amsterdam Avenue and West 156th Street; Riverside Drive West and 158th Street

Bx19 to West 145th Street and Riverside Drive

Bx15 to West 125th Street and 12th Avenue; St Clair Place and West 125th Street

M79 to West 79th Street and Amsterdam Avenue, walk west 3 blocks

M104 makes regular stops along Broadway from 72nd Street to Martin Luther King Boulevard

6 RIVERBANK STATE PARK

Riverbank State Park is located between Riverside Drive and the Hudson River from 137th to 145th Streets; the entrance is at Riverside Drive and West 145th Street

Riverbank State Park is a busy place. There are indoor and outdoor pools; a covered skating rink; multiple gyms; a running track; soccer, football, and softball fields; tennis courts; grassy picnic spots; and a cultural facility offering classes of every kind. And yet, this spacious, 28-acre site in West Harlem didn't even exist some 20 years ago. The surface that the park occupies was created when the North River Wastewater Treatment Plant was built over the Hudson River and completed in 1978. While swimming, running, skating, or just standing still, visitors find it hard to believe that

Riverbank State Park is located on the roof of the North River Wastewater Treatment Plant. Here a sludge vessel, one of four operated by the New York City Department of Environmental Protection, Marine Section, is being filled with liquid sludge to be transported from the plant. The George Washington Bridge is visible in the background.

they are atop a treatment plant. Only the large ventilation pipes at the park's entrance serve as industrial reminders that there is something else going on beneath the surface.

The advantages of Riverbank State Park's location, wedged between the Hudson River and the West Side Highway, are manifold. First, because the park is west of the West Side Highway, there is no visual barrier between the park and the water. There's a spectacular view of the George Washington Bridge to the north and unobstructed views of the Palisades from the park's western edges. Second, because the highway runs below grade along the eastern edge of the park, automotive sounds from the road are muffled. And third, because the park is built out over the Hudson River and rests some 69 feet above it, breezes are strong and refreshing.

The park's distinct location creates some disadvantages too. Though public buses from the Bronx and Manhattan discharge visitors right at the entrance, the walk from the 1 train at 145th Street can take about 10 minutes. Drivers, who are required to get a permit at the park's entrance to

A damaging fire inside the plant in July 2011 left it inoperable for three days, and raw sewage had to be pumped into the Hudson River. In spite of the tremendous heat, the main structural steel girder, wrapped in concrete fireproofing, remained sound. The roof held and the park reopened several days later.

park in an outdoor area below the complex, must negotiate a convoluted set of roads and cross under the West Side Highway at West 138th Street to find the lot. And then there is the question of the smell. The treatment plant processes about 125 million gallons of wastewater on dry days, almost triple that when the weather is wet. Happily, the answer is that for the most part the park doesn't smell. The breezes help, of course, but sometimes, yes, there is an odor.

Opened in 1993, Riverbank State Park is one of the most heavily used parks in the state system, attracting over 2 million visitors a year in this densely populated part of town. The ice-skating rink morphs into a roller rink in the summer; the Olympic-size indoor pool holds 835 people in the pool and on the deck; the athletic complex seats 2,500; and the cultural arena accommodates 800. Packed with kids after school and people of all ages on weekends and throughout the summer, the facilities are well used. Beware, though, there are lots of state regulations: no bike riding, no dogs, no grilling.

Designed by Dattner Architects and Abel Bainnson Butz Landscape Architects, this platform is an early example of a green roof, and it's still the largest one in New York City. The wastewater facility itself sits on a reinforced concrete platform supported by 2,300 caissons pinned into bedrock, some to a depth of 230 feet beneath the river.

The park's design relies to a great degree on hard materials—concrete, brick, and metal—that can accommodate heavy use and require minimal maintenance. Don't look for this park to resemble Central Park, even as it serves as the neighborhood's central outdoor facility. There are no hills and dales, rock outcroppings, or wilderness areas. No running barefoot through the grass.

But given that the whole park is on a platform, its design is an impressive sleight of hand, allowing one to forget its rooftop status. There's even a series of garden plots for visitors who want to get their hands dirty. And elevated picnic areas receive welcome shade from medium-size trees.

The first thing visitors see when they enter the park is a huge, green, synthetic sports surface with a 400-meter, eight-lane running track around it. Its vast size, bright color, and openness make the park appear to stretch on and on, which in fact it does, extending from 145th Street south to 137th Street.

A running track on the roof of the North River Wastewater Treatment Plant encircles one of the park's playing fields. The ice skating rink, which serves as a roller rink in warmer weather, is the covered structure on the upper left.

A carousel in the northwest corner adds just the right degree of whimsy.

Riverbank State Park's design appears dated today, particularly in relation to the fashionable landscape of the far smaller West Harlem Piers Park (p. 92), directly south of it. There are no grasses planted in metallic planters or cutting-edge street furniture here. But that's not the point. This park isn't designed for strolling; it's for stretching, playing, and moving. It's an action-packed place. —R.L.

HOURS: General: 6 am–11 pm daily

Athletics Complex: Monday–Friday 6:30 am–10 pm

Carousel: summer weekends 1–6 pm

RESTROOMS: Located throughout the park, including at the playground and tennis courts

REGULATIONS: No pets allowed, no bike riding, no grilling

Smoking is prohibited

Free WiFi is available

MAP & FURTHER INFORMATION AVAILABLE AT:
nysparks.state.ny.us/parks/93/details.aspx

BY SUBWAY: 1 to 145th St, walk west 2 blocks

BY BUS: Bx19, M11 to Riverbank State Park

M4, M5 to Broadway and West 145th Street, walk west 2 blocks

7 WEST HARLEM PIERS PARK

West Harlem Piers Park is located along the Hudson River, west of Riverside Drive from St. Clair Place and West 135th Street to West 125th Street; the entrance is at West 125th Street

The small, 2-acre West Harlem Piers Park includes the first new public piers built on the Hudson River in over 40 years. It represents a major civic improvement in this uptown neighborhood, the Manhattanville section of Harlem, which had long had restricted access to its own waterfront. Dedicated in spring 2009, its opening was a victory for the more than 40 community groups that had worked with the city's Economic Development Corporation since 2001 to realize its creation.

The master plan, produced by W Architecture & Landscape Architecture, Barbara Wilks, principal, with Archipelago Architecture & Landscape Architecture, reconfigured the space, a portion of which had been used as a parking lot. They compensated for its relatively small size through inventive

A whole range of elevated structures is visible from the water: one of the piers, elevated above the Hudson River, in the foreground; the elevated section of the Henry Hudson Parkway, in the middle ground; and the giant steel arches of the elevated viaduct that connects the two sides of the Manhattanville Valley, in the background.

design; the pleasing geometry of the piers reflects a thoughtful meeting of land and water. The finger pier jutting straight out over the water offers walkers unimpeded views of the George Washington Bridge to the north and panoramic views of the Hudson River to the south. Two other piers— one straight, the other diagonal—intersect, forming a triangular crib that fills with river water. The sloshing noise beneath these promenades—the sound of water hitting the piers—is a pleasing reminder that one is offshore.

The other challenge was to provide access: the area is separated from the Harlem community by a giant viaduct that connects the 80-foot-high cliffs on the north and south sides of the Manhattanville valley. Train tracks laid out parallel to the Hudson River in the 19th century, though hidden today in their own tunnel, create a psychological barrier. A final barrier is the elevated Henry Hudson Parkway, which stands between the river and the railroad tracks. Is there any wonder that community access to the Hudson River was impeded, even though Harlem's major thoroughfare,

A solitary figure among the grasses in West Harlem Piers Park, view looking south. *Photo by Alison Cartwright*

125th Street, ends at the water's edge?

The West Harlem Master Plan and Waterfront Park study (2002) initially looked at a 40-block area, from Broadway to the Hudson River between 125th and 135th Streets, to assess how to reattach the community to the waterfront and create an economic development plan for the area. A solution was to narrow the roadway coming off the West Side highway so that pedestrians could access the park without having to traverse a wide exit ramp. It works; the transitional space is marked by pavers that set off the area and create a pleasing passageway.

West Harlem Piers Park represents the final phase of the Hudson River Greenway, a continuous bike route from Battery Park to Dyckman Street. The bike path here links Cherry Walk in Riverside Park to the south with Riverbank State Park to the north. And taking a cue from the design of Central Park, which pioneered the separation of vehicular functions, the bike path remains distinct from pedestrian areas.

Other park users also have their own dedicated areas. Close to the water's edge, the piers are equipped with cleaning tables for fisherman. Walkers have a variety of paths to choose from, both on the piers and on

The bike path along the eastern edge of West Harlem Piers Park completed the Hudson River Greenway, linking Battery Park to Dyckman Street in Upper Manhattan in one continuous, traffic-free ride.

shore. And there is a designated spot for kayakers to put their craft into the river.

Explanatory panels installed at intervals along the walkway, written by neighborhood historian Eric K. Washington, tell the story of the area's past, when ferries docked there to take passengers to Palisades Amusement Park in New Jersey and trolley cars stopped nearby to bring passengers to excursion boats.

Here's a tip for all the park's users—pedestrians, bikers, kayakers, and fisherman: stop at Fairway, the great food emporium located directly across from the piers at West 132nd Street and 12th Avenue, buy a sandwich, and then have a picnic on the park's granite benches, artfully situated among a carefully composed landscape of grasses and granite rocks. The grasses move with the slightest ripple of wind coming down the river and provide a visual and aural buffer from the traffic rushing past on the Henry Hudson Parkway. The granite has been recycled from the historic bulkheads that were once located here.

Other fun design features include good-looking boulders, seemingly a requisite feature in all new waterfront parks, strewn about to convey a sense of age and permanence. Likewise the granite cobblestones, part of the paving material, show a regard for recycling materials that speak to New York's history.

There's also a lovely contrast in color between the silvery railing of the walkways, the granite slabs, and the grasses. Enhancing the composition are the triangular steel planters that hold the grasses, a sloped lawn, and nautical-themed metal sculpture by artist Nari Ward, installed as part of the City of New York Department of Cultural Affairs Percent for Art Program, which requires that 1 percent of the capital costs of publicly funded projects be spent on art.

There is still an element of suspense related to the West Harlem Piers Park that doesn't affect it directly but that involves the fate of its near neighbor to the north, the decommissioned New York City Department of Sanitation Marine Transfer Station at 135th Street. This unused structure was once the repository of voluminous amounts of garbage that was unloaded there before being sent to landfills. The regeneration of the Marine Transfer Station, now in its earliest stages, is part of a design competition, The Harlem Edge/Cultivating Connections, sponsored by the Emerging New York Architects Committee of the AIA. The ideas generated by that competition may someday further beautify the shoreline.

Just north of the transfer station is Riverbank State Park, built on the giant roof of a waste treatment plant (p. 88). Both the transfer station and the waste treatment plant are reminders of an earlier era when West Harlem was more a dumping ground than an area lauded for park design. The award-winning West Harlem Piers Park represents a new era, one in which the city is distributing environmental functions, some less desirable, among many neighborhoods and shorelines. —R.L.

RESTROOMS: Riverside Park at the 138th Street Tennis Courts

Claremont Dolphin Playground near Tiemann Place

REGULATIONS: Smoking is prohibited

For more info: www.nycgovparks.org/parks/M376/

BY SUBWAY: 1 to 125th Street and Broadway, walk northwest 3 blocks on West 125th Street, cross under the Henry Hudson Parkway (HHP) to reach the park

BY BUS: M4 to West 131st Street and Broadway, walk west 2 blocks, cross under the HHP

M5 to Riverside Drive and Tiemann Place, walk north 2 blocks on Riverside Drive to West 125th Street, turn left, walk northwest 1 block, and cross under the HHP

Bx15 to West 125th Street and 12th Avenue, walk northwest 1 block on 125th Street, and cross under the HHP

BROOKLYN

BROOKLYN BRIDGE PARK 8

Brooklyn Bridge Park stretches along the water's edge for more than a mile, from
its John Street site, just north of the Manhattan Bridge, to its Pier 6 sites at Atlantic
Avenue, the main southern entrance to the park. Currently, Piers 1 and 6, Fulton
Ferry Landing, Main Street, and Empire-Fulton Ferry are open, but many more piers,
as well as upland areas, are under construction. Check the Web site for up-to-date
information.

Brooklyn's East River waterfront, from Greenpoint south to Bay Ridge,
was once one of the most active port and industrial complexes on
earth. In the section between the Manhattan Bridge and the blocks
just south of the Brooklyn Bridge, in the neighborhoods now known as
DUMBO (Down Under the Manhattan Bridge Overpass) and Fulton Ferry,
stood the factories and warehouses—some 19th-century timber-frame

The city is part of the action: visitors hear the sound of water lapping the shoreline
and the buzzing of cars and rumbling of trains crossing the Manhattan Bridge.

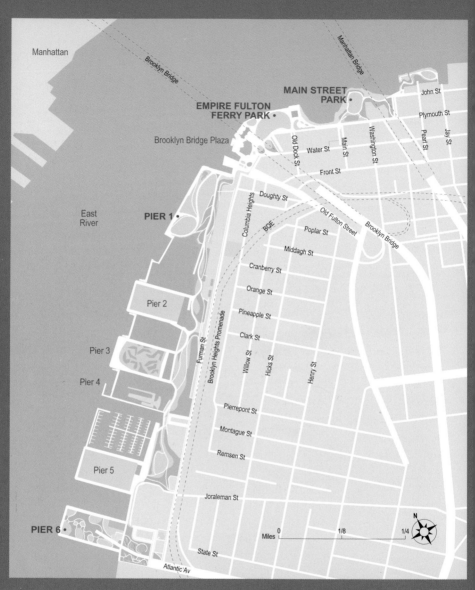

Manhattan

Brooklyn Bridge

Manhattan Bridge

MAIN STREET PARK •

EMPIRE FULTON FERRY PARK •

Brooklyn Bridge Plaza

John St

Plymouth St

Pearl St

Jay St

Washington St

Main St

Water St

Old Dock St

Front St

East River

PIER 1 •

Columbia Heights

Doughty St

BQE

Old Fulton Street

Brooklyn Bridge

Poplar St

Middagh St

Cranberry St

Orange St

Pier 2

Pineapple St

Furman St

Clark St

Brooklyn Heights Promenade

Willow St

Hicks St

Henry St

Pier 3

Pier 4

Pierrepont St

Montague St

Remsen St

Pier 5

Joraleman St

PIER 6 •

Miles 0   1/8   1/4

N

State St

Atlantic Av

BROOKLYN BRIDGE PARK

Map by John Hill,
Courtesy of Michael Van
Valkenburgh Associates

structures, others pioneering early-20th-century examples of reinforced-concrete construction—of such industrial concerns as Gair Manufacturing (the world's largest maker of cardboard boxes), Bliss Machine Works, and Squibb Pharmaceuticals. Here, too, once upon a time, at the foot of Fulton Street, was the terminal of the Fulton Ferry, the original steam ferry service connecting Manhattan and Brooklyn 69 years before the Brooklyn Bridge opened. Today, the site of the ferry terminal is Fulton Ferry Landing Pier, designed by Mathews Nielsen and completed in 1995. The 20,000-square-foot pier nestles between two old barges. The barge to the south now houses Bargemusic, a nationally renowned chamber music venue. The one to the north is home to the famous River Café. Both Bargemusic and the River Café opened in 1977, which was also the year the New York City Landmarks Preservation Commission designated a small Fulton Ferry Historic District to preserve the historic buildings along Old Fulton Street—the bit severed from the rest of Fulton Street in the 1950s by the vast Cadman Plaza urban renewal project—and Water Street. The wood-decked pier has metal railings inset with lines from Walt Whitman's "Crossing Brooklyn Ferry." (The fence is similar to the one with quotes from Whitman and Frank O'Hara that Siah Armajani created for World Financial Center Plaza, p. 44, in 1989.) Bronze plaques feature images and maps relating the history of the site. Not only did Walt Whitman come here to catch the ferry, but from this location George Washington miraculously ferried his troops across the East River to Manhattan under cover of fog on the night of August 29, 1776, to evade capture by the British in the Battle of Brooklyn. George Washington and Walt Whitman: the American history conjured by that pairing of names makes this spot on the Brooklyn shore one of the most hallowed sites in New York. Mathews Nielsen Landscape Architects wisely took the approach of utmost simplicity in their pier design. The openness to the prospect before you—of river and harbor and a Manhattan skyline that from here, more than from any other point along this shore, you feel you can reach out and touch—is magic, the feeling of holding the world in the palm of your hand. At the eastern end of the pier is an old marine fireboat station that now houses the justly renowned Brooklyn Ice Cream Factory. The pier also serves as a stop on the New York Water Taxi. Oh, and that's the Brooklyn Bridge looming directly overhead. American history indeed.

To the north of the pier runs Water Street, lined with 19th-century warehouses on its river side between Dock and Main Streets. The Tobacco Inspection Warehouse, or Fulton Stores (ca. 1860), originally stood five stories high and served as the grading station for western and southern tobacco barged in from the railroad termini on the New Jersey shore. A few years ago (and some years after its top three stories were removed), the warehouse's roof collapsed. Today it's a ruin: four brick walls open to the sky. Some have proposed reroofing it and turning it into a performance venue, but at this writing it appears that the warehouse will remain an ornamental ruin, a folly, within its new context of Brooklyn Bridge Park (see below). Next to it are the broodingly majestic warehouses known as the Empire Stores. The four-story group to the west went up in 1870, the five-story group to the east in 1885. Waterfront warehouses such as these once gave Brooklyn its sobriquet, "walled city." The Empire Stores lent their name to Empire-Fulton Ferry State Park. "State park" conjures images of Adirondack wilderness, not of urban warehouses. Yet in 1978 the patch of waterfront land on the north side of the Empire Stores became a state park, the result of a concerted effort by community groups and civic organizations to prevent the city from relocating the ancient Fort Greene Meat Market to this spot. It is another stark example of the desolate, postindustrial waterfronts of New York being so undervalued that the city regarded them as suitable out-of-the-way locations for noisome uses. (The wholesale meat market ended up on the waterfront in Sunset Park, where local residents lacked the resources to prevent its relocation.)

Thus, up until a few years ago the only access to this magnificent waterfront was at Fulton Ferry Landing Pier and Empire-Fulton Ferry State Park. To the east, at Main Street, another old ferry terminal had been converted into a parking lot. Beyond that was Washington Street, which terminated at the riverfront under the majestic (if rather noisy, because of the trains rattling back and forth on it) Manhattan Bridge. In 2003 a delightful small park opened at the foot of Main Street. Here granite boulders cascade down to the water. Granite steps and a bluestone-paved plaza provide space for waterfront strolling and sitting. Native grasses sway in the river breezes. A winsome, nautically themed playground proved a godsend to the many young families moving into the adjacent DUMBO neighborhood. The small, inviting park bore a sign: Brooklyn Bridge Park. This was the first section of an eagerly anticipated new park that would stretch from the Manhattan Bridge south all the way to Atlantic Avenue.

For years those words resounded in the press and contentious neighborhood meetings and official hearings. Hailed as the city's most significant park project since the 19th century, Brooklyn Bridge Park promised the transformation of the postindustrial waterfront into a 21st-century pleasure ground. In New York, however, nothing is easy.

From the beginning, controversy engulfed Brooklyn Bridge Park. Most of the contending parties were in favor of it, though some Brooklyn Heights residents were not, fearing the influx into their neighborhood of too many outsiders. The issues involved what kind of park it

Swimmers entered the East River from the "Cove Between the Bridges" for the Brooklyn-to-Manhattan swim on September 11, 2010, sponsored by NYC Swim. *Courtesy of Giacomo Curradi*

would be. Some wanted only the simplest of greenswards for passive recreation—something akin to the simple but charming Empire-Fulton Ferry State Park. Others championed active uses—a swimming pool, a skating rink. Some saw this as an opportunity for a major design statement—as Prospect Park once was. And then came the questions of funding. Could a cash-strapped city bear the full cost of building and maintaining such a park? (Protecting piers built on piles from marine borers is very expensive.) The city required Brooklyn Bridge Park to be self-sustaining. Revenues from concessions would help. So, too, would assessments on private housing developments built along the park's rim—and that "privatization" of park space set off a firestorm of controversy. The venerable Brooklyn Heights Association backed the private housing solution. The Project for Public Spaces and the Cobble Hill Association, however, objected both to the housing component and to what they said was a too-elaborate and insufficiently people-centric design. At this writing, it appears that the city plans to use a dedicated property-tax stream from previously tax-exempt former Jehovah's Witnesses properties in the adjacent neighborhood to fund the park and obviate the need for part, if not all, of the housing component in the park itself.

The design comes from Michael Van Valkenburgh Associates (MVVA), the firm responsible for Teardrop Park, in Battery Park City (p. 33), and the Chelsea Cove section of Hudson River Park (p. 67). But neither of those projects quite compares in scale or impact to Brooklyn Bridge Park. Van Valkenburgh is one of the biggest names in contemporary landscape architecture. Born in 1951, he received a B.S. in landscape architecture from Cornell University. (Gilmore David Clarke and Michael Rapuano, who designed the Brooklyn Heights Promenade, see below, were also Cornell graduates.) Van Valkenburgh received an M.L.A. from the University of Illinois, and has taught at Harvard since 1982. From 1991 to 1996, he chaired Harvard's Graduate School of Design. Today he is Charles Eliot Professor in Practice of Landscape Architecture. (The first to hold that professorship was Frederick Law Olmsted, Jr., planner of Forest Hills Gardens.) Matthew Urbanski, MVVA principal and lead designer on Brooklyn Bridge Park, had a horticultural background before he attended Harvard's Graduate School of Design. Also the lead designer on Teardrop Park and Chelsea Cove, Urbanski co-owns a New Jersey nursery that cultivates hard-to-find plant species. MVVA maintains offices in Cambridge, Massachusetts, and Brooklyn. It came on as a consultant to Brooklyn Bridge Park in 1998 and received the design commission in 2004. Both Van Valkenburgh and Urbanski are proponents of Landscape Urbanism, as even a cursory glance at Brooklyn Bridge Park, with its wild grasses, restored wetlands, and derelict pilings, attests.

Planners project the completed park will comprise 85 acres and extend 1.3 miles (at the shoreline), with an upkeep cost of $16 million a year. (Central Park, ten times the size, costs about $37 million a year.)

Empire-Fulton Ferry State Park became part of Brooklyn Bridge Park in 2011. Here one finds Jane's Carousel, built in 1922 by the Philadelphia Toboggan Company and purchased in 1984 by Jane and David Walentas. David Walentas is the person principally responsible for the transformation of surrounding DUMBO from a gritty industrial neighborhood into a very chic (and very expensive) residential neighborhood. The carousel operates inside a sleek steel-and-glass pavilion designed by the celebrated French architect Jean Nouvel. (In 1999, Walentas proposed a plan to develop both sides of the Manhattan Bridge with a hotel, stores, and a multiplex cinema, all designed by Jean Nouvel. It didn't happen.)

To the south of Fulton Ferry Landing Pier lies a series of piers. Use of Piers 1 through 6 (at Atlantic Avenue) for cargo shipping ceased in 1983, and they are now part of Brooklyn Bridge Park. Pier 1 is the largest of the park piers, at 9.5 acres (about the size of Washington Square). It opened as part of the park in 2010. It is the only park pier built on landfill, rather than piles, and thus can withstand the greatest weight. A hill occupies the center of the pier; flanking it are two ovoid lawns. On the water edge of the southern lawn (Harbor View Lawn), we find the Granite Prospect, a series of steps affording stunning views of the river and the Manhattan skyline. To the south of Harbor View Lawn is a salt marsh, one of several wetland features incorporated into the park. This beautiful arrangement of murky water, marsh grasses, granite boulders, and old pilings ranks as one of the most pleasing elements in the whole park design. There is also a kayak launch. A bridge connects Squibb Park, on Columbia Heights and Middagh Street, to Pier 1.

Pier 2 fronts the northern edge of the Brooklyn Heights Promenade. The Promenade opened in 1950–51 Bowing to community concerns (not something he usually did), Robert Moses built most of the Brooklyn Heights portion of his Brooklyn–Queens Expressway near the water's edge (and not, as originally planned, along Hicks Street), and designed it as a "triple cantilever": the southbound roadway, the northbound roadway, and a pedestrian promenade are cantilevered, one atop the other, off the high bluff that rises behind the old piers. The Promenade, designed by Gilmore D. Clarke

Children enjoying the water features in the 1.6-acre park at Pier 6 at the foot of Atlantic Avenue.

and Michael Rapuano, is a masterpiece of its kind. Graceful, bench-lined, with the backyards of the fine houses of Columbia Heights forming a backdrop, the Promenade does not get you anywhere near the water, but it does offer unobstructed views of river and harbor and Manhattan and the Brooklyn Bridge (and even, on a clear day, the Verrazano-Narrows Bridge). It also offers the thrill of height, of being suspended on high. From the park below, it is equally thrilling to turn your back to the water and gaze up at the triple cantilever in all its infrastructural dazzle. There is no direct access from the Promenade to the park, and that is doubtless how many Heights residents want it. Recreational uses dominate Pier 2: basketball, handball, bocce, and in-line skating.

The Brooklyn–Queens Expressway is extremely noisy, and to mitigate the noise, MVVA proposed a large earthen berm. Critics charged that the berm would unnecessarily usurp potentially usable park space and called for the long-overdue reconstruction of the triple cantilever to incorporate noise-reduction features (possibly including full enclosure of the expressway).

Piers 3 and 4 are not, at this writing, open. In the spring of 2012, philanthropist and bicycling enthusiast Joshua P. Rechnitz donated an astonishing $40 million to Brooklyn Bridge Park for the construction of an enormous 115,000-square-foot field house on Pier 5. To put it in perspective, Rechnitz's gift ranks as the largest—by far—ever given to a park in New York City (Barry Diller and Diane von Furstenberg gave half that amount to the High Line). The proposed structure will include facilities for basketball, tennis, volleyball, and gymnastics, but its principal feature will be a velodrome for track cycling. Though a large, state-of-the-art, centrally located velodrome fulfills one of the fondest dreams of New York's avid but small track-cycling community, opponents object to its proposed size and feel that it is too specialized a use for such a significant chunk of public land.

Just beyond Pier 5, at the foot of Joralemon Street, stands a massive warehouse built in 1928 by the New York Dock Company, which once owned property all up and down the Brooklyn waterfront. Designed by Russell G. Cory, the 14-story building later became a distribution warehouse for Jehovah's Witnesses publications. It is now a luxury condominium complex called One Brooklyn Bridge Park, with 449 units—part of the park's private housing component.

Pier 6, which one may enter from Atlantic Avenue under the Brooklyn–Queens Expressway viaduct, features active recreation in the form of three sand volleyball courts, as well as a children's playground. There is also an outdoor food court, a dog run, and a dock for the ferry to Governors Island

(p. 145). Future plans include two 15,000-square-foot lawns planted with native plants and trees.

Brooklyn Bridge Park is not complete. Like Central Park, Hudson River Park, and the High Line, however, the design allows each section to open as soon as it is finished. By now, enough of the park has been completed to make clear that it is, indeed, one of the most ambitious park projects ever undertaken in New York City. Its detractors may never warm to it. But that it utterly transforms a recently derelict waterfront, that it shows the city can still take on lofty projects, and that it is, with the High Line, one of the two most visible examples of Landscape Urbanism in America, is undeniable. —F.M.

HOURS: 6 am–1 am daily

RESTROOMS: The base of Pier 6; Furman & Doughty Streets on Pier 1

REGULATIONS: Smoking is prohibited

MAP & FURTHER INFORMATION AVAILABLE AT: www.brooklynbridgepark.org or www.brooklynbridgeparknyc.org

PIER 1, FURMAN STREET AND OLD FULTON STREET:

BY SUBWAY: A, C to High Street and Brooklyn Bridge, take Cadman Plaza West exit, walk north 2 blocks on Cadman Plaza West, continue north on Old Fulton Street for about 5 blocks

2, 3 to Clark Street and Henry Street, walk north 5½ blocks on Henry Street, turn left, and walk west 4 blocks on Old Fulton Street

F to York Street and Jay Street, walk west 4 blocks on York Street, turn left on Front Street, walk under the Brooklyn Bridge to Old Fulton Street, turn right, and walk approximately 3 blocks to Pier 1 entrance

BY BUS: B25 to Fulton Ferry Landing

BY WATER TAXI: Shuttle service available seasonal weekends from Pier 6 and South Street Seaport

PIER 6, ATLANTIC AVENUE AND FURMAN STREET:

BY SUBWAY: 2, 3, 4, 5, N, R to Borough Hall and Court Street, walk south 4 blocks on Court Street, turn right on on Atlantic Avenue, and walk west 5 blocks

A, C, F, R to Jay Street-Metro Tech and Fulton Mall, walk west 1 block on Fulton Street, turn left on Boerum Place, walk south 4 blocks, turn right on Atlantic Avenue, and walk west 6 blocks

BY BUS: B63 to Atlantic Avenue and Columbia Street, walk west 1 block on Atlantic Avenue

FULTON FERRY LANDING, OLD FULTON STREET AND WATER STREET:

BY SUBWAY: A, C to High Street and Brooklyn Bridge, take the Cadman Plaza West exit, walk north 2 blocks on Cadman Plaza West, walk northwest 5 blocks on Old Fulton Street (toward the river)

BY BUS: B25 to Fulton Ferry Landing

MAIN STREET AND PLYMOUTH STREET:

BY SUBWAY: A, C to High Street and Brooklyn Bridge, walk north 6 blocks on Washington Street, turn left on Plymouth Street, and walk west 1 block

F to York Street and Jay Street, walk north 3 blocks on Bridge Street, turn left on Plymouth Street, and walk west 4 blocks (under the Manhattan Bridge)

BY BUS: B25 to Fulton Ferry Landing, walk east 3 blocks on Water Street, walk north 1 block on Main Street to Water Street (weekdays), same walking directions as above

BY WATER TAXI: East River Commuter to Fulton Ferry Landing (seasonal)

9 WILLIAMSBURG WATERFRONT

East River State Park is located at 90 Kent Avenue and North 7th Street in Williamsburg, Brooklyn

Grand Ferry Park is located at Grand Street and River Street in Williamsburg, Brooklyn

Bushwick Inlet Park is located just north of, and adjacent to, East River State Park

What does Brooklyn's industrial waterfront have in common with El Camino Real de Tierra Adentro National Historic Trail in New Mexico or Hialeah Park Race Course in Florida? All three appear on the National Trust for Historic Preservation's 2007 list of the eleven most endangered historic sites in America. "Brooklyn's industrial waterfront," a once-mighty concentration of factories, warehouses, railways, and piers, ranges south from Greenpoint to Sunset Park. Following a 2005 rezoning, Greenpoint and Williamsburg represent a particularly endangered swath of historic waterfront.

Though the economic downturn slowed redevelopment, expect to witness the further transition of this waterfront from a gritty industrial environment to phalanxes of shiny residential towers with riverfront esplanades and the occasional park. The L train penetrates to the heart of Northside, epicenter of Williamsburg's dramatic, and rapidly outward-spreading, gentrification. A short walk from the Bedford Avenue station along North 7th Street takes you to the waterfront, at Kent Avenue, where you'll find, on the left, the new luxury developments called Northside Piers and The Edge, and, on the right, East River State Park, which opened in 2007.

"State park" conjures visions of pristine mountain trails. In Williamsburg we have something different: seven acres of mostly lawn, with a kind of beach, allowing users to go right up to the water. In addition, the park preserves remnants of the site's past industrial use. It formerly was part of the Eastern District Terminal, a node in the Rube

Looking north from East River State Park. Its shoreline
allows users to go right up to the water.

Goldberg-esque network of dock and railway facilities that once dominated the Brooklyn and Manhattan waterfronts. Begun in the 1870s, the
terminal received the Eastern District name (once a commonly used
moniker referring to Williamsburg, Greenpoint, and Bushwick) in 1906.
Barges and carfloats came from New Jersey, Staten Island, and the Bronx.
Major docks operated between North 4th and North 10th Streets. The
park occupies the waterfront from North 7th to North 9th Street. To
the south, Northside Piers and The Edge occupy old carfloat docks
where the Eastern District Terminal facilitated the transfer of cargo
from the barges to several major national and regional freight railroads.
Waterfront trains carried supplies, raw materials, and manufactured
goods to such vast industrial facilities as the Domino Sugar refinery and
the Austin, Nichols food warehouse. Declining industry and the port's
reconfiguration following the postwar introduction of container shipping
caused the terminal to close by 1983. In industrial days, the public had
scant access to Williamsburg's busy waterfront. That began to change in
1998 with the opening of Grand Ferry Park on the site of a former ferry
landing at the foot of Grand Street, seven blocks to the south of East
River State Park.

Though it is only 1.5 acres, Grand Ferry Park helped pioneer the new
waterfront park aesthetic in New York. Here we find, years before Gantry
Plaza State Park (p. 119) or Brooklyn Bridge Park (p. 97), such elements
as preserved industrial archaeology (a smokestack from a former Pfizer

Just to the north of East River State Park is a surprisingly beautiful soccer field in the small portion of Bushwick Inlet Park that has been completed.

pharmaceutical plant), the use of riprap (boulders along the shoreline that protect against erosion and provide places for park users to sit in intimate proximity to the water), and native plantings. To the immediate south of Grand Ferry Park stands the vast Domino Sugar refinery complex, which closed in 2003, making 2004 the first year in 275 years in which a sugar refinery did not operate within the present five boroughs of New York City. Some of the refinery buildings won designated landmark status. But developers plan to replace others with high-rise housing that threatens to cast Grand Ferry Park in shadow.

Just north of East River State Park is the newest public space on the Williamsburg waterfront, Bushwick Inlet Park. New York City promised this park—an ambitious project, planned to extend from North 9th Street for several blocks to Quay Street, encompassing Bushwick Inlet (the onetime site of Charles Pratt's Astral Oil Works)—to the people of Williamsburg in exchange for the rezoning that cleared the way for construction of luxury high-rise apartments along the waterfront. However, only a small portion of the park, from North 9th to North 10th Streets, has been completed to date. The rest has fallen victim to the city's massive budget shortfalls in the wake of the economic downturn. It will presumably be built, but when is anyone's guess. The park consists thus far of an athletic field, but if it is ever completed, it will feature much in the way of active recreation, as well as facilities like a dog run and a bike path that are not permitted in state parks such as East River State Park next door.

Needless to say, the views from these parks are peerless: to the south, the Williamsburg Bridge, spanning the East River like a giant steel lizard; across the water, Manhattan—if that's your sort of thing. —F.M.

East River State Park

HOURS: 9 am–dusk (subject to change)

RESTROOMS: There are no bathrooms at this park

REGULATIONS: Pets are not allowed

Permits are required for picnics

Smoking is prohibited

MAP & FURTHER INFORMATION AVAILABLE AT:
nysparks.state.ny.us/parks/155/details.aspx

BY SUBWAY: L to Bedford Avenue and North 7th Street, walk northwest 4 blocks (toward the river) on North 7th Street, and northeast 1 block on Kent Avenue

G to Metropolitan Avenue, walk north 2 blocks on Union Avenue, turn left, walk under the Brookllyn-Queens Expressway (BQE) and cross Meeker Avenue to North 8th Street, walk northwest 7 blocks (toward the river)

BY BUS: B62 to Bedford Avenue and North 9th Street, walk northwest 4 blocks on North 9th Street

B24 to Metropolitan Ave and Macri Square, walk north 2 blocks on Union Avenue, turn left, walk under the BQE and cross Meeker Ave to North 8th Street, walk northwest 7 blocks

Q59 to Metropolitan Ave and North 5th Street, walk northwest 6 blocks on North 5th Street, turn right on Kent Avenue, walk north 3 blocks to North 8th Street

GRAND FERRY PARK:
HOURS: 6 am–1 am

RESTROOMS: There are no restrooms at this park

REGULATIONS: Smoking is prohibited

MAP & FURTHER INFORMATION AVAILABLE AT: www.nycgovparks.org/parks/B401/

BY SUBWAY: L to Bedford Avenue and North 7th Street, walk southwest 6 blocks on Bedford Avenue to Grand Street, and west 3 blocks on Grand Street

G to Metropolitan Avenue, walk west 9 blocks on Metropolitan Avenue, turn left on Kent Avenue, walk 2 blocks, turn right on Grand Street

J, M, Z to Marcy Avenue and Broadway, walk north 6 blocks on Marcy Avenue, turn left on Grand Street, and walk northwest 8 blocks (toward the river)

BY BUS: Q59 to Kent Avenue and South 1st Street, walk north 1 block on Kent Avenue, turn left on Grand Street

B62 to Bedford Ave and Grand Street, walk northwest 4 blocks on Grand Street

ABOVE AND FACING PAGE Erie Basin Park has a nearly one-mile-long waterfront esplanade. The Swedish company IKEA erected a giant store in the Red Hook neighborhood and was allowed to fill in a 700-foot-long dry dock—a place for ship repair—for its parking lot. The park itself, built and paid for by IKEA, was designed by landscape architect Lee Weintraub, who incorporated elements of the area's nautical past, such as its four giant gantries, in addition to new elements, such as the park's furniture.

10 ERIE BASIN PARK

The park is located between Columbia and Otsego Streets, behind IKEA at 1 Beard Street, Red Hook, Brooklyn

The decision by the Swedish home-furnishings giant IKEA to build its first New York City store on the site of the old Todd Shipyards in Red Hook, Brooklyn, upset a great many people. Todd had played a major role in the maritime history of New York. For many, the vanishing reminders of that history cast a pall on a number of the city's waterfront redevelopment schemes. At Todd, in particular, we lost one of the most historic dry docks for ship repair in the country. The 19th-century dry dock was 700 feet long, and was used as recently as 2005. Some critics, such as James Howard Kunstler, contend that in the coming age of "peak oil" and diminish-

ing resources generally, we might well find we were foolish to dismantle so much of our marine infrastructure, which we might need again one day. Then there was the big-box IKEA store itself, 346,000 square feet, in the company's trademark blue and yellow, hardly the sort of waterfront landmark worth losing a historic graving (dry) dock for. The store opened in 2008.

All along, IKEA promised that in addition to the new store, Red Hook would receive a finer waterfront park than it had ever had before. No New York neighborhood enjoys a more intimate relationship with the harbor than Red Hook. Back in the halcyon days of New York shipping, Red Hook's Atlantic Basin and Erie Basin ranked among the largest and busiest dock and warehouse complexes in the world. This was a congested and bustling neighborhood of tough longshoremen and stevedores (and, as the movie *On the Waterfront*, which was based on newspaper articles about Red Hook, attests, gangsters), where the waterfront meant work, not play. When the postwar container revolution devastated Brooklyn shipping, once densely populated Red Hook rapidly became a ghost town. But the tide began to turn in the 1990s. With its unique charms—the harbor views, quaint, narrow streets, intriguing old housing stock, even the air of isolation (no subway penetrates into the neighborhood)—Red Hook became red hot. Still, its glorious waterfront afforded as little access as formerly industrial waterfronts elsewhere in New York. And, as elsewhere in New York, that is no longer the case.

IKEA followed through on its promise. The park surrounding the big box, designed by the estimable Lee Weintraub, won plaudits even from some of IKEA's harshest critics. In the manner of many contemporary landscape designers, Weintraub decided to make the park about the history of its site—the very history that IKEA displaced. He made extensive use of materials that had belonged to Todd Shipyards, including four gantry cranes—which sometimes seem as common as riprap and wild grasses in many of the city's new waterfront landscapes. In addition, Weintraub incorporated old bollards, old tools (wrenches, winches, hoists, vises, chains), and even heaps of old rope that he found on the shipyard site. The site of the graving dock is now the IKEA parking lot. Weintraub outlined the dry dock in stone paving. And concrete blocks throughout the site bear the names of ships repaired at the Todd Shipyards. Thus, Weintraub's design serves as a memorial to the Brooklyn industrial waterfront. The gantry cranes here, more than at Gantry Plaza State Park (on which Weintraub worked with Thomas Balsley, see p. 119), stand starkly against the sky, transforming those most muscular machines of the old working waterfront into monumental sculpture. The renowned firm of Fisher Marantz Stone designed the nighttime lighting of the cranes. Lots of trees, native plantings, and Balsley-like chaises longues round out the major design elements. Erie Basin Park is only seven acres, but it seems much larger because it is spread along the waterfront and wraps around IKEA and its parking lot. Its extent, remarkably, is about a mile. It rates in all ways as a major waterfront amenity, and may take its place on the roll of honor with Brooklyn Bridge Park, Gantry Plaza State Park, Hudson River Park, and the others.

The park lies on the site of the old Erie Basin. Completed in 1864 by the developer William Beard, it was the largest dock and warehouse complex on the East Coast. Its name derives from the Erie Canal: Erie Basin handled goods shipped from the Midwest via the Erie Canal, including grain sent out from Red Hook to points around the world, as well as grain destined for the many breweries for which Brooklyn was once famous. Many old grain silos still stand around here. The marine function of Erie Basin continues in the form of the Erie Basin Bargeport, visible from the park, "the largest private commercial marine berthing facility in the Northeast," with more than "4,000 linear feet of modern bulkhead for wharfing of tugs, barges, and other vessels."

While in the neighborhood, be sure to take a look at Red Hook Park, just across Columbia Street from the IKEA site. This is a classic, 58-acre, Robert Moses–era recreational park laid out in the 1930s by Gilmore D. Clarke and meant to serve the active recreation needs of a mostly poor neighborhood. It is home to the Sol Goldman Pool, designed by Aymar Embury II (1880–1966). Now a designated landmark, the pool is one of the many improbably large and elaborate municipal swimming pools that Robert Moses built in the city in the mid-1930s. Today, the area of Red Hook to the west of Red Hook Park is wealthier than it has ever been. To the north of the park stand the vast Red Hook Houses, a 27-building public housing project completed in 1939. On weekends from late spring to early fall, Latin American food vendors congregate at Red Hook Park, offering some of the best "street eats" and authentic Latin cuisine in New York. They are a legend among New York foodies.

The visitor should also go to Valentino Pier, off Coffey Street, just north of Ferris Street. The old Pier 39 was rebuilt for passive recreation and fishing in 1997 by di Domenico & Partners, the firm of John di Domenico, one-time partner of Lee Weintraub. As Weintraub & di Domenico, they designed the delightful Washington Market Park on Chambers Street (p. 71). The gardens at Valentino Pier are by Lynden B. Miller. Standing out on the end of the pier, you feel as though you are right in the bay. —F.M.

HOURS: Dawn–Dusk

RESTROOMS: Inside IKEA

REGULATIONS: Smoking is prohibited

MAP & FURTHER INFORMATION AVAILABLE AT:

www.ikea.com/us/en/store/brooklyn/activities or

info.ikea-usa.com/Brooklyn/pdf/IKEABklynWaterTaxiSept2011.pdf

BY SUBWAY: 2, 3, 4, 5, N, R to Court St-Borough Hall, take free shuttle bus to IKEA

F, G to Smith and 9th Street

F, D, G, N, R to 4th Avenue and 9th Street, take free shuttle bus

Shuttle buses run weekdays every half hour, 3 pm–9 pm, weekends every 20 minutes, 11 am–9 pm

BY BUS: Free shuttle buses run from Court St-Borough Hall, Smith and 9th Street, 4th Avenue and 9th Street

B61 to Beard Street and Ostego Street

BY WATER TAXI: From Pier 11, East River

Weekdays every 20 minutes, 12 pm–9 pm, $5

Weekends every 40 minutes, 11:20 am–9 pm, free

11 NEWTOWN CREEK NATURE WALK

The entrance to the Newtown Creek Nature Walk is located at the eastern end of Paidge Avenue in Greenpoint, Brooklyn

The Newtown Creek Nature Walk in Greenpoint, Brooklyn, is located at the least likely spot in all of New York City to find a successful open space: beside Newtown Creek, once a busy industrial waterway where factories spewed waste. In 2010 the U.S. Environmental Protection Agency designated the area as a Superfund site and committed agency resources from its Federal Superfund Program to clean up this contaminated area. The nature walk is on the grounds of the Newtown Creek Wastewater Treatment Plant, a giant facility that transforms New York's sewage into vast amounts of sludge, methane gas, and other byproducts.

The Wastewater Treatment Plant, one of 14 in the city, underwent a $3 billion upgrade in the late 1980s to deal with the more than 1.3 billion gallons of wastewater generated by New Yorkers on a daily basis. Clearly visible from the nature walk are eight large, futuristic, egg-shaped stainless-steel-clad digesters designed by Polshek Partnership (now known as Ennead Architects). These forms, in which the raw material is treated, are the most easily recognizable features in the area; the ethereal blue lights illuminating the eggs at night were designed by artist Hervé Descottes of L'Observatoire International, an American/French company. The digesters are equally impressive by day because of their shape, size, and shiny surface finish.

And the nature walk? It was developed under the New York City Department of Cultural Affairs Percent for Art Program mandating that 1 percent of the first $20 million of a city-funded construction project be spent on art, and at least one half of 1 percent on amounts over $20 million. That's a considerable sum when a facility of this magnitude is upgraded. So the question is: What sort of work of art would be right for an outsized industrial site that is literally on the urban edge?

Enter George Trakas, an artist who has navigated the waterways of New York for over 45 years in his own vessels, and was more than familiar with the waters of Newtown Creek, the 4-mile-long fouled waterway separating western Queens from northern Brooklyn. Trakas, an environmental sculptor, saw potential.

Initially the plan called for open space—a waterside park—to serve the city workers employed there. The plan was expanded, with support from

The surprise is that no barriers prevent visitors from approaching Newtown Creek on the giant steps. Jack Eichenbaum, Queens Borough historian and urban geographer, leads a Municipal Art Society tour to the water's edge in fall 2010.

the local community, to make the site accessible to anyone interested in the intersection of art, industry, and nature. (Trakas attended monthly community meetings for 10 years). The Polshek firm asked Trakas to create a distinctive vocabulary that would be in keeping with its own unusual design work. Now visitors from throughout the city, in addition to community residents, come to experience this one-of-a-kind nature walk and urban artwork, opened in 2007 as part of a working plant run by the city's Department of Environmental Protection.

Greenpoint, Brooklyn, is a working-class community that has seen gentrification in recent years. But this facility is in the industrial precincts of Greenpoint, not the gentrified areas. It is about a half-hour walk from the subway to the northwestern corner of the wastewater property, at the east end of Paidge Avenue. One enters through an inconspicuously located gate (locked at night), over what looks like a gangplank, and then down a narrow, open-air, concrete-lined corridor known as the "vessel." The bowed shape

Urban canoeing, with the Manhattan skyline, across the East River, as the backdrop.

of the concrete walls is reminiscent of a ship's keel; the round openings resembling portholes that pierce the concrete walls complete the nautical imagery. "Is this a nature walk?" one inquires. "Keep going," others say, "it turns into one."

And sure enough, by following the concrete walkway, turning left, and continuing down another corridor, one encounters, a mere 740 feet from the entrance gate, the softly flowing Newtown Creek. Surprisingly, nothing separates the visitor from the water's edge. Stone steps lead directly down into the water like the ghats in Benares, India, that descend right into the Ganges River.

The granite steps are carved with names of geologic eras (Triassic, Oligocene), life forms (protozoa, mammalian), and Newtown Creek marine life (shad, angler fish). The handholds on the tops of the handrails are in the shape of spheres representing the H_2O molecule—two small spheres representing the hydrogen atoms and a large one for the oxygen atom.

Imaginative attempts to evoke the area's past are met at every turn. The walkway, which at first runs parallel to the creek only to veer away from it at a right angle, is planted with a selection of indigenous trees and plants that are identified on freestanding plaques. There's a pitch pine tree (*pinus rigida*): "Resinous wood used for dock pilings, lodge ribs, ridgepoles and rafters. Boiled bark used as tonic for stomach pain and applied to cuts and sores to ward off infection." And there's *Equisetum hyemale*, commonly known as

In this heavily industrialized section of Greenpoint, Brooklyn, the Newtown Creek Nature Walk, on the grounds of the Newtown Creek Wastewater Treatment Plant, also serves as a jogging path.

scouring rush, dating back to the Carboniferous period (354 to 290 million years ago). Quennell Rothschild & Partners served as the landscape architects (see Green-Wood Cemetery, p. 165.)

All of this is revealed against a backdrop, across the creek, of a mountain of rusted cars whose metal parts are being moved about by giant jaws. Yet surprisingly, because the nature walk is in a distant corner of the wastewater facility, away from the street and the large trailer trucks that rumble through Greenpoint, and by a creek now underused by ships, the setting is quiet and contemplative. Through the imaginative use of fencing, lighting, landscaping, and planting, one is indeed on a nature walk.

A final surprise is revealed on the return walk: the Empire State Building, across the East River, is directly on axis with the path of the concrete-lined, keel-like corridor. It's just another one of the details that lend a unique character to an open space where one doesn't expect to find either nature or art. —R.L.

HOURS: Dawn–dusk, weather permitting

RESTROOMS: There are no bathroom facilities at the park. Restrooms can be found at the Newtown Creek Visitors Center, located on the opposite side of the Newtown Creek Wastewater Treatment Plant (on the north side of Greenpoint Avenue at its intersection with Humboldt Avenue), open to the public Fridays, noon–4 pm

REGULATIONS: Biking, rollerblading, skateboarding, swimming, and diving are prohibited

Pets are not allowed with the exception of guide dogs

Smoking is prohibited

FURTHER INFORMATION AVAILABLE AT:
www.nyc.gov/html/dep/html/environmental_education/newtown.shtml

BY SUBWAY: G to Greenpoint Avenue and Manhattan Avenue, use Greenpoint-Manhattan Avenue exit, walk east 1 block on Greenpoint Avenue, cross McGuiness Boulevard, continue 2 blocks to Provost Street, turn left on Provost, walk north 8 blocks, and turn right on Paidge Avenue

7 to Vernon Boulevard-Jackson Avenue, walk east 1 block, turn right on 11th Street heading south, cross the Pulaski Bridge, take the staircase before the end of the bridge to street level, walk east on Ash Street under the bridge, cross McGuinness Boulevard, walk south less than 1 block to Paidge Avenue

BY BUS: B62 to McGuinness Blvd and Freeman Street, walk east 1 block on Freeman Street, turn left on Provost Street, and walk north 2 blocks, turn right on Paidge Avenue

B24 to Greenpoint Avenue and Provost Street, walk north 8 blocks on Provost Street, turn right on Paidge Avenue

B43 to Box Street and Manhattan Avenue, walk east 1 block on Box Street, cross McGuinness Boulevard, and walk to end of Paidge Avenue

QUEENS

12

GANTRY PLAZA STATE PARK

The park is located on Center Boulevard between 47th Road and 50th Avenue in Long Island City, Queens

For the last 25 years Long Island City, Queens, has been the "next hot neighborhood." Its tantalizing proximity to midtown (one subway stop on the 7 train to Grand Central), its spectacular views (the view of Manhattan is better than that from Brooklyn), and its robust industrial architecture combined with row houses all made Long Island City seem a natural for hotness. Yet only recently has it started to take off, and it has taken a public authority, the Empire State Development Corporation, in the guise of the Queens West Development Corporation, to make it happen. The corporation has planned a multiphase project along the waterfront between

One of the two gantries in the park, with the United Nations Secretariat Building and the Chrysler Building, across the East River, as a backdrop.

A finger pier reimagined.

Anabel Basin (on the line of 45th Road) on the north, Newtown Creek on the south, Fifth Street on the east, and the East River on the west. Though still a work in progress, there are now several apartment buildings and, most important, Gantry Plaza State Park, one of the most elaborate of the city's recent spate of waterfront parks.

The dominant visual features of the park are two gigantic old Long Island Railroad gantries, which were used in carfloat operations when this waterfront was a crucial node in the city's once vast and intricate port and terminal system. The gantries date from 1925 and linked to the freight line of the Long Island Railroad. These structures testify to the success of industrial archaeologists in getting us to value artifacts of our industrial past. Here the gantries feel right at home in a 12-acre postmodern park consisting of long, snaking piers, promenades, the now-obligatory cascading boulders that allow a dip of the toe in river water, and a children's playground. It's beguiling in itself, and for its superb views. Right across the river stands the United Nations Secretariat Building, and the Chrysler Building stands out from this vantage point as it does from no other. To the right, the lovely Queensboro Bridge warrants dreamy appraisal. A nice touch is the preservation of the popular neon Pepsi-Cola sign (made in 1936 by the neon pioneers Artkraft Strauss), vestige of an old bottling plant. The park also provides facilities for active recreation, including basketball and handball courts and even a fishing pier.

In 2005, New York Water Taxi, a commercial operator of local ferry boats, contributed 400 tons of sand to create Water Taxi Beach just south of the gantries. The Project for Public Spaces praised the project for its simplicity and tremendous magnetism. It had a volleyball area, some seating, and a bar, and for a few years it seemed like the most popular place to go in the summer in New York. However, as of 2012, Water Taxi Beach has relocated to Governors Island (p. 145) and to the South Street Seaport.

The Queens-side backdrop comprises a group of dramatically tall apartment towers, including Citylights by Cesar Pelli & Associates, two Avalon Bay developments by Perkins Eastman, and two buildings by Miami-based Arquitectonica.

The first 2.5-acre section of Gantry Plaza, which is to the south and includes the gantries, opened in 1998. Its designers, Weintraub &

The chaise longue has become increasingly popular in parks. Thomas Balsley, responsible for designing the first section of Gantry Plaza State Park, has been at the forefront of a movement to bring new kinds of furniture to New York's public spaces.

di Domenico and Thomas Balsley, have left huge imprints on the New York City of their time. Born in 1943, Balsley founded his landscape architecture firm in New York in 1971. His credits include Thomas F. Smith Park, at Chelsea Piers, and Riverside Park South (p. 67). He has been at the forefront of two trends. One is the incorporation of historic industrial artifacts into his parks. The other is his use of unusual park furniture, such as chaises longues. Because a park user can easily fall asleep in one of these, they symbolize a new spirit in New York City in which people have lost all fear. It's impossible to imagine Gantry Plaza State Park existing in the 1970s. It's very much a product of the New York of its time. Weintraub & di Domenico gave us, in 1983, the lovely Washington Market Park, on Chambers Street (p. 71). More recently, Lee Weintraub designed Erie Basin Park in Red Hook, Brooklyn (for more on Weintraub, see Erie Basin Park, p. 110). Neither Balsley nor Weintraub & di Domenico, however, designed phase 2 of the park, the part that replaced the Pepsi-Cola bottling plant (closed in 1999) to the north, where the sign has been preserved. Opened in 2009, that 6-acre section was the handiwork of Abel Bainsson Butz, the firm responsible for the dramatic Pier 45, at Christopher Street, in Hudson River Park (p. 67).

I do lament the infelicitous alteration of McKim, Mead & White's beautiful old Pennsylvania Railroad powerhouse (1909) at Fifth Street and 50th Avenue, a landmark-worthy structure that sported high smokestacks once rendered by Georgia O'Keeffe. —F.M.

HOURS: 8 am–10 pm daily

REGULATIONS: Dogs and other pets are not allowed

Smoking is prohibited

MAP & FURTHER INFORMATION AVAILABLE AT:
nysparks.state.ny.us/parks/149/details.aspx

BY SUBWAY: 7 to Vernon Boulevard-Jackson Avenue, walk west 2 blocks, follow Center Boulevard north

G to 21st Street and Jackson Avenue, walk west 3 blocks

BY BUS: Q103 to Vernon Boulevard and Jackson Avenue, walk west 2 blocks, follow Center Boulevard north

B62 to 11th Street and Jackson Avenue, walk west 3 blocks on 49th Avenue

BY TRAIN: LIRR trains to Long Island City station, walk north 2 blocks on 2nd Street and another 2 blocks north on Center Boulevard

BY WATER TAXI: Weekday evenings, East River commuter service to Long Island City, walk north 1 block on 2nd Street and a further 2 blocks north on Center Boulevard

BRONX

CONCRETE PLANT PARK

13

Stretches along the west bank of the Bronx River between Westchester Avenue and Bruckner Boulevard in the Bronx; one entrance at Westchester Avenue, the other at Bruckner Boulevard

Concrete Plant Park is more than just another park with an industrial past. Its presence demonstrates that a community organization can be the driver behind creating new public space. At its dedication in 2009, former New York City Parks Commissioner Adrian Benepe said that the park is "an example of what happens when the community leads and the government is smart enough to follow."

Located in the South Bronx, the park's seven acres are sandwiched between the Bronx River to the east and AMTRAK railroad tracks to the

The linear park was designed by James Mituzas of the Bronx landscape team of the New York City Department of Parks and Recreation.

Concrete Plant Park is bordered on its southern edge by train and subway tracks. The abandoned 1908 railroad station by Cass Gilbert looms precariously over the AMTRAK rail lines.

west, Bruckner Boulevard to the south and Westchester Avenue to the north. An elevated subway line and the Sheridan Expressway are close by—and audible. The backs of industrial buildings are visible across the Bronx River. The area had been an active concrete plant from 1945 to 1987 and was an unlikely park site; the city had proposed a truck route for its next use.

Alexie Torres-Fleming, founder and executive director of Youth Ministries for Peace and Justice (YMPJ), a community organization in the southeast Bronx, had other ideas when she first saw the area. Though there were still squatters living on the site, submerged cars in the Bronx River, and thousands of unused tires littering the property, the group's persistence and collaboration with allied community organizations resulted in the transfer of the land to the Parks Department in 2000. Over the next ten years, and with continual community involvement, the park was transformed into a welcoming, functional space.

Walkway along the western shore of the Bronx River in the industrial South Bronx.

Today the 1,900-foot-long waterfront park provides open space in a community with too little of it. The towering forms of the concrete-mixing machines are still there, but now they're painted pink and are sculptural highlights. The cars have been extracted from the river, and a canoe/kayak launch has been installed along the river's edge. There is even a beaver named José, who returned to the Bronx River, representing the first beaver to swim in the New York waterways in 200 years.

The park is part of the Bronx River Greenway, a consortium of unexpected green sites along the southern end of the Bronx River, including tiny 1.4-acre Hunts Point Riverside Park and Starlight Park, on the site of a former contaminated goal gasification plant cleaned up by Con Ed. The river itself is 23 miles long, beginning in the wealthy precincts of lower Westchester County and passing through the South Bronx, the poorest congressional district in the United States, before emptying into the East River. Kayak tours from Concrete Plant Park often include tidal trips south through reclaimed salt marshes along the industrial corridor.

The long, narrow park, designed by James Mituzas of the Bronx landscape team of the New York City Department of Parks and Recreation, features a paved path running close to the water, with concrete benches, a shade awning, and chess tables and chairs, as well as a lawn area located closer to the railroad tracks. The two entrances on either end of the park, one at Westchester Avenue and the other at Bruckner Boulevard, run slightly downhill. This descent into the park provides a sense of being removed and sheltered from the congestion at street level. Though the park is surrounded by subway and train tracks, overhead bridges, and highways, urban cacophony is held at arm's length.

Mituzas deliberately left the concrete plant's silos, hoppers, and conveyor structures to reflect the area's past and to create a visible presence from the Sheridan Expressway. Just as visually arresting is the decaying but jewel-like train station designed by Cass Gilbert (architect of the iconic Woolworth Building in lower Manhattan) in 1908, which is elevated over the AMTRAK train tracks. Its decrepit condition, a victim of weather, vandals, and time, gives visitors an idea of the decay that defined this area, and the uphill fight to arrest a neglected industrial area and design a 21st-century park.

The park is popular with school groups—it's common to see a science class testing the river's water quality—residents taking advantage of the area's brisk winds to fly kites, and couples walking along the water's edge. For those who live nearby, the park is a welcome respite, and for those coming from outside the neighborhood it's a satisfying destination. —R.L.

HOURS: 6 am–1 am, subject to change

RESTROOMS: None

REGULATIONS: Smoking is prohibited

MAP & FURTHER INFORMATION AVAILABLE AT:
www.nycgovparks.org/parks/concreteplantpark

BY SUBWAY: 6 to Whitlock Avenue

BY BUS: Bx4, Bx27 to Westchester Avenue and Longfellow Avenue, walk northeast 1 block on Westchester Avenue

STATEN ISLAND

14

NORTH SHORE WATERFRONT ESPLANADE, ST. GEORGE

The esplanade and Staten Island September 11 Memorial is located on Bank Street, on the waterfront just north of the St. George Ferry Terminal and the Richmond County Bank Ballpark

Staten Island's St. George waterfront has undergone a major makeover, beginning in the 1990s with the development of the North Shore Waterfront Esplanade. From here, dramatic harbor views rival those from any other vantage point. In 2005 the new St. George Ferry Terminal, designed by HOK (formerly Hellmuth Obata + Kassabaum), opened, relieving this waterfront of the grimy, forbidding, utterly charmless ferry terminal of old. The new facility is bright, wide, open, and high ceilinged—a perfectly

Masayuki Sono's *Postcards*, Staten Island's memorial to the World Trade Center attacks, with a view of the lower Manhattan skyline.

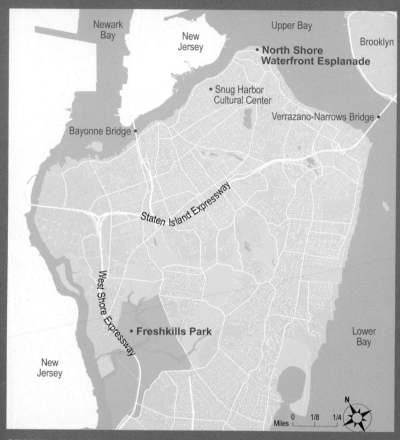

STATEN ISLAND

Map by John Hill

pleasant place to hang out while waiting for your boat. Big windows afford views of the water and of the ferryboats, and two large tropical fish tanks, maintained by the Staten Island Zoo, provide waiting commuters with an unexpected contemplative pleasure. Best of all, the terminal has, in addition to its exits onto a parking lot and bus ramps, an exit directly onto the esplanade to the north. The many people, including tourists, who ride the ferry for fun now have no excuse not to disembark in St. George and spend some time there. One may choose to walk across Richmond Terrace to view Carrère & Hastings's Borough Hall (1904–6) and Richmond County Courthouse (1919), which present a monumental face to the world beyond Staten Island, or to visit Hyatt Street, where the high clock tower at the back of Borough Hall gently commands an urban space that almost reads as (and perhaps should be) a village green or town square. Or the visitor may prefer to spend most of his or her time right on the water. The exit from

Visitors to *Postcards* looking at the individual plaques dedicated to Staten Island victims of the 1993 and 2001 attacks.

the terminal leads directly to the northern esplanade, but one may also visit its southern extension via a bridge from the bus ramp.

On the extension of the esplanade to the south of the ferry terminal we find a 65-foot-long bridge and a 65-foot-high tower, designed by Minneapolis-based artist Siah Armajani and completed in 1996. The top of the tower lights up at night, referencing a lighthouse that stood on this site for more than a century until the 1970s. The work also strikingly evokes the tower and bridge Armajani designed for the 1996 Olympics in Atlanta and calls to mind the lantern he created for the World Financial Center Plaza (1989) in Battery Park City (p. 33). Armajani is famous for incorporating the words of poets he admires into his public installations. At the World Financial Center Plaza, he embedded in the fence lines from Frank O'Hara and Walt Whitman. For a pedestrian bridge in Minneapolis, Armajani commissioned a poem from John Ashbery. Here, the tower incorporates lines from Wallace Stevens's controversial poem "Like Decorations in a Nigger Cemetery" (1934):

> The cloud rose upward like a heavy stone
> That lost its heaviness through that same will,
> Which changed light green to olive then to blue.

From the tower a walkway takes one south to a plaza neatly nestled among buildings on three sides and open to the harbor on the east. Set with bright red bollards, tables inlaid with chess boards, and honey locust trees, the plaza is the handiwork of Johansson & Walcavage. Johansson & Walcavage, or Donna Walcavage on her own, have quietly left a big imprint on New York in recent years, with such works as their elaborate playground in Rockefeller Park in Battery Park City (p. 36) and Stuyvesant Cove Park on the East River waterfront (p. 65).

The site of the bridge, tower, and plaza was originally the property of the U.S. Coast Guard, which gave it to the City of New York in the 1970s. At the time the city lacked the resources to do anything with the site, and its cluster of 19th-century buildings and the surrounding lots deteriorated precipitously—right at the point where the ferry enters Staten Island. Little wonder that the tourists aboard the ferryboats felt no desire to get off and explore St. George.

To the north of the terminal, between Wall Street and Hamilton Avenue, is the Richmond County Bank Ballpark, designed by HOK Sport and completed in 2001. This ballpark has almost a cult following among New Yorkers. One of the great things to do on summer evenings is to take the Staten Island Ferry to St. George and walk the short distance from the terminal to this home of the New York Yankees' Class A minor league affiliate. Not only does one experience the pleasure of watching professional players at the beginning of their careers—such Yankees as Robinson Cano and Chien-Ming Wang once called this ballpark home—but does so in extraordinary surroundings, from seats with views of the verdant playing field and, beyond, the harbor and Manhattan.

Just to the north of the ballpark is Staten Island's memorial to September 11, 2001. Staten Islanders accounted for 270 of those killed in the attacks on the World Trade Center. The memorial, entitled *Postcards*, by Masayuki Sono, dates from 2004, and ranks among the most affecting of all 9/11 memorials. The fiberglass composition evokes two letters, or postcards, or envelopes, twisting in the wind and framing a view of lower Manhattan. It also reads as an elegant biomorphic sculpture evoking birds' wings—a bit in the spirit of Eero Saarinen's TWA Terminal (1962) at Kennedy Airport. The Japanese-born sculptor, who is also a painter and architect, cites among his diverse influences the painter Andrew Wyeth and the architect Oscar Niemeyer.

It is uplifting to see the St. George waterfront take shape as it has, as St. George slowly and almost silently takes its rightful place among New York City's most captivating neighborhoods. —F.M.

RESTROOMS: Located in the St. George Ferry Terminal

REGULATIONS: Smoking is allowed outside

MAP & FURTHER INFORMATION AVAILABLE AT:
www.statenislandusa.com/pages/memorial.html or

www.preserve.org/stgeorge/stgeorge.htm

BY RAIL: Staten Island Railway to St. George, walk north along the water (water on your right) to the memorial

BY BUS: S40, S42, S44, S46, S48, S51, S52, S61, S62, S66, S74, S76, S78, S81, S84, S86, S90, S91, S92, S94, S96, S98 to St. George Terminal, walk north along the water (water on your right) to the memorial

BY FERRY: Staten Island Ferry to St. George Terminal, walk north along the water (water on your right) to the memorial (ferry service runs 24/7, every 15–20 minutes during weekday rush hours, every 30–60 minutes at all other times)

FERRY SCHEDULES AVAILABLE AT: www.siferry.com/SIFerry_Schedules.aspx

BY CAR: Alert the guard that you are coming to see the September 11 Memorial for free parking in the lot opposite the memorial

FROM FRESH KILLS LANDFILL 15
TO FRESHKILLS PARK

Freshkills Park is located on the west shore of Staten Island, along the Arthur Kill, the waterway separating Staten Island from New Jersey. The 2,200-acre park is under construction, and will be for decades to come, so public access is controlled for reasons of safety. The public is invited to visit during the annual fall "Sneak Peek" and for a wide variety of seasonal tours and special events.

How's this for an ambitious undertaking: Close the world's largest landfill and transform it over a period of 30 years into New York City's largest park and most notable reclamation project. On March 22, 2011, Freshkills Park celebrated the 10th anniversary of the landfill closure. Nothing about the project has been fast or easy. Despite delays and difficulties, the results of years of work behind the scenes are now becoming visible.

From April through November, small groups tour the site. And every fall, Freshkills opens its gates for a "Sneak Peek" of the ongoing transformation. Boats from Manhattan and shuttle buses from the St. George Ferry Terminal provide convenient transportation. Thousands turn out. They fly kites from the top of a grass-covered mound, safe from power lines and nearby trees. Kayakers ply pristine creeks in the company of ducks, while red-tailed hawks ride thermals overhead. Birders keep an eye out for ospreys and meadowlarks. From the top of the engineered hills, visitors enjoy extraordinary vistas that include New Jersey's mountains and Manhattan's skyline. For Staten Islanders, it's already quite a change.

When the landfill was operational, "Fresh Kills" sounded like a bad joke. One could well believe that the stench was related to some sort of kills, but "fresh" seemed a misnomer. Actually, kill is Dutch for stream or channel. The narrow Kill van Kull and Arthur Kill separate Staten Island from New Jersey. Before it became a landfill, Fresh Kills was a beautiful tidal marsh, fed by fresh streams. In the 20th century, it was considered little more than a breeding ground for mosquitoes.

In 1948 Robert Moses turned Fresh Kills into a landfill, which he promised to close within three years. He didn't. By the 1990s, the tallest of the four mounds had grown to over 200 feet. And the taller the mounds, the more easily the odors were dispersed. During the summers, water trucks sprayed deodorizer throughout communities near the landfill, but the stench still kept adults and children inside. The landfill was the only thing most non-Staten Islanders knew about the borough and a source of dismay and anger for those who lived there.

In 1993 Rudolph Giuliani ran for mayor. He lost Manhattan but carried Staten Island by a wide margin, making him the first Republican to be elected mayor since 1965. As former borough resident Lee Weintraub commented, "Staten Island was very nice to Rudy Giuliani, and Rudy Giuliani was very nice to Staten Island."[1]

In 1996 Governor George Pataki, with the mayor and the Staten Island borough president at his side, announced Fresh Kills would close no later than December 31, 2001. The closure had been helped along by a federal lawsuit brought by Staten Island elected officials, but political will was

Aerial view looking south toward the waterways and four mounds of Freshkills Park, with the William T. Davis Wildlife Refuge in the foreground. Prior to 1948, Fresh Kills was an equally beautiful wetland. *Alex MacLean. Courtesy of City of New York.*

required to make it happen. After all, the city's garbage had to go somewhere, and some 150 million tons went to Fresh Kills. Since 2001, it has been transported out of state at considerable cost.

Landscape architect Lee Weintraub lived close enough to Fresh Kills to smell the noxious odors, hear the raucous gulls, and see the windblown plastic bags caught in nearby trees. But unlike others, he had always considered Fresh Kills an asset as well as a nuisance, a 2,200-acre "bulwark against complete development."

In 2000 Weintraub was driving by the landfill, thinking about both the closure of Fresh Kills and the upcoming 150th anniversary of Central Park. It struck him that Fresh Kills could become a great park and that "a process that explored its potential . . . Would be an incredible way to celebrate" Central Park's anniversary.

Weintraub turned to Brendan Sexton, then president of the Municipal Art Society (MAS), a nonprofit with a long history of advocacy. Sexton also knew Fresh Kills: he was a former commissioner of sanitation, then living on Staten Island himself. Weintraub invited Sexton over for breakfast. Sexton's reaction to Weintraub's idea: "This was brilliant."

Sexton had grown up across the street from Flushing Meadow Park, once the smoking wasteland described in F. Scott Fitzgerald's *The Great Gatsby*. He knew of Pelham Bay Park and other reclaimed sites, but he had experienced Flushing Meadow Park "viscerally." It was where he had played as a boy. "I knew it could be done."

Weintraub already had in mind a design competition, like Central Park's, but international in scope. Weintraub and Sexton agreed on three ideas: one, Fresh Kills could be a spectacular park, an opportunity that New York City would not have again; two, a competition was the way to attract talent and first concepts; and three, as Sexton put it, "These ideas—if we were lucky . . . Would attract capital . . . At least enough capital to get the idea one step further. There was a chance, in other words. A chance."

At MAS, Ellen Ryan, director of planning issues, joined the Weintraub-Sexton team and helped move the idea forward. The trio made calls on the major entities in the city involved with the landfill, from Planning and Parks and Sanitation to Cultural Affairs. It was an educational effort, said Ryan. Most had never actually seen Fresh Kills. They needed to understand, she said, that it was "more than a mound of garbage with seagulls." Half of Fresh Kills was free of garbage. It comprised "pristine waterways with great

Spectacular views abound at Freshkills. Here, looking north to the Bayonne Bridge and the Manhattan skyline. *Garrett Ziegler*

vistas." It was also more than two and a half times the size of Central Park, a scope that was nearly "unfathomable."

Once the concept had the support of the city, MAS began raising money. Sexton believed that an early $50,000 Public Works grant from the National Endowment for the Arts was especially important: "It showed the city that . . . serious people took this crazy notion seriously."

In all, MAS raised nearly $200,000 in seed money, used largely to educate the public about the project and to facilitate the public's response. The outreach included public programs, open meetings on Staten Island, a photographic display, and a traveling exhibition of the finalists, which was available in a digital version on the Fresh Kills competition Web site.

MAS had advanced what Sexton viewed as a "marvelous, game-changing idea," but then it was up to the city, which owned the property and would be assuming the political risk and the cost. "They put in immeasurable hours and effort and plain cash . . . [i]t's all about follow-through. . . ." The follow-through was there, from Mayor Bloomberg to all affected departments of the City of New York. City Planning led the way.

The competition, entitled Fresh Kills: Landfill to Landscape, drew nearly fifty entries, from which six interdisciplinary teams were chosen. They visited the site on September 5, 2001, six days before the attack on the World Trade Center (WTC). Fresh Kills became the site for the terrible task of sifting through a ton of WTC debris for remains and personal effects. The WTC material is now kept in an undisturbed area until it is incorporated into an earthwork memorial.

Field Operations, with a team led by James Corner, won the competition. On his first visit to Fresh Kills, Corner found himself "just blown away by the beauty and scope of the place." He felt the first priority was to retain the openness, the green expanses so hard to come by in any metropolitan area. "These are views and vistas that most people in a city would have to drive three or four hours to see."

Unlike the other finalists, Corner's team dealt explicitly with the trash heaps, making "the old dump part of the new park, by acknowledging it, reclaiming it, recycling it. " Field Operations envisioned a remediated landscape of native plants, trees, and wildflowers. That vision was not universally endorsed. Some expressed a preference for a starker approach, with more emphasis on the realities of trash and the reclamation process. Corner's view: "I think landscape can be edifying, but there are joyous and optimistic ways. "

Following the competition, Field Operations drafted a master plan that became the basis for subsequent design. Fittingly, the park is to be a model of sustainable strategies, in ways small and large. And the neighbors are being invited in. The park's future will depend on attracting the next generation of New Yorkers.

The first areas open on a daily basis are found along the periphery of the site. Schmul Park, on the western edge of Freshkills, is neighborhood focused, with a playground, basketball and handball courts, and a wildflower meadow. Owl Hollow Fields, on the southern perimeter, features four synthetic-turf soccer fields and a state-of-the-art comfort station, complete with green roof, wind turbine, and geothermal heating and cooling. The New Springville Greenway, along the eastern edge, is funded by a federal Congestion Mitigation and Air Quality (CMAQ) grant. It will feature a 3.3-mile bike and pedestrian path connecting to existing sidewalks and paths.

During the ten years of Phase I, the two remaining landfill mounds will be capped. It's a complicated process that requires layers of soil, synthetic textile, plastic, and grass, plus the collection of landfill gases and elaborate drainage systems to control the liquid run-off called leachate. Each mound will become a separate park (East Park, West Park, North Park, and yes, South Park) with its own identity and recreational, educational, and cultural activities: biking and trail running, horseback riding, public art projects, and cultural programming. Water recreation will expand, with additional put-ins and docks. More deer, foxes, and muskrats will take up residence; woodlands will spread and native plants will replace invasive species.

The challenges are substantial. First, there is the money. Some $100 million in city funds are needed to complete Phase I, plus $420 million in Department of Sanitation monies for closure and post-closure costs. The final price tag on the park will exceed $1 billion. It will require exceptional financial and political commitment.

Once completed, operating costs are expected to run at least $33 million per year at a site that can support no residential development and very little commercial development. Methane harvesting now brings upward of $12 million a year (sold to National Grid to heat Staten Island homes). Those profits may continue for another ten to fifteen years, but the money is understandably credited to the Department of Sanitation and goes into the city's General Fund.

To explore the potential for the generation of alternate energy, the NYC Department of Environmental Protection is issuing an RFP (request for proposal) for wind and solar projects. The recently created nonprofit Freshkills Park Alliance will likely be a fundraising source in the future.

Freshkills is difficult to reach by public transportation. When everything goes right, it takes two hours from Midtown Manhattan by subway, ferry, and bus. The good news is that it takes only an hour by boat—and what an hour! It's a trip into the industrial heart of the metropolitan region. Along

One of the best ways to see Freshkills Park is from the water, on a kayak tour. *Robert S Johnson*

the way are container ships the size of apartment buildings, bustling dry docks, tank farms, boneyards of scuttled vessels, the port of Howland Hook, and great bridges. The past, present, and future of New York passes before your eyes.

Perhaps in 2040 a fleet of solar-powered boats will ferry New Yorkers and tourists alike to the just-completed, world-famous Freshkills Park. Some of the visionaries who conceived, planned, and designed it may miss the grand finale, but fortunately they were present at the creation. —T.C.

HOURS: As scheduled. Specially organized group tours for 15–23 people may be arranged for Wednesdays and alternate Saturdays, from April to November

RESTROOMS: Eltingville Transit Center. No public restrooms on site. Portable toilets available during Sneak Peek and public programs.

REGULATIONS: Freshkills Park is under construction; access to the center of the park is allowed only for scheduled events

Smoking is prohibited

MAP & FURTHER INFORMATION AVAILABLE AT: www.nycgovparks.org/park-features/freshkills-park/

BY SUBWAY: No subway

BY BUS: For public programs and group tours: express buses from Manhattan or S74 from St. George Ferry Terminal to Eltingville Transit Center. During annual fall Sneak Peek: free shuttle buses from St. George Ferry Terminal to site, or S64 from the St. George Ferry Terminal to Victory Boulevard and Glen Street, walk south on Beresford Avenue to Wild Avenue, enter on foot or wait for the shuttle bus

BY BOAT: During Sneak Peek, free waterborne transportation from Manhattan is usually available, or take free Staten Island Ferry to St. George and bus to site (see above)

ISLANDS

FRANKLIN D. ROOSEVELT FOUR FREEDOMS PARK and SOUTHPOINT PARK, ROOSEVELT ISLAND

16

Franklin D. Roosevelt Four Freedoms Park is located at the southern tip of Roosevelt Island

Southpoint Park is located just north of Four Freedoms Park on the southern end of Roosevelt Island

The two parks on the southern end of Roosevelt Island—Franklin D. Roosevelt Four Freedoms Park and Southpoint Park—are separated only by the ruins of an 1850s smallpox hospital, yet they are

Aerial photograph of Franklin D. Roosevelt Four Freedoms Park under construction. *Amiaga, www.amiaga.com, Courtesy of Franklin D. Roosevelt Four Freedoms Park, LLC.*

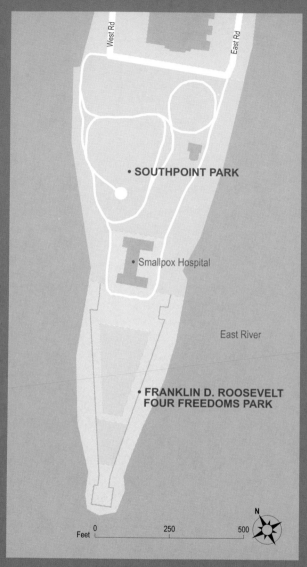

West Rd

East Rd

• SOUTHPOINT PARK

• Smallpox Hospital

East River

• FRANKLIN D. ROOSEVELT
FOUR FREEDOMS PARK

N

Feet 0   250   500

SOUTHERN END OF ROOSEVELT ISLAND

Map by John Hill,
Courtesy of Mark K.
Morrison Landscape
Architects

The "room" under construction in early 2011.
"Untapped Cities by Augustin Pasquet"

far apart in terms of design and philosophy. One has defined vistas and an architectural pedigree; the other is a humbler green space. Although each uses the concept of "rooms" to draw visitors into and through their spaces, the similarities end there.

Franklin D. Roosevelt Four Freedoms Park occupies a 4-acre triangular wedge at the southern tip of the 2-mile-long, cigar-shaped island in the middle of the East River. The 72-foot-square "room" with its bronze head of FDR at the southern end of the park is open to the sky and the water, yet enclosed on its east, west, and north sides by giant, silvery gray, 12-foot-high granite blocks weighing 36 tons each. The famed modernist architect Louis I. Kahn designed the memorial in the 1970s, his sole work in New York City.

To reach the focal point of Kahn's symmetrical design—the room—one must walk the length of the triangle-shaped site. Gina Pollara, executive director of the Franklin D. Roosevelt Four Freedoms Park, says that the beauty of the design is the "shifting perspective as you walk." The design "plays on viewpoints and perspectives. As you move, your viewpoint shifts."

The room can be accessed in one of two ways: by passing a line of five copper beech trees, ascending a broad staircase, walking the length of a sloping lawn lined with linden trees (the garden in Kahn's design), and proceeding along a crushed-gravel path toward a forecourt; or by promenading along the water's edge on paths situated to either side of the sloping lawn, and then walking slightly uphill to reach the forecourt. The memorial park, a formal composition, is inviting. The public can lounge on the grassy lawn, sit in the forecourt, and walk along the promenades, taking in the river views.

The bronze head of FDR by sculptor Jo Davidson is placed in a niche at the entrance to the room. The Four Freedoms that Roosevelt named in his 1941 State of the Union address—Freedom of Speech, Freedom of Worship, Freedom from Want, and Freedom from Fear—are inscribed on the tall granite blocks on the north wall of the room. With the United Nations complex visible across the East River to the west, the visitor has a composite view of FDR through his words, the sculptural representation, and his work for world peace as expressed through the presence of the U.N.

That the visitor can take this stately walk at all is a testament to patience and persistence. After all, it was back in the 1960s that Governor Nelson Rockefeller proposed developing Roosevelt Island, then known as Welfare Island, into a mixed-income, handicapped-accessible residential community. The memorial became part of the development plan and Kahn was commissioned; the island was renamed for FDR. In September 1973, Mayor John Lindsay held a public groundbreaking.

But fiscal crises prevented the housing from being completed, and the FDR memorial from being built at all. (The project was among Kahn's last works: a drawing of it was found in his pocket after he died in Pennsylvania Station in 1974 on his way home to Philadelphia from Bangladesh, where he was designing a complex in Dhaka.) Time passed. Thirty-six years. And yet, to the surprise of many, the memorial project had been successfully kept alive by the Franklin and Eleanor Roosevelt Institute (FERI) and its then president, now chairman, Ambassador William vanden Heuvel, who originally developed the project. Construction began in 2010, and the memorial opened in fall 2012.

Southpoint Park, the 7.2-acre green park developed by the Trust for Public Land with the Roosevelt Island Operating Corporation, opened in August 2011. Its site is just north of the ruins of the Gothic-style smallpox hospital by James Renwick, who also designed St. Patrick's Cathedral. (The New York City landmark is in need of rehabilitation, even if it's an officially designated ruin. The stern stone building clearly expresses a time when Welfare Island, now Roosevelt Island, housed the poor, the sick, and the incarcerated.)

The park has plenty of curved roadways on which one can meander among landscaped "green rooms" planted with native grasses and other vegetation. The elevated lawns are lined with granite pavers quarried from the island's demolished City Hospital. An appealing hill that visitors like to climb was formerly an island garbage mound. In late summer the landscape is awash in Black-eyed Susans. There's a lack of shade now because the trees that have been planted are still immature, but hopefully time will make the difference. The Trust for Public Land hired former Riverside Park adminis-

The dramatic East Side skyline provides the backdrop for Roosevelt Island's Southpoint Park, separated from Manhattan by the East River.

trator Charles McKinney and the landscape architecture firm of Mark K. Morrison to prepare a master plan; Wallace Roberts & Todd of Philadelphia served as the landscape architects.

The terrain is mostly flat—all the better to take in the unobstructed panoramic views of Manhattan's East Side to the west or the Queens landscape stretching to the east. And though the roadways seem a bit too wide, more like traffic lanes than paths, they are conducive to meditative walks. An extant older structure is the 19th-century Strecker Memorial Laboratory, the first laboratory for pathological and bacteriological research in the nation, which one can look at but not enter. The Metropolitan Transportation Authority controls the building and houses a power conversion substation there; they completely restored its façade so that it looks newer than it really is. A shame.

The greatest difference between the two Roosevelt Island parks may not be their contrasting landscapes—one formal, one informal—but their depictions of FDR. In Southpoint Park there's a room—a protected grove— where a statue of FDR by sculptor Meredith Bergmann will be placed, showing the president in a wheelchair greeting a disabled child. The citizens of Roosevelt Island, many handicapped, worked with the Roosevelt Island Operating Corporation and the Trust for Public Land to commission this work. The bronze head in the Four Freedoms Park portrays FDR as he wished to be seen, without emphasis on his body.

Southpoint Park under construction in winter 2011, with the 1892 Strecker Memorial Laboratory, where doctors once conducted pathological and bacteriological research, seen in profile. *"Untapped Cities by Augustin Pasquet"*

To reach Franklin D. Roosevelt Four Freedoms Park one must pass by Southpoint Park, so comparisons of the sculptures and the spaces in which they are placed are inevitable. Seeing such contrasting approaches to the urban landscape side by side is reason enough to visit Roosevelt Island.

And finally, as this book goes to print, there are promises of more unusual green spaces to come on Roosevelt Island. In December 2010, the team of Cornell University and Technion–Israel Institute of Technology won the city competition to build an applied engineering campus on city land, with the NYC government providing $100 million to subsidize infrastructure costs. The $2.2 billion Cornell NYC Tech Campus, south of the Ed Koch Queensboro Bridge and just north of Southpoint Park, on a 12-acre parcel of land once occupied by Goldwater Hospital, will be designed as a net-zero-energy facility, powered largely by solar and geothermal energy. It also promises to be "one of New York City's largest green spaces open to the public," with over 500,000 square feet, according to the Cornell Chronicle. Cathy Dove, Vice President, Cornell NYC Tech Campus, spoke at a town meeting on Roosevelt Island and described the vision for the project: to create an "open, interconnected campus," encouraging "a symbiotic cycle between outdoor and indoor spaces," with a "diverse collection of active open spaces," accessible to the public. Early plans include a campus tech walk along a north–south pedestrian spine. Keep your eye on Roosevelt Island for the foreseeable future—the first buildings are scheduled to be completed in 2017—to see what's new, open, and green in New York. —R.L.

FRANKLIN D. ROOSEVELT FOUR FREEDOMS PARK, ROOSEVELT ISLAND

HOURS: Thursday–Sunday, 9am–5pm

RESTROOMS: Southpoint Park

REGULATIONS: Franklin D. Roosevelt Four Freedoms Park became the newest New York state park upon its dedication on October 17, 2012. No climbing, eating, picnicking, biking, smoking, fishing, or amplified sound

MAP & FURTHER INFORMATION AVAILABLE AT: www.fdrfourfreedomspark.org/

BY SUBWAY: F to Roosevelt Island, walk south under the Queensboro Bridge and along the promenade to East Gate, the eastern entrance to Southpoint Park (roughly equivalent to 10 blocks), continue south to Four Freedoms Park

BY TRAM: Tramway car (59th Street and 2nd Avenue) to Roosevelt Island. Follow directions above (roughly equivalent to 8 blocks)

SOUTHPOINT PARK, ROOSEVELT ISLAND

HOURS: Dawn to dusk

RESTROOMS: On site

REGULATIONS: Grilling is prohibited

Smoking is prohibited

MAP & FURTHER INFORMATION AVAILABLE AT: www.rioc.com/southpoint.htm

BY SUBWAY: F to Roosevelt Island, walk south under the Queensboro Bridge to the entrance on the west side of the island (roughly equivalent to 6 blocks)

BY TRAM: Tramway car (59th Street and 2nd Avenue) to Roosevelt Island. Follow directions above (roughly equivalent to 6 blocks)

GOVERNORS ISLAND   17

Governors Island is offshore from lower Manhattan and is accessible only by ferry

Governors Island sits about half a mile off the southern tip of Manhattan and just across Buttermilk Channel from Red Hook, Brooklyn, in the Upper Bay of New York Harbor. (Though the island is closer to Brooklyn, it is officially part of Manhattan.) The 172-acre island was the site of the first European settlement in what is now New York; representatives of the Dutch West India Company settled there in 1624. Once called by some Dutch, English, or Native American variation of "Nut Island," it has a long and illustrious history, though limited space precludes a full account here. Suffice it to say that it served as home, farmland, or retreat for various Dutch directors and English governors (hence its eventual name). In 1776 the Continental Army

ABOVE AND FACING PAGE The 172-acre Governors Island, with its close-up views of the Statue of Liberty and lower Manhattan, is a major destination along the water's edge for New Yorkers. When the next phase of development is completed by the fall of 2013, there will be 40 new acres of gardens, lawns, and play areas, including a hammock grove and two ball fields, designed by Dutch landscape architecture firm West 8 with New York architects Diller Scofidio + Renfro and Rogers Marvel, at the southern end.

built a fortification there, but lost the island to the British following the Battle of Brooklyn. The British held control for the war's duration, until 1783. The island did not again serve a military purpose until 1794, when the first Fort Jay was constructed. That began the island's 202-year continuous run as a military installation. It became headquarters of the U.S. First Army in 1939. The Army held the island until 1966, when the U.S. Coast Guard took over for the next 30 years.

Because of the island's splendid location, New York mayors and others long dreamed of taking it over and using it for something besides a military base. Mayor Fiorello La Guardia proposed transforming it into a municipal airport. The island may have suited the airplanes of the 1930s, but the airport would have rapidly become obsolete. Mayor William O'Dwyer later proposed it as a site for the new United Nations, which had rejected the offer of a site in Queens and almost ended up in Philadelphia for want of a suitable Manhattan location.

The Coast Guard ceased operations on the island in 1996 as a budget-cutting measure. In 2003, the federal government sold 150 acres of the island to the State of New York for one dollar. (The other 22 acres are under the control of the National Park Service.) Today, the city-run Trust for Governors Island administers the 150 acres. About 92 acres in the northern part of the island are now open to the public from late spring to early fall, as are Picnic Point, on the southern tip, and the circumferential roadway, which serves as a bike trail (bikes can be rented on the island).

A number of historic structures, forming both a historic district, as designated by the New York City Landmarks Preservation Commission, and a National Historic Landmark, define the northern public area. Within this area, Fort Jay, right in the center, and Castle Williams, in the northwest corner, dominate. The present Fort Jay was built in 1806–9; Castle Williams, in 1807–11. Both served in the harbor defense system that seemed imperative in the days when the Napoleonic Wars routinely disrupted American shipping. Both later served as military prisons, an important part of the story told in the excellent Park Ranger tours on offer. Other interesting structures include St. Cornelius Chapel, a Gothic Revival church, at the southern end of Nolan Park. Built by Manhattan's Trinity Parish, it was designed by Charles Coolidge Haight and erected in 1905. Liggett Hall, the barracks structure that spans the island from east to west, demarcates the southern end of the public area. Designed by McKim, Mead & White, the Army erected Liggett Hall in 1929 supposedly to thwart any notion of turning the island into an airfield—by bisecting the island, the barracks blocked any landing route.

Major areas include Nolan Park, on the east, and, to its west, the Parade Ground. On the northern edge of the island, adjacent to Soissons Dock (serving the ferries to and from the Battery Maritime Building) is Water Taxi Beach. Like the original Water Taxi Beach that once operated at Gantry Plaza State Park (p. 119) in Long Island City, the one at Governors Island comprises imported sand, volleyball courts, and a food concession. Because you can't go in the water, the "beach," as commenters on Yelp like to point out, is more of an adult sandbox. It is, nonetheless, wildly popular. The Project for Public Spaces, usually right about such matters, praised the original Water Taxi Beach for the simplicity of its conception and for being a people magnet. In addition to Water Taxi Beach, food and drink are available at a food court and picnicking area on King Avenue at the eastern end of Liggett Hall, and at Picnic Point. Be advised that on the entire island at present the only indoor public restrooms are located in Building 110, across the road from Water Taxi Beach. Portable toilets are scattered throughout the rest of the island.

The future of most of the island is still being worked out, and will definitely include a 40-acre park at the southern end designed by the Dutch landscape architecture firm West 8 with New York architects Diller Scofidio + Renfro and Rogers Marvel. We may now add West 8 to the formidable roster of globally acclaimed landscape architecture firms that make New York perhaps the single hottest destination in the world for a survey of that hot field. Basically, in future the northern part that is now open to the public will not change. Private development (you know, to pay for the whole thing) will take place along the west and east sides. And there will be a circumferential esplanade.

Today, there is plenty to see and do at Governors Island, even as its future entices. The warmer months bring an impressive schedule of art and historical exhibitions, concerts, and dance performances, special events such as the all-day, weekend-long Jazz Age Lawn Parties featuring live music and swing dancing, and Park Ranger tours. Free ferries operate from Manhattan from the beautiful Battery Maritime Building (1909, Walker & Morris, architects), operated by New York Waterway; and for $4 from DUMBO, Williamsburg, and Greenpoint in Brooklyn via New York Waterway. —F.M.

HOURS: Governors Island closes for the winter in late September and reopens each year in late May or early June. The Island is open Friday–Sunday and all holiday Mondays. Check the ferry schedule for days and hours of access

RESTROOMS: Public restroom in Building 110, across the road from Water Taxi Beach, and portable toilets scattered throughout the rest of the island

REGULATIONS: Dogs and other pets are not allowed on Governors Island

Smoking is prohibited

MAP, FERRY SCHEDULES, AND FURTHER INFORMATION AVAILABLE AT:
www.govisland.com/html/home/home.shtml

BY FREE FERRY FROM MANHATTAN: Departing from the Battery Maritime Building at 10 South Street, near the Staten Island Ferry

BY FREE FERRY FROM BROOKLYN: Departing from Pier 6 in Brooklyn Bridge Park, located at the foot of Atlantic Avenue (corner of Columbia Street)

BY SUBWAY TO THE FREE MANHATTAN FERRY: 1 to South Ferry

4, 5 to Bowling Green, walk east 1 block and south 5 blocks

N, R to Whitehall Street-South Ferry, walk south 2 blocks

BY BUS TO THE FREE MANHATTAN FERRY: M5, M20, X8, X14 to State Street and Whitehall Street, walk south 1 block

M6 to South Street and Whitehall Street

M15 to Broad Street and Water Street, walk south 1 block

BY SUBWAY TO THE FREE BROOKLYN FERRY: 2, 3, 4, 5, R to Borough Hall and Court Street, walk south on Court Street toward Atlantic Avenue, make a right on Atlantic Avenue, continue toward the East River, cross under the Brooklyn-Queens Expressway (BQE), and continue to the end of Atlantic Avenue to Pier 6 park entrance across Furman Street

A, C, F to Jay Street-Metro Tech, walk west on Fulton Street toward Borough Hall, turn left on Boerum Place, continue south toward Atlantic Avenue, cross under the BQE to Pier 6 park entrance across Furman Street

BY BUS TO THE FREE BROOKLYN FERRY: B63 to the terminus of Atlantic Avenue (at Columbia Street)

BY NEW YORK WATERWAY EAST RIVER FERRY TO GOVERNORS ISLAND: Leaves from East 34th Street/Midtown; Hunters Point South/Long Island City; India Street/Greenpoint; North 6th Street/N. Williamsburg; Schaefer Landing/S. Williamsburg; Brooklyn Bridge Park/DUMBO; Wall Street/Pier 11. Cost: $4 one way plus $1 per bike; $12 all-day pass or $15 all-day pass with bike

MAP, FERRY SCHEDULES, AND FURTHER INFORMATION AVAILABLE AT:
www.nywaterway.com/EastRiverSchedule.aspx?schl=1

18 RANDALL'S ISLAND

The island is located between the Harlem and East Rivers; the park is located on the north side of the island

Pole vaulting in New York City? Why not?

The Carl Icahn Stadium on Randall's Island is a state-of-the-art facility for track and field events, among them pole vaulting. It hasn't always been that way. As recently as the 1990s Randall's Island was a down-at-the-heels site with second-rate everything, from a decaying track facility to neglected ball fields. Jesse Owens, the black Olympic athlete, may have run qualifying races at Downing Stadium, the predecessor to Carl Icahn Stadium, before winning four gold medals at the 1936 Olympics while Hitler looked on, but that wasn't going to keep the stadium from falling into decay over the ensuing decades.

The key to transforming 273-acre Randall's Island into a first-class destination was the formation of a public-private partnership in which the city worked with the Randall's Island Sports Foundation (RISF) to create plans for the park. The foundation, established in 1992, sought not only city dollars but also funds from the private sector to upgrade the island's facilities. Upgrading city parks, with a massive infusion of private capital, was still a relatively new phenomenon at that time.

The transformation of Carl Icahn Stadium is a case in point. The city contributed $20 million from its capital budget toward the $42 million proj-

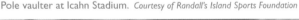

Pole vaulter at Icahn Stadium. *Courtesy of Randall's Island Sports Foundation*

Playing lacrosse in the shadow of the Robert F. Kennedy Bridge.

ect. The RISF sought private funds to cover the rest; the final $10 million came from philanthropist Carl Icahn, for whom the stadium is named. The stadium boasts a 400-meter Mondo running track and a covered seating area for more than 5,000 spectators.

Today this East River island is a case study in "before and after." Once there was plenty of trash strewn among the dilapidated ball fields and now there are over 60 pristine sports fields. A bike and pedestrian path has been created along the water's edge; a salt marsh and freshwater wetlands have been rehabilitated. In addition to the renovated track and field stadium, there is a new a golf driving range and a 20-court tennis center.

And there has been controversy too.

This island, hiding in plain sight in the East River under the approach to the RFK Bridge, is geographically accessible from its nearby communities: the South Bronx, Astoria, East Harlem, and the Upper East Side. Twenty private schools in the city, wanting playing fields for their students, offered to pay $52 million to upgrade the fields in exchange for the right to use two-thirds of them during the after-school hours of 3–6 pm. Citizen groups from the poorer nearby communities fought back, saying that this was giving land to a privileged group without going through the land review process. The courts agreed.

The city kept building the fields anyway while the lawsuits made their way through the courts. Even though the private schools eventually lost, and the fields remained accessible for all during the after school hours, the results were pretty much the same. Because the private schools can provide direct, dedicated private transportation to Randall's Island, and the public school children have to make a number of public transit connections to get there, the private schools still use many of the fields during the after-school hours.

But no one can argue with the quality of the improvements or even that the facilities are available to all, if not always easily accessible.

In May 2010 the RISF announced the conclusion of its 3-year-long, $130 million campaign to transform the 60 ball fields into state-of-the-art facilities and restore the natural area. More than half of the ball fields in Manhattan are now on Randall's Island, which has some of the best views in the city. There are now 4.5 miles of bike and pedestrian pathways running along the island's edges. There's the golf center, a miniature golf course, and the tennis center. More than 9 acres of salt marsh and freshwater wetlands have been restored, creating a habitat for wildlife while reducing water pollution.

The arts play a role too. In the summers of 2011 and 2012 the work of five contemporary artists was installed along the shoreline to emphasize the connection between art and the environment. The FLOW exhibition (www.flow12.org), in conjunction with the Bronx Museum of the Arts and Made Event, calls attention to the island beyond its reputation as a sports destination and helps attract visitors to an island that too few people know.

When visitors arrive, they find a sufficient number of well-designed rest-rooms spread out among the 60 playing fields. This is not a minor achieve-

Wetlands with Icahn Stadium in the distance; the elevated roadway is just beyond the tollbooth of the Robert F. Kennedy Bridge. *Courtesy of Randall's Island Sports Foundation*

Gardens on Randall's Island—used to teach schoolchildren about growing vegetables and healthy eating habits—are located next to the mighty 1916 steel-arch Hell Gate Bridge, which carries freight and Amtrak passengers. *Courtesy of Randall's Island Sports Foundation*

ment. Prior to the work of the RISF, Randall's Island was a very difficult place to visit because of a lack of facilities. The distinctive orange bathroom sheds, visible from any distance, combine high design with great tile work and good-looking stainless-steel toilets and sinks.

And the Carl Icahn Stadium offers much more than pole vaulting. There are concerts and events of all types during the summer, and plans are in the works for ferry service to and from the island.

John Randal, the surveyor and father of New York's grid system, for whom the Randall's Island is named (although with a different spelling) would be pleased to know that this area is a haven from the grid. He spent years roaming Manhattan, laying out the groundwork for its development with his 1811 survey. Manhattan island was his playground; now Randall's Island is ours. —R.L.

HOURS: The footbridge and island are accessible twenty-four hours a day

REGULATIONS: Smoking is prohibited

MAP & FURTHER INFORMATION AVAILABLE AT:
www.nycgovparks.org/parks/randallsislandpark or http://randallsisland.org/

24-hour fields hot line: 212.860.1830

BY FOOT: 103rd Street Pedestrian Bridge

BY BUS: M35 to Main Roadway and Parks & Recreation; Main Roadway and T.B.T.A. (Robert Moses Building); Ward's Island; Main Roadway and After Exit Ramp; Main

The High Line: one mile long, thirty feet wide, and very, very popular.

Inland

RECLAIMED

19 HIGH LINE

The High Line stretches from Gansevoort Street to West 34th Street between 10th and 11th Avenues

Access points are located at: Gansevoort Street; 14th Street (elevator access); 16th Street (elevator access); 18th Street; 20th Street; 23rd Street (elevator access); 26th Street; 28th Street; 30th Street (elevator access)

The High Line is, today, one mile long. What is more important, it is 30 feet high. "The High Line," wrote Adam Gopnik in the *New Yorker* in 2001, long before the viaduct's transformation into a park, "does not offer a God's-eye view of the city exactly, but something rarer, the view of a lesser angel: of a cupid in a Renaissance painting, of the putti looking down on the Nativity manger." When the High Line's first section opened in June 2009, *New York Times* architecture critic Nicolai Ouroussoff

BELOW AND FACING PAGE   Clearly elevated, but just three stories above the ground.

wrote, "As mesmerizing as the design is, it is the height of the High Line that makes it so magical, and that has such a profound effect on how you view the city. Lifted just three stories above the ground, you are suddenly able to perceive, with remarkable clarity, aspects of the city's character you would never glean from an office window. At some points, billboards and parking structures dominate the foreground. At others, you are directly below the cornice line, so that you seem to be floating among the rooftops."

In other words, a putto's-eye view.

For many visitors to the High Line, this view is the park's most salient feature. However, there is much more to the High Line than just the view.

In the second half of the 19th century and the first half of the 20th, the West Side waterfront of Manhattan was one of the busiest port and terminal complexes on earth. Great steamships docked at Chelsea Piers and elsewhere along the riverfront. Countless barges, lighters, and carfloats came across the Hudson River from New Jersey. A freight railroad then transported their cargoes to the warehouses and factories

up and down the riverbank. For most of its history, this railroad ran at street level. Persistent calls from those who lived and worked nearby to make the railroad less obtrusive and less dangerous by moving it or elevating it or submerging it finally bore fruit as part of the vast West Side Improvement conceived in the 1920s and guided to completion by the master planner Robert Moses in the 1930s. This project doubled the size of Riverside Park (in part by building a giant box around the grade-level tracks of the New York Central Railroad north of 72nd Street), created the Miller Elevated Highway (since dismantled) and the world-famous Henry Hudson Parkway, and gave us the "High Line"—the elevated tracks used by the freight trains of the New York Central Railroad south of 34th Street. (The 1980s' dismantling of the elevated highway, deteriorated beyond repair, removed a psychological as well as a physical barrier to pedestrian waterfront access.)

The High Line opened in 1934, connecting the vast freight yards (now known as Hudson Yards) at 34th Street to the St. John's Park Freight Terminal, at Spring Street. So that it could serve the factories and warehouses along its path as efficiently as possible, planners threaded the elevated railroad amid the buildings along the waterfront and, dramatically, cut right through some buildings. Among the great industrial concerns that the High Line served were the National Biscuit Company factory, once the world's largest bakery, where the Oreo cookie was invented, and the Bell Laboratories, where work was done on many of the defining inventions of the 20th century, including the transistor and the laser. Today, the Nabisco plant (bounded by Ninth and Eleventh Avenues and 15th and 16th Streets) has been transformed into a wonderful food market and TV studio complex called Chelsea Market, and the Bell Labs have become Westbeth (bounded by Washington, West, Bank, and Bethune Streets), a subsidized housing complex for artists.

What about the High Line? As a result of the decline in waterfront commerce, the trains stopped running in 1980. The part south of Gansevoort Street had already been decommissioned and demolished in the 1960s. The rest awaited demolition. Even though some local business owners considered the hulking structure a blight on the neighborhood, there was no real urgency to take it down. (Among other things, CSX Corporation—which had taken over Conrail, which had in turn taken over the freight operations of the New York Central—and the city dithered over who would pay the costs of dismantling it.) Over the years, many people grew fascinated by the structure: by its history, by its ghostly presence, and by how nature had claimed it, as riotously colorful wildflowers had crowded the old train bed. Though it was illegal to

The walkway snakes among older industrial buildings, with the prominent exception of the Standard Hotel, which was built over the High Line, between 13th Street and Little West 12th Street.

climb up for a look, many people did. The renowned photographer Joel Sternfeld became particularly obsessed, and his 2002 book, *Walking the High Line*, drew attention to the potential of the forlorn viaduct more than perhaps anything else.

In 1999, 30-year-old West Village resident Robert Hammond, an artist, and 36-year-old Chelsea resident Joshua David, a freelance writer, both fascinated by the elevated structure, met at a Community Board hearing and soon thereafter formed a group called Friends of the High Line. Inspired by the Washington, D.C.–based Rails to Trails Conservancy, a nonprofit organization that advocates for the conversion of disused railroad rights-of-way into walking trails, and by the Promenade plantée, the three-mile-long park built in the 1990s atop an obsolete railroad viaduct in the 12th arrondissement of Paris, Hammond and David fought vigorously for the preservation of the High Line. They faced opposition from the administration of Mayor Rudolph W. Giuliani, who sided with the property owners who wanted the structure removed. Nevertheless,

Hammond and David persevered, demonstrating a genius for publicity. Gradually, their idea gained traction not only with the public but also with Mayor Michael R. Bloomberg and such deep-pocketed backers as InterActive Corporation's Barry Diller and his wife, fashion designer Diane von Furstenberg, and hedge-fund director Philip Falcone and his wife, Lisa Maria Falcone. Hammond and David saved the High Line. In 2003 Friends of the High Line held a competition for the park's design. The architects Diller Scofidio + Renfro, landscape architects James Corner Field Operations, and garden designer Piet Oudolf won the competition and created the dazzling park we see today.

In his 2001 piece in the *New Yorker*, Adam Gopnik noted that the photographer Joel Sternfeld wanted the High Line to become a park but only if its overtaken-by-nature state ("what spring in New York actually looks like when it's left up to Spring") was kept as undisturbed as possible and not gussied up into what passes for a park. Gussied up the High Line is. There is no getting around it. But there's also no getting around that it is gussied up—"a construct," as Joel Sternfeld said of Central Park, "made for an effect"—in a way very different from Central Park or any but the most recent generation of New York City parks. It is an example of what many call Landscape Urbanism.

James Corner, whose firm co-designed the High Line, is a principal figure in Landscape Urbanism. Born in 1961, Corner has been the chair of the Department of Landscape Architecture at the University of Pennsylvania since 2000, and he is one of the most influential figures in contemporary landscape design. (The firm of James Corner Field Operations operates out of New York City and Philadelphia.) Landscape Urbanism seeks, among other things, to restore the primacy of landscape to urban design, and to do so at a level that is more "archaeological" than what is usually meant by "urbanistic." Another important figure in Landscape Urbanism, Charles Waldheim of the Harvard Graduate School of Design, wrote, of another Corner project:

> Corner's proposition here would be that the shape of the public realm, the shape of the parks and the plazas and the open spaces, would not be derived by urban precedent from models of the 19th century, would not be derived by walking radii of transit oriented development or other principles. It would be derived from a mapping of the plumes of the toxicity subsurface onsite.

That may at first sound opaque. But the first sentence tells us that the Landscape Urbanist is not particularly interested in fitting his design into the existing context of the surrounding city—that's what the "New

Urbanists" want to do. The second sentence tells us that the design is generated by the deep history of the site—the "plumes" of its past. In so many of our contemporary urban landscape designs we find these combinations (threatening to become a cliché!) of industrial archaeology and native ecology—of, at the High Line, the carefully preserved industrial-strength steel trestle and the sort of native wildflowers and trees and shrubs that took spontaneous root on the rail bed in the years of abandonment. This is what makes the High Line different from Central Park, which was an idealized landscape design imposed upon as much of a tabula rasa as the park's creators could make of its unprepossessing site. Calvert Vaux and Frederick Law Olmsted did not in any way try to tease from their 843 acres the essences of what had been there in the past—although a number of outcrops of Manhattan schist did get in the way. The High Line is largely about what the High Line has been throughout its history. Even the putto's-eye view is part of that: it's the view that Joel Sternfeld and a host of urban adventurers enjoyed for all those years, as did the trainmen before them.

The experience of the High Line, thus, is that of a walkway in the sky, snaking among old industrial buildings, tunneling here, sideswiping there, ever slithering. It unexpectedly has in common with Central Park a sinuousness, an ever-shifting perspective that yields roller coaster–like surprises. And along the way you look not only outward from the elevated structure, but also at it itself, at the plantings, the wild grasses, the shrubs and trees and wildflowers, including such native species as Eastern redbud, sumac, amelanchier, sassafras, magnolia, swamp rose mallow, joe-pye weed, and on and on. (Of the 210 plant species used in the first section of the High Line, 161 are native to New York.) In the second section, which opened in June 2011, at the very northern end, at 30th Street, is the Cut-Out, where a transparent floor has replaced a 15-by-35-foot section of the concrete decking to expose the viaduct's steel skeleton of beams, girders, and columns. Framed by native sassafras, birch, and juniper, the Cut-Out makes plain the site's combination of manufactured structure and native ecology.

The relationship of the High Line to new architecture in its neighborhood is also an important part of the experience. The Standard Hotel, designed by Todd Schliemann of Polshek Partnership Architects and opened in 2009, has the most direct connection to the park. Located at 13th Street, the 20-story hotel, comprising two great concrete and glass slabs that evoke an open book, straddles the High Line on giant concrete haunches. These haunches—or pilotis in the language of Le Corbusier, whose spirit informs Schliemann's design—raise the main body of the building some 56 feet from the street (and thus about 26 feet above the High Line). It's a remarkably contextual design in the way it evokes the sorts of reinforced-concrete industrial buildings through which the trains once rumbled.

In the past few years the nearby streets have experienced—in large measure because of the High Line—a frenzy of development. In a city long criticized for its insular architectural culture and for its failure in recent decades to build much in the way of attention-grabbing buildings, the new architecture along the High Line signals a new era for New York. The new buildings include the IAC (InterActive Corporation) Building (2007), Frank Gehry's first building in New York, and Jean Nouvel's 100 Eleventh Avenue (2008), on either side of 19th Street from each other on Eleventh Avenue; the Metal Shutter Houses (2010) by Shigeru Ban and Dean Maltz, on 19th Street between Tenth and Eleventh Avenues; and the Porter House (2003) by SHoP, on 15th Street between Eighth and Ninth Avenues. It's been said of Landscape Urbanist landscapes that they are ideally suited to setting off "object buildings," the context-defying, often showy buildings we've come to expect from jet-setting "starchitects" for whom what New York has in common with, say, Hong Kong as a global city is more important than what the physical fabric of one lot in West Chelsea may have in common with that of an adjoining lot. The streets surrounding the High Line have become a kind of architectural theme park; as chic new buildings vie with one another for attention, only the High Line, threading its way, holds them all together. A new 200,000-square-foot Whitney Museum of American Art, designed by Renzo Piano, is scheduled to open in 2015 at Gansevoort and Washington Streets, right at the southern terminus of the High Line, in the ultra-fashionable Meatpacking District, near the Alexander McQueen boutique and the Apple Store.

The first two sections of the High Line cost $152 million. A great deal is also expended in the meticulous upkeep of the park. Much of the funding comes from private sources. The Friends of the High Line manages the park in an arrangement with the city similar to those of the Central Park Conservancy and the Bryant Park Restoration Corporation. The only existing stretch of High Line not yet incorporated into the park is the part extending north from 30th to 34th Streets—the bit that is in the train yards. At this writing, that section has just been acquired for conversion to park use.

Adam Gopnik said in 2001 that the "High Line is a place where the discordant encounters of its city are briefly resolved." He was referring to the pre-park High Line. But it is just as true of the High Line today. —F. M.

HOURS: 7 am–11 pm daily, last entrance 10:45 pm

RESTROOMS: West 16th Street, wheelchair accessible

REGULATIONS: Dogs, skateboards, scooters, and bicycles are not allowed on the High Line

Smoking is prohibited

MAP & FURTHER INFORMATION AVAILABLE AT:
www.thehighline.org/about/park-information

BY SUBWAY: L, A, C, E to 14th Street and 8th Avenue, walk west 2 blocks

C, E to 23rd Street and 8th Avenue, walk west 2 blocks

1, 2, 3 to 14th Street and 7th Avenue, walk west 3 blocks

1 to 18th Street and 7th Avenue, walk west 3 blocks

1 to 23rd Street and 7th Avenue, walk west 3 blocks

BY BUS: M11 to W 14th Street and Washington Street, walk west 1 block; 9th Avenue and 16th Street, walk west 2 blocks; 9th Avenue and 19th Street, walk north 1 block to 20th Street and west 2 blocks

M14 to Hudson Street and Horatio Street, walk north 1 block and west 2 blocks

M20 to 8th Avenue and 14th Street, walk west 2 blocks

M23 to 23rd Street and 10th Avenue, walk south 3 blocks and west <1 block

M34 to 34th Street and 10th Avenue, walk south 4 blocks to 30th Street

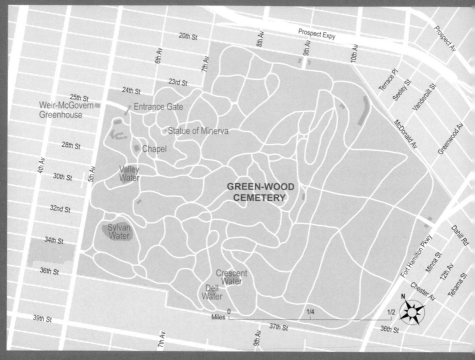

GREEN-WOOD CEMETERY

Map by Jonathan Richman
Jerry Kelly, and John Hill

CEMETERIES

GREEN-WOOD CEMETERY, BROOKLYN

20

The main entrance is located at 5th Avenue and 25th Street in Brooklyn; alternate entrances are located at 4th Avenue and 35th Street; 20th Street and Prospect Park West; and Fort Hamilton Parkway

Geologically and historically, Brooklyn has three main sections. To the west lie the neighborhoods of the original City of Brooklyn, established by state charter in 1834. For the most part, these neighborhoods are now known as "brownstone Brooklyn"—Brooklyn Heights, Fort Greene, Bedford-Stuyvesant, Cobble Hill, Carroll Gardens, Park Slope. To the east lie the old towns of Flatbush and Flatlands. Straddling the borough between these two sections is a terminal moraine. One may follow it on a map by drawing a line connecting a number of big green spaces: from Owl's Head Park, in Bay Ridge, through Green-Wood Cemetery and Prospect Park, to the Cemetery of the Evergreens hard by the border with Queens. In 1839, when Green-Wood Cemetery began, only the parts of the City of Brooklyn nearest the East River and the ferry landings from which the Brooklyn resident commuted to a job in Manhattan possessed an urban character. Farther inland, all was rural, at least until the 1860s, when the extension of horse streetcar lines began to bring neighborhoods such as those near the new Prospect Park (1865–73) into the metropolitan orbit. Flatbush and Flatlands, however, remained dominated by farms until the end of the 19th century.

Atop the moraine, though, neither urbanization nor farming was an option. As geologist Anita Harris told the writer John McPhee in 1983, "In glacial country, all you have to do is look for cemeteries if you want to find the moraine. . . . A moraine is poor farmland—steep and hummocky, with erratics and boulders. Yet it's easy ground to dig in, and well drained."

Green-Wood Cemetery is, in a manner of speaking, the original urban landscape of New York. Mount Auburn Cemetery in Cambridge, Massachusetts, opened in 1831. It was the first "rural cemetery" in America. Before Mount Auburn and its immediate followers, including Philadelphia's Laurel Hill and Brooklyn's Green-Wood, we buried our dead in graveyards. Of varying dimensions, they were located primarily in churchyards and town centers. Many of the squares and small parks of old American cities—in New York, think of

Washington Square, Bryant Park, Madison Square—originally served as "potter's fields," where the poor and indigent who could not afford proper burials were placed in unmarked graves. However, in the 19th century, as cities grew rapidly, so did their stores of dead bodies. The graveyards filled up. In addition, as little-understood contagious diseases took a horrible toll in lives, many people came to believe that all the putrefying bodies so close to the surface of the earth somehow contributed to the "miasmas" held to be responsible for so much disease. In 1830 a group of prominent New Yorkers established the New York Marble Cemetery, on Second Avenue between 2nd and 3rd Streets. Here the deceased spend eternity in 156 large underground vaults constructed of Tuckahoe marble—a bulwark against miasma. (A year later, a companion New York City Marble Cemetery opened on 2nd Street between First and Second Avenues.)

Henry Evelyn Pierrepont (1808–1888) had another idea. The son of Hezekiah Pierrepont, the principal early developer of Brooklyn Heights, Henry Pierrepont was as prominent a man as lived in Brooklyn. He conceived of Green-Wood Cemetery, high atop the moraine at the farthest edge of the City of Brooklyn. As a contemporary observer put it, "The idea of a rural cemetery, sufficiently remote to be beyond the range of city improvements, yet so near as to be of convenient access, seemed to reach, at once, all the necessities of the case." As an owner of the Union Ferry Company, which had a monopoly on the passage between Brooklyn and

FACING PAGE AND RIGHT Green-Wood, located in the City of Brooklyn when it opened in 1838, was part of the rural cemetery movement. In addition to offering a magnificent final resting place for New Yorkers, its rolling hills and splendid lookouts attracted picnickers, promenaders, and tourists.

Manhattan, Pierrepont established a ferry landing at Hamilton Avenue, in Red Hook. From there, it was a two-mile coach ride to Green-Wood. (A byproduct of Pierrepont's new ferry was the development of the neighborhood of Carroll Gardens.) On land purchased between 1838 and 1840, Pierrepont built a 175-acre landscaped cemetery (expanded to its present 478 acres between 1844 and 1895), laid out by a military engineer named David Bates Douglass (1790–1849). The designers of America's early landscape parks often were engineers, experienced in such matters as building retaining walls and drainage systems that were thought to be beyond the expertise of the American gardeners of the time. (Douglass, by the way, resigned from Green-Wood in 1841 to become president of Kenyon College in Ohio.)

The first burials at Green-Wood took place in 1840. Like Mount Auburn, it was a great rural park, kin to the great country parks of England. (Emphasis on rural: the cemetery's promoters did not wish for it to be called a necropolis, not because of necro, but because polis conjured an image of cities.) In a country, let alone a city, where few places of its kind existed, Green-Wood was a sensation. The romantic grounds, pathways winding among hills and lakes and trees, broad lawns, attractive monuments, breathtaking views from high atop the moraine, and hospitableness to carriages all made Green-Wood a destination not just for the dead and their grieving families, but for picnickers, Sunday strollers, nature lovers, and amorous couples.

In an 1847 guidebook called *Green-Wood Illustrated*, Nehemiah Cleaveland wrote:

> Now you pass over verdant and sunny lawns,—now through park-like groves,—and now by the side of a tangled, unpruned forest. At one moment, you are in the dell, with its still waters, its overhanging shade, and its sweet repose. At the next, you look out from the hill-top, on the imperial city, with its queenly daughter—on the bay, so beautiful and life-like—down into the quiet, rural hamlet—or beyond it, on the distant ocean.

Two years later, the Newburgh, New York–based landscape gardener Andrew Jackson Downing wrote in *The Horticulturist* (July 18, 1849):

> The great attraction of these cemeteries is not in the fact that they are burial places ... All these might be realized in a burial ground planted with straight lines of willows and sombre avenues of evergreens. The true secret of the attraction lies in the natural beauty of the sites, and in the tasteful and harmonious embellishment of these sites by art.... Hence to the inhabitant of the town a visit to one of these spots has the united charm of nature and art—the double wealth of rural and moral associations. ... Indeed, in the absence of great public gardens, such as we must surely one day have in America, our rural cemeteries are doing a great deal to enlarge and educate the popular taste in rural embellishment.

Downing went on: "The passion for rural pleasures is destined to be the predominant passion of all the more thoughtful and educated portion of our people, and any means of gratifying their love for ornamental or useful gardening will be eagerly seized by hundreds of thousands of our countrymen."

In fact, the rural cemeteries did not attract pleasure-seekers by accident. Like any new service or product, the cemeteries had to build a market. People who were used to burying their dead in churchyards might not at first go in for the idea of a big cemetery miles from town. So Green-Wood and the other cemeteries played up the experience of a day's outing in a magnificently landscaped setting. Once the public fell in love with the setting, then they might wish to bury their dead there.

"The time inevitably came," wrote park historian M. M. Graff, "as Downing foresaw, when the underground population, prominently represented by sorrowing angels and whiskered effigies in marble frock coats, outweighed the festive atmosphere of a notable collection of flowering shrubs and trees." Today, some 560,000 people lie buried in Green-Wood Cemetery. (You could say it's the second largest city in New York State.)

Downing was one of the two principal advocates for the creation of a proper public park for New York City (the other was nature poet and newspaper editor William Cullen Bryant). In fact, if Downing had not died tragically in a steamboat accident in 1852, he undoubtedly would have designed Central Park. In his stead, the job went to Frederick Law Olmsted, a long-time avid reader of Downing's *Horticulturist*, and English architect Calvert Vaux, who had been Downing's assistant in the Newburgh practice. Their Greensward plan of 1858 won the competition for the design of Central Park. Brooklyn soon hired them to design Prospect Park a stone's throw from Green-Wood. But make no mistake: the success of Green-Wood paved the way for New York's two greatest public parks.

Today, Douglass's layout remains largely intact, and the additions, which extend south and east to Fort Hamilton Parkway and McDonald Avenue, basically follow the style of the original section, though the topography is not nearly as dramatic as in the original, northwestern section of the cemetery—the part just inside the Fifth Avenue and 25th Street gate. (The present gate dates from 1861–65.) The layout of paths in squiggly lines around amoeboid plots makes Central Park's layout look like a grid. But Green-Wood preserves far more of the original contours of the land than Central Park. The bodies of water are glacial kettles; the hills are original. Douglass even worked around most of the trees that were already on the site. In con-

Minerva and the Altar to Liberty was erected in 1920 to commemorate the Battle of Brooklyn, fought on August 27, 1776, on land that is now part of Green-Wood Cemetery. The monument stands on Battle Hill, where Minerva's raised hand is waving to the Statue of Liberty, which faces Battle Hill 3.5 miles to the west.

trast, Olmsted and Vaux treated the Central Park site as a tabula rasa. As mausoleums appeared at Green-Wood, they resembled the garden follies on the great English country estates, and that is how visitors experienced them.

Of the view from atop Green-Wood's Ocean Hill, the highest point in Brooklyn, Nehemiah Cleaveland wrote:

> Toward the east the view is unobstructed and wide. From the base of the hill stretch far away the plains of Flatbush and New Utrecht. Below, a short mile distant, lies the little village of Flatbush,—an image of quiet life,—with its white dwellings and simple spire [that of the Flatbush Reformed Dutch Church that still stands at Flatbush and Church Avenues]; the Pavilion at Rockaway, some ten miles off, is clearly seen; while the sea itself, with here and there a sail, terminates the view.

The views alone—no less breathtaking today than in 1847—drew countless visitors to the cemetery.

One of the most startling architectural and landscape experiences in New York can be had by going to the intersection of Fifth Avenue and 25th Street in Brooklyn. On the west side of Fifth Avenue stands the great glass-domed Weir-McGovern Greenhouse, built in 1895, a superb specimen of 19th-century greenhouse architecture, and one of the few greenhouses to be seen in the city today (neither Central Park nor Prospect Park retains the greenhouses they once had). Today it is in a pitiably deteriorated condition. But it has recently been purchased by Green-Wood Cemetery, which plans to restore it—something some of us look forward to eagerly. Across Fifth Avenue from the greenhouse is the main entrance to the cemetery, announced by a great Gothic gate of the 1860s, designed by Richard Michell Upjohn, who with his father, Richard Upjohn, the architect of Manhattan's Trinity Church, helped spread the Gothic gospel that affected so much of Victorian architecture in America. From the gate, Landscape Avenue curves gracefully a short distance to the chapel, faced in Indiana limestone, one of the loveliest churches in New York. Designed by Warren & Wetmore and completed in 1911, its design draws upon Sir Christopher Wren's Tom Tower (1682) at Christ Church, Oxford. But whereas Tom Tower is monumental, the Green-Wood chapel is intimate, a miraculous transmutation, by great architects, of a historical precedent. (The little-used chapel closed in the 1980s but was restored and reopened in 2000.) Beyond lay the hills and valleys, aqueous bodies and snaking paths among the gravestones and mausoleums. The Manhattan-based landscape architecture firm Quennell Rothschild & Partners is in charge of master planning and continuing preservation at Green-Wood.

Schoolchildren at the William Holbrook Beard Memorial, looking at the new bronze sculpture by renowned animal artist Dan Ostermiller, installed in 2002 by the Green-Wood Historic Fund. Beard was himself an animal painter, best known for his satiric canvas *Bulls and Bears in the Market* (1879), which poked fun at Wall Street.

Of course, many people visit Green-Wood to see the final resting places of the countless famous (and infamous) New Yorkers interred there. The best book on Green-Wood, including information on the illustrious persons buried there, is Jeff Richman's *Brooklyn's Green-Wood Cemetery: New York's Buried Treasure* (1998). Among those you will find at Green-Wood are New York's greatest mayor, DeWitt Clinton; Henry Ward Beecher, the Brooklyn Heights preacher once said to be the most famous man in America; James Gordon Bennett, founder of the *New York Herald*, the first truly modern newspaper; conductor and composer Leonard Bernstein; industrialist and philanthropist Peter Cooper; the great lithographers Nathaniel Currier and James Merritt Ives; financier Leonard Jerome, who was Winston Churchill's grandfather; Lola Montez, mistress to King Ludwig of Bavaria; father and son Henry and William Steinway, who built the greatest piano company in the world; James S. T. Stranahan, the "Baron Haussmann of Brooklyn"; jewelry baron Charles Lewis Tiffany and his artist son Louis Comfort Tiffany (in the plainest of graves); the notorious Tammany Hall leader William "Boss" Tweed;

and on and on it goes—including all four of the Brooks brothers. Leading sculptors and architects designed many of the memorials and mausoleums.

On a personal note, many know me as a leader of architectural tours in New York. Some wonder why I never lead tours of Green-Wood Cemetery. I do not for two reasons. First, Green-Wood offers its own excellent tours, and I do not want my tours to piggy-back on the research of others, such as Green-Wood's historian Jeff Richman. Second, Green-Wood is my own oasis. When I am down, or when I need to think through a problem, or even if it's just a nice day, I walk the 20 or so blocks from my home to the great Gothic gate and then wander through the grounds, just as though I had come by coach in the 1850s. If I knew it as I know the places where I lead tours, I'd perhaps know it better. But I would not know it as personally. —F.M.

HOURS: 25th Street entrance: 8 am–5 pm daily, with extended summer hours

4th Avenue entrance: 8 am–4 pm daily

20th Street and Prospect Park West, and Fort Hamilton Parkway: 8 am–4 pm weekends only

NOTE: Entrances may be closed due to inclement weather. Call ahead.

RESTROOMS: 25th Street arches, near the information kiosk

REGULATIONS: Biking, jogging, filming, food, beverages, and pets (with the exception of service animals) are prohibited

Smoking is prohibited

MAP & FURTHER INFORMATION AVAILABLE AT: www.green-wood.com

BY SUBWAY: R to 25th Street and 4th Avenue, walk southeast 1 block on 25th Street (25th Street entrance)

D, N, R to 36th Street and 4th Avenue, walk northeast 1 block on 4th Avenue (4th Avenue entrance)

F, G to 15th Street-Prospect Park and Prospect Park West, walk northwest 1 block to Prospect Park West and southwest 6 blocks on Prospect Park West (Prospect Park West entrance)

BY BUS: B63 to 5th Avenue and 24th Street, walk southwest 1 block to 25th Street (25th Street entrance)

B70 to 36th Street and 4th Avenue, walk northeast 1 block on 4th Avenue (4th Avenue entrance)

B67, B69 to 20th Street and Prospect Park West (Prospect Park West entrance)

B61, B67, B69 to Prospect Park West and 19th Street, walk southwest 1 block (Prospect Park West entrance)

B67, B69 to McDonald Avenue and Fort Hamilton Parkway, walk west 2 blocks on Fort Hamilton Parkway (Fort Hamilton Parkway entrance)

B16, B67, B69 to Caton Avenue and McDonald Avenue, walk west 1 block on Caton Avenue, continue west 1 block on Fort Hamilton Parkway (Fort Hamilton Parkway entrance)

The Woodlawn Cemetery entrances are at Webster Avenue and East 233rd Street and at Jerome Avenue and Bainbridge Avenue

Woodlawn Cemetery opened in lower Westchester County in 1863. Its part of the present Borough of the Bronx was not annexed by New York City until 1874. Like Brooklyn's Green-Wood Cemetery, older by a quarter century (see p. 165), Woodlawn was one of the pioneering rural cemeteries in America. Before such cemeteries, city people tended to be buried in one of two ways. The well-off were buried in churchyards, just like out in the country. In Manhattan, there are celebrated church graveyards at Trinity Church, on Broadway and Wall Street, dating to the 17th century, and at St. Paul's Chapel, on Broadway and Fulton Street, dating to the 18th century. In the 1840s, when the present Trinity Church building, designed by Richard Upjohn, was being built, a new and larger Trinity burial ground opened on part of the old estate of John James Audubon, at Broadway and 155th Street. The poor, on the other hand, were buried in potter's fields, such as those at the present sites of Washington Square, Madison Square, and Bryant Park. (Fields of soil mixed with "potter's clay" were not suited to

When it opened in 1863, Woodlawn Cemetery was in a rural setting in the Bronx, and a rail link was built to connect visitors with the developed city to the south. Today, the borough's residential buildings are visible from the sloping grounds on the cemetery's eastern perimeter.

ABOVE AND FACING PAGE Woodlawn Cemetery was designated a National Historic Landmark in 2011 in recognition of the notable figures buried there and the quality of its landscape design.

farming but made fine graveyards. Hence the term potter's field, which came to be used even for paupers' burial grounds in which there was no clay.)

The rural cemeteries were an entirely new concept. Not only were they vast burial fields that no one could imagine ever filling up, but they were also among the first of America's great landscaped parks. Green-Wood became so popular as a pleasure destination that it helped inspire the creation of Central Park. Central Park was under construction, and important sections of it had already opened when Woodlawn Cemetery came into being.

Woodlawn was originally laid out by James Charles Sidney (ca. 1819–1881), an English-born surveyor and architect who had worked in Philadelphia on, among other projects, an expansion of Laurel Hill Cemetery. Sidney moved to New York in 1855 and in 1860 formed a partnership with Frederick C. Merry, a fellow Englishman. The partnership lasted until 1864, through the planning and opening of Woodlawn. About 1850, Sidney laid out Oakwood Cemetery, a great rural cemetery in Troy, New York. Later, he would be well known for house and landscape designs in Cape May, New Jersey.

Sidney designed Woodlawn with the requisite picturesque curving lanes, lake, and ovoid lawns. It is important to remember, however, that in time, cemeteries bear scant resemblance to their original designs. To some extent, this is true of all planted landscapes: things grow. But at least theoretically, through vigilant maintenance, most landscapes can be kept much as their designers intended. Cemeteries are different. They exist to

be filled with memorials and mausoleums, and with each passing decade take on a dramatically different appearance—here a giant mausoleum, there a statue where yesterday there was none. Sometimes, and this has happened at Woodlawn, configurations of lanes and lawns are altered to accommodate bigger or better plots. Thus we may say that David Bates Douglass laid out Green-Wood, and J. C. Sidney laid out Woodlawn, but how much of these talented men's handiwork survives? Today's Woodlawn comprises 400 acres. Some 310,000 people are buried there, and there are a staggering 1,300 private mausoleums, perhaps more than in any other cemetery in the world. To the south the cemetery stretches down almost all the way to Gun Hill Road, to the west it abuts Van Cortlandt Park along Jerome Avenue, to the north it reaches 233rd Street, and to the east it is bordered by Webster Avenue.

There are many unique sights at Woodlawn, including one of only two executed designs in America by Britain's greatest 20th-century architect, Sir Edwin Lutyens. It is a modest but affecting memorial to James Keteltas Hackett, once a famous actor of stage and silent screen, who died in 1926. (Lutyens's other American work is the British Embassy in Washington, D.C.) The grounds of the memorial were laid out by none other than Ellen Biddle Shipman (1869–1950), an American landscape gardener who had been strongly influenced by renowned British landscape designer Gertrude Jekyll, who in turn often worked with Lutyens. Around the time Shipman was working at Woodlawn she bought and renovated a dilapidated old row house on the northeast corner of Beekman Place and 50th Street in Manhattan. She was among the first wave of residents to "gentrify" what had been a very down-at-the-heels neighborhood. She operated her landscape gardening firm—which employed only women—out of that house. Another eminent American landscape gardener who worked at Woodlawn was Beatrix Jones Farrand, niece of the novelist Edith Wharton. Farrand landscaped the grounds surrounding the mausoleum of philanthropist Edward Stephen Harkness (1874–1940). The beautiful Gothic mausoleum, set in a gated courtyard landscaped by Farrand, was designed by James Gamble Rogers, who also designed Harkness's house on Fifth Avenue and 75th Street, as well as the Harkness Quadrangle at Yale University.

Other architects of note designed mausoleums at Woodlawn, including Carrère & Hastings, McKim, Mead & White, and John Russell Pope. And important sculptors such as Sally James Farnham, Paul Wayland Bartlett, and Daniel Chester French contributed statuary. Among the notable New Yorkers buried at Woodlawn are Herman Melville, Gertrude Vanderbilt Whitney, David Glasgow Farragut, Fiorello La Guardia, Elizabeth Cady Stanton, Jay Gould, R. H. Macy, Isidor Straus, Robert Moses, Joseph Pulitzer, Duke Ellington, W. C. Handy, Miles Davis, Madame C. J. Walker, Irving Berlin, Irene and Vernon Castle, George M. Cohan, and Florence Mills. If Green-Wood is the final resting place for a good many of the mid-19th-century elite (including the South Street merchant princes and the early baseball greats), as well as Brooklynites of all times, Woodlawn, which truly came into its own in the late 19th century, was the final destination of choice for the Gilded Age elite as well as many famous 20th-century entertainers. —F.M.

HOURS: 8:30 am–5 pm

RESTROOMS: At the entrance gates

REGULATIONS: Leashed dogs are permitted

Jogging and biking are prohibited

Photography permits are required

MAP & FURTHER INFORMATION AVAILABLE AT: www.thewoodlawncemetery.org

BY SUBWAY: 4 to Woodlawn Station, walk north <1 block to Jerome Street entrance

2, 5 to 233rd Street, walk west 3 blocks on 233rd Street, cross Webster Avenue

BY TRAIN: Metro North Harlem Line local from Grand Central to Woodlawn Station, turn right at top of exit stairs, cross Webster Street

BY BUS: Bx16, Bx31 to East 233rd Street and Webster Avenue

Bx16, Bx34 to Bainbridge Avenue and Jerome Avenue

BOULEVARDS

EASTERN PARKWAY AND OCEAN PARKWAY, BROOKLYN

22

The Eastern Parkway pedestrian mall runs from Grand Army Plaza east to Ralph Avenue in Brooklyn

Ocean Parkway runs through Brooklyn from the Prospect Park area to Coney Island

Think "boulevard," and Paris comes to mind—or maybe Chicago. But New York, too, is a city of boulevards. Broadway on the Upper West Side comes closest to the typical boulevards of central Paris, lined by stately apartment blocks with stores, restaurants, cafés, bakeries, and so on at street level. The Grand Concourse in the Bronx is different. It is the boulevard sans commerce. Even before zoning codes, developers respected Americans' predilection for streets and neighborhoods that are exclusively residential, free of the moral taint of business. We share this predilection with the English. The French are different—hence the lively boulevards mixing residences and businesses.

Frederick Law Olmsted and Calvert Vaux were responsible for designing both Ocean Parkway and Eastern Parkway. More accessible than Ocean Parkway, Eastern Parkway became a sought-after address both for residences and institutions.

Though built in the 19th century, Ocean Parkway adapted to the automotive age without missing a beat. The north–south boulevard, over 5 miles long, is also a great pedestrian favorite because walkers have their own path.

Brooklyn has boulevards, too. Frederick Law Olmsted and Calvert Vaux laid out Eastern Parkway and Ocean Parkway in the 1870s as part of the same project that gave us the glorious 585-acre Prospect Park. Eastern Parkway extends from the park's northeast corner, at Grand Army Plaza (p. 197), and runs a little more than two miles through Crown Heights to Ralph Avenue. (A later Eastern Parkway Extension brought the road up to Atlantic Avenue.) Vaux and Olmsted intended it to be part of a network— never completed—of "parkways" (their coinage) linking parks throughout the metropolis. More accessible than Ocean Parkway to the old, established parts of Brooklyn, Eastern Parkway became a sought-after address both for residences and for institutions. Notably, the Brooklyn Museum opened in 1897 at 200 Eastern Parkway, at Washington Avenue.

Ocean Parkway, which begins at the southern end of Prospect Park, connects that park to Seaside (now Asser Levy) Park in Coney Island. It is New York's most finely realized boulevard.

Ocean Parkway had a Parisian model—Avenue de l'Impératrice. So where are the cafés? In fact, Napoleon III built that stately boulevard between the

Arc de Triomphe and the Bois de Boulogne as a strictly residential thoroughfare with fine houses, allées of chestnut trees, and a carriage drive. The emperor was an Anglophile, and Avenue de l'Impératrice (now called Avenue Foch) was an English-style drive. Olmsted had visited Paris and met Adolphe Alphand, the engineer and park designer Napoleon III put in charge of the renovation of the Bois de Boulogne and the Bois de Vincennes, the former royal hunting grounds. The emperor told Alphand to make them more English than French. Alphand also laid out Avenue de l'Impératrice.

Ocean Parkway may be lacking cafés and have stretches of undistinguished architecture, but it remains a model of sound urbanism. Our traffic planners should take note.

Though built in the 19th century, Ocean Parkway adapted to the automotive age without missing a beat. That is because a true boulevard is flexible and perfectly accommodates a wide range of quotidian human activities—swift movement, slow movement, sitting, kibitzing, children's play, group knitting, exercise, reading, people watching. The center lane of Ocean Parkway serves through, or "express," automobile traffic—it originally served carriages out on pleasure drives. (Robert Moses also made it a connector road between the Prospect Expressway and the Belt Parkway.) On either side of the express lane are tree-lined pedestrian malls. These are not just medians like those on Broadway. The pedestrian accesses them across the flanking "local" drives; thus the pedestrian does not have to cross the central express lane to reach the malls.

In 1894 the City of Brooklyn established the first dedicated bicycle lanes in the present boundaries of New York City (and perhaps in the United States) on Ocean Parkway, and the fast, level surface remains a bicyclist's delight. Some call the 1890s the Golden Age of bicycling. Safe, affordable, mass-produced bicycles seemed poised to become a dominant form of commuting. Soon, however, the automobile arrived on the scene, relegating the bicycle to the plaything of suburban children. Bicycle commuting returned with the oil shocks of the 1970s, and has only grown since then. Today, amid concerns about climate change and energy scarcity, municipalities the world over seek to increase bicycle ridership. The Danish urban planner Jan Gehl is a global leader in this movement. So, too, is the current New York City transportation commissioner, Janette Sadik-Khan, who took a page from the Jan Gehl playbook when she set out, soon after her appointment by Mayor Michael R. Bloomberg in 2007, to establish a series of new bike lanes in the city. For a look at her handiwork, go to Prospect Park West, which runs from 15th Street on the south to Flatbush Avenue and the western terminus of Eastern Parkway on the north. A lane of cars parked not at the curb but several feet from the curb, making room for the bikes, protects the bike lane on the east side of the broad roadway. Sadik-Khan has placed several such protected bike lanes throughout the city. Ocean Parkway's "protected" bike lane predates Sadik-Khan's by well more than a century. An iron railing separates cyclists from pedestrians (the elderly, who are often terrified of illegal sidewalk cyclists, feel more comfortable in their protected lane on Ocean Parkway than they do just about anywhere else), and a row of trees separates cyclists from motorists. It may be the best setup in the whole city. Bridle paths also operated on the parkway as late as the 1970s and one wishes they still did.

In their excellent *The Boulevard Book: History, Evolution, Design of Multiway Boulevards* (2002), Allan B. Jacobs, Elizabeth Macdonald, and Yodan Rofé extol the virtues of boulevards like Ocean Parkway, calling them "wonderful, human, community places." Modern traffic planners tend to separate the various modes of transportation in the wholly mistaken belief that such separation increases safety and efficiency. In the automobile age, we routinely allowed traffic engineers to eviscerate swaths of city. As we enter the post-automobile age, we can, and must, do better. Boulevards knit together a community's varied activities with safety, efficiency, comeliness, and responsiveness to elemental human needs—that is to say, with everything that is missing from the Brooklyn–Queens Expressway. —F.M.

EASTERN PARKWAY

REGULATIONS: Smoking is prohibited on the pedestrian mall

MAP & FURTHER INFORMATION AVAILABLE AT: www.nycgovparks.org/parks/B029/

BY SUBWAY: 2, 3 to Eastern Parkway-Brooklyn Museum; Franklin Avenue and Eastern Parkway

4 to Eastern Parkway-Brooklyn Museum; Franklin Avenue and Eastern Parkway; Nostrand Avenue and Eastern Parkway; Kingston Avenue and Eastern Parkway; Crown Heights-Utica Avenue and Eastern Parkway

5 to Franklin Avenue and Eastern Parkway

BY BUS: B41, B69 to Flatbush Avenue and Grand Army Plaza, walk east to Eastern Parkway

B49 to Bedford Avenue and Eastern Parkway; Rogers Avenue and Eastern Parkway

B44 to Nostrand Avenue and Eastern Parkway

B43 to Brooklyn Avenue and Eastern Parkway

B17 to Troy Avenue and Eastern Parkway; Schenectady Avenue and Eastern Parkway; Utica Avenue and Eastern Parkway

B17, B46 to Utica Avenue and Eastern Parkway

B14 to Rochester Avenue and Eastern Parkway; Buffalo Avenue and Eastern Parkway

Residents gather under the tree-lined mall to socialize and play cards or board games.

OCEAN PARKWAY

REGULATIONS: Smoking is prohibited on the Parkway malls

MAP & FURTHER INFORMATION AVAILABLE AT: www.nycgovparks.org/parks/B065/

BY SUBWAY: F to 18th Avenue, walk northeast 4 blocks on 18th Avenue; Avenue I, walk east 5 blocks on Avenue I; Avenue N, walk east 5 blocks on Avenue N; Avenue P, walk east 5 blocks on Avenue P; Kings Highway, walk east 5 blocks on Kings Highway; Avenue U, walk east 7 blocks on Avenue U; Avenue X, walk east 9 blocks on Avenue X; Neptune Avenue, walk east 2 long blocks on Neptune Avenue

B, Q to Avenue U, walk west 10 blocks on Avenue U

Q to Ocean Parkway

BY BUS: B11 to Avenue I and Ocean Parkway

B6 to Avenue J and Ocean Parkway

B9 to Avenue M and Ocean Parkway; Avenue N and Ocean Parkway

B82 to Kings Highway and Ocean Parkway

B3 to Avenue U and Ocean Parkway

B4 to Avenue Z and Ocean Pkwy; Ocean Parkway and Shore Parkway North

B36 to Avenue Z and Ocean Parkway; Ocean Parkway and Shore Parkway; Ocean Parkway and West Avenue

B1 to Avenue X and Ocean Parkway; Ocean Parkway and Shore Parkway; Ocean Parkway and West Avenue; Ocean Parkkway and Neptune Avenue; Ocean Parkway and Ocean View Avenue; Brighton Beach and Ocean Parkway

B68 to Brighton Beach Avenue and Ocean Parkway

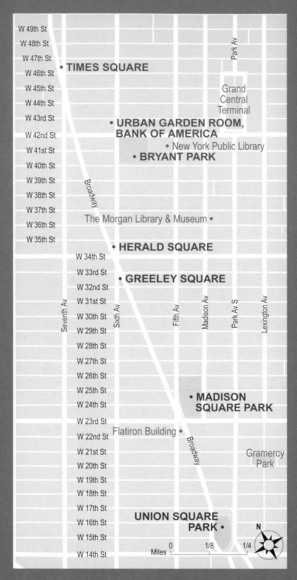

W 49th St
W 48th St
W 47th St
W 46th St · **TIMES SQUARE**
W 45th St
W 44th St
W 43rd St
W 42nd St · **URBAN GARDEN ROOM,**
BANK OF AMERICA
W 41st St · New York Public Library
W 40th St · **BRYANT PARK**
W 39th St
W 38th St
W 37th St
W 36th St The Morgan Library & Museum ·
W 35th St

Broadway

Park Av

Grand
Central
Terminal

W 34th St · **HERALD SQUARE**
W 33rd St
W 32nd St · **GREELEY SQUARE**
W 31st St
W 30th St
W 29th St
W 28th St
W 27th St
W 26th St
W 25th St
W 24th St · **MADISON**
SQUARE PARK
W 23rd St
W 22nd St Flatiron Building ·
W 21st St
W 20th St
W 19th St
W 18th St
W 17th St
W 16th St **UNION SQUARE**
W 15th St **PARK** ·
W 14th St

Seventh Av
Sixth Av
Fifth Av
Madison Av
Park Av S
Lexington Av

Broadway

Gramercy
Park

N

Miles 0   1/8   1/4

BROADWAY AND VICINITY   Map by John Hill

BROADWAY

23

Madison Square is between 5th and Madison Avenues and 23rd and 26th Streets

Herald and Greeley Squares form a bowtie along Broadway; Herald Square is bounded by Broadway, 6th Avenue, and 34th Street; Greeley Square is bounded by Broadway and 6th Avenue and 32nd and 33rd Streets

Times Square consists of the area around the intersection of Broadway and 7th Avenue between 42nd and 47th Streets; the Times Square TKTS booth is located in Father Duffy Square at Broadway and 47th Street

B roadway, New York's most fabled thoroughfare, runs almost the entire length of Manhattan, from Bowling Green, near the southern tip of the island, to the Harlem River. It adheres to the rectilinear grid until it gets to East 10th Street, where it begins its sharp diagonal cut—southeast to northwest—across the grid. The diagonal ends at West 77th Street. In that section—10th to 77th Streets—we find the famous crossings of Broadway with the north–south avenues. More on those in a bit. From West 77th Street to West 108th Street, Broadway follows a kind of squirmy, drunken path, but does not touch any of the avenues until it lurches westward at West 106th Street to rub against West End Avenue

Today's Madison Square is what remains of a large, open space—bounded on the east and west by Third and Seventh Avenues and on the south and north by 23rd and 34th Streets—that was labeled the "Grand Parade" on the Commissioners' Plan of 1811.

A perfect day to relax in Madison Square, overlooked by the strikingly beautiful MetLife tower on the right, and the former northern annex of MetLife to the left.

at lovely Straus Park. From West 108th to West 168th Streets Broadway sobers up and follows a ramrod-straight path. Beyond 168th, it again falls off the wagon.

Our focus is on the diagonal section, from 10th to 77th Street, where Broadway forges a series of openings in the grid. When Broadway crosses an avenue, it makes an X in the street plan, creating two triangular plots of land that form a bowtie—a delightful diversion from the foursquare grid. Look at 23rd Street, where Broadway crosses Fifth Avenue. In the resulting X, the triangle to the south (22nd to 23rd Streets) holds the famous Flatiron Building, designed by Daniel Burnham (1902), a triangular-plan skyscraper. In the triangle to the north (24th to 25th Streets), called Worth Square, we find the 1857 monument to (and burial place of) General William Jenkins Worth, Mexican War hero. (Adjacent Madison Square actually has nothing to do with the spatial consequences of this crossing.)

At 34th Street, the next avenue crossing to the north, where Broadway intersects Sixth Avenue, the triangles are rather different. Greeley Square, on the south, and Herald Square, on the north, serve as public open spaces. For many years both "squares" (they are actually triangles) suffered deferred maintenance and became scruffy patches with broken benches, cracked pavements, and no plantings, inviting only to the homeless. In 1999, however, the 34th Street Partnership—a public-private association through which assessments levied on local businesses supplement city services—completely renovated both squares according to the principles, laid down by William H. Whyte, that had worked so well in Bryant Park (p. 234). (The 34th Street Partnership and the Bryant Park Restoration Corporation are

This formerly barren triangular patch of land at the intersection of Fifth Avenue and Broadway has been transformed.

Greeley Square is a small triangular park south of
34th Street, where Broadway intersects Sixth Avenue.

sister organizations.) In came the movable chairs and tables, the planters
and perennials and shade trees, fancy automated public toilets, food kiosks,
and live entertainment. Immediately, the squares pulsed with life as neighborhood workers and tourists and Macy's shoppers alike flocked to the
refurbished spaces.

At 42nd Street, Broadway crosses Seventh Avenue. In 1904, the city
named the lower triangle (42nd to 43rd Streets) Times Square. Like the
Flatiron Building, the triangular-plan Times Tower filled its site. Today, that
onetime headquarters of the *New York Times* serves purely as a support
for giant advertising signs, though it remains the scene of the annual New
Year's Eve ball drop. The upper triangle (46th to 47th Streets) is Father
Duffy Square (named for Francis Patrick Duffy, a hero priest of World War
I and later pastor of Holy Cross Church on West 42nd Street). Father
Duffy Square hosts the TKTS booth, where same-day half-price tickets
to Broadway and Off-Broadway shows are for sale. Designed by Perkins
Eastman with Choi Ropiha, the structure dates from 2008. It replaced a

The Bell Ringers' Monument by French sculptor Antonin Jean Paul Carles is a focal point of the small, smartly designed Herald Square, across from Macy's.

temporary structure, of canvas, that went up in 1973. (Sometimes things take a long time in New York.) The new structure ingeniously sports a sloping, south-facing roof in the form of grandstand-style seating, where people (primarily tourists) can sit and view the whole panorama of Times Square.

What do you see when you view that panorama? It is, to be sure, a spectacle. It is not, however, your father's spectacle. A center of nightlife and theater since the beginning of the 20th century, Times Square was always raffish. As the 1957 movie *Sweet Smell of Success* attests, raffish could easily sidle up to seamy. By the 1970s and 1980s, words like raffish and seamy were too mild. Times Square in those decades was a place primarily of sex-related businesses (as depicted in the 1976 movie *Taxi Driver*). It all changed in the 1990s, largely through zoning amendments. And it had less to do with "cleaning up" a municipal shame than with relieving development pressure on the East Side, where office skyscrapers began replacing modest tenements in the 1950s, at the very moment that transit access disappeared with the dismantling of the elevated railroads. With each passing decade the situation grew more unbearable. The city was desperate to get office development to shift westward. Times Square was not then, nor had it ever been, an office center. It was a low-rise area. The new zoning permitted tall buildings, and also sent the X-rated businesses packing. (Developers would not build there if those businesses did not leave.) It seemed to many a New Yorker that, virtually overnight, Times Square changed from massage parlors and peep shows to Disney's *The Lion King* and the world headquarters of Ernst & Young.

Amid the changes, many New Yorkers, including distinguished civic organizations such as the Municipal Art Society of New York, feared that the traditional carnival atmosphere of Times Square, particularly its electric signs, would go the way of the X-rated businesses. At the beginning of the 20th century, Times Square glowed with white incandescent bulbs, earning it the sobriquet "Great White Way." In the 1920s, colored neon

Buy discounted tickets to Broadway and Off-Broadway shows at the TKTS booth, then sit on the red steps atop the booth and take in the Times Square scene.

Some traffic lanes in Times Square have been given over to pedestrians and furnished with movable chairs and small tables.

came in, and Times Square was a greater spectacle than ever. Even in its tawdriest years, it blazed in neon glory. Responding to these concerns, the city amended the zoning yet again: today, all new Times Square buildings must devote their lower façades to large electric billboards. This makes Times Square the only place in the world where the law does not merely permit large advertising signs but requires them. In the new Times Square, neon has yielded to various types of computer animation, light-emitting diode displays, and the like, and tourists flock as never before to these newly family-friendly streets to take in a sight like no other in the world.

The consequent crowding led the city to close Broadway to automobiles between 42nd and 47th Streets. Transportation commissioner Janette Sadik-Khan, appointed in 2007 by Mayor Michael R. Bloomberg and inspired by the renowned Danish urban planner Jan Gehl, who is credited with making Copenhagen one of the world's friendliest cities for walkers and bikers, basically used paint and planters to indicate where cars were no longer welcome. Then the movable chairs and tables came in—and, voilà, at shockingly little expense, and virtually overnight, the pedestrian experience in Times Square changed dramatically.

Voices rose in protest: Some businesses complained that this hindered truck deliveries. Cab drivers hated it. In fact, all motorists hated it. (That, of course, was part of the point: to get people to drive less!) And then there are those New Yorkers who pride themselves on their disdain for tourists. The new malls were for the benefit of tourists—New Yorkers be damned. Who thought up this stupid idea of people sitting and sunning themselves right in the middle of Broadway, anyway?

But Sadik-Khan was not done. She extended her malls up and down the Broadway diagonal, and elsewhere. She as much as said that she planned to do what the city found itself unable to do when it established the grid in 1811: eliminate Broadway. Or more precisely, hand it over to the walkers and bikers. At 23rd Street, the mall divides in two. One part is between 23rd and 24th Streets, in the crook to the south of Worth Square and to the west of Madison Square, and the other part is between 22nd and 23rd Streets along the east side of the Flatiron Building. There are plenty of tourists here, too—they go to Shake Shack in Madison Square and to Eataly, the vast Italian food emporium at the northwest corner of Fifth Avenue and 23rd Street. Still, there are fewer tourists than at Times Square, and here they mix in about equal numbers with locals. In this writer's opinion, to sit on a nice afternoon in the mall next to the Flatiron Building is, quite simply, one of the most pleasurable things one can do in New York today. You are right in the middle of Broadway, seeing the city as neither you nor anyone has ever seen it before. It is intoxicating.

The glory of the malls is their utter simplicity. Their simplicity and inexpensiveness may also be their tragedy: a future transportation commissioner could, to placate a constituency (motorists come to mind), as easily dismantle them as Sadik-Khan built them. Enjoy them while you can.

On the Upper West Side, Broadway crosses Amsterdam Avenue (the uptown extension of Tenth Avenue) at West 72nd Street. Between 72nd and 73rd Streets, Verdi Square provides an opening that, unlike most of the other Broadway openings, architects could take full advantage of. That is, the foursquare city grid tends to limit architectural effects requiring dramatic views. The Flatiron Building, to be sure, brings drama to the crossing at 23rd Street. Nothing of scenic drama unfolds at Greeley and Herald Squares. Times Square's drama comes from the signs on buildings, not the buildings themselves. Columbus Circle (p. 194), where Broadway crosses

Eighth Avenue at 59th Street, is perhaps New York's single greatest lost opportunity for architectural grandeur. At Verdi Square, however, the architects Graves and Duboy designed the Ansonia Hotel (1899–1904), on the west side of Broadway between 73rd and 74th Streets, to take full advantage of the open view made possible by Verdi Square. The block-long, 18-story apartment building hovers majestically over the square, a cliff of rich ornamentation, of brackets and balustrades and cabuchons and scroll frames, of filigreed ironwork and grotesque masks. Similarly, the magnificent limestone pile of York & Sawyer's Central Savings Bank (1926–28; now home to the Apple Bank for Savings) commands the north side of Verdi Square. Be sure to go inside.

Verdi Square has a colorful history. The statue of the composer Giuseppe Verdi, by the Sicilian sculptor Pasquale Civiletti, was dedicated in 1906. Figures of characters from Verdi operas—Falstaff, Aïda, Otello, and Leonora (from La Forza del Destino) surround the composer, rendered in Carrara marble. More than any other group, Italian Americans wished upon New York a bounty of statues and took up campaigns to erect them—which explains why New York has a disproportionate number of statues of famous Italians!

In the 1960s and 1970s, the Upper West Side experienced many problems, including high crime. Verdi Square became "Needle Park," a hangout of heroin addicts—and setting of the 1971 film The Panic in Needle Park, starring Al Pacino. The 1980s, however, brought to the Upper West Side, as to so many other parts of New York, a great wave of gentrification that soon made Needle Park a murky memory. Even in the Needle Park days, though, decades before Janette Sadik-Khan set about to transform Broadway into one long mall, the Upper West Side stretch of the broad boulevard had a mall running down its center. Never much to look at, this mall proffered its wooden benches to the elderly Central European denizens of the neighborhood, who whiled away their afternoons in conversation and newspaper reading and people watching. In his beautiful essay "Shadow Cities," which appeared in the New York Review of Books in 1997, the writer André Aciman described "the elderly ladies who sat, not in the park, but along the benches outside," as they

> had probably learned to do on sunny, windy summer days in Central Europe, and as they still do in those mock-England spots in Paris that the French call petits squares, where people chat while their children play. Some of these ladies spoke with thick accents. I pictured their homes to myself, lots of lace, many doilies, Old World silverware, mannered Austro-Hungarian everything, down to the old gramophone, the black-and-white pictures on the wall, and de rigueur schnapps and slivovitz.

This, decades before Thomas Balsley festooned the waterfronts with chaises longues.

In a project completed in 2003, the city vastly expanded Verdi Square to the west, usurping part of the Broadway roadbed. This extension accommodated a large new subway kiosk designed by Gruzen Samton Architects and Richard Dattner & Partners. The modern design defers to the older subway kiosk on the south side of 72nd Street, designed by Heins & LaFarge for the city's original Interborough Rapid Transit subway line in 1904. As part of the expansion and refurbishment of Verdi Square, the city restored the Verdi Monument and installed new landscaping, designed by Lynden B. Miller. —F.M.

HOURS:

MADISON SQUARE:
6 am–midnight

THE TKTS BOOTH:
Monday, Thursday, Friday: 3–8 pm
Wednesday, Saturday: 10 am–2 pm (matinees); 3–8 pm
Tuesday: 2–8 pm
Sunday: 11 am–3 pm (matinees); 3 pm–30 minutes before curtain

RESTROOMS: Madison Square: Pay toilet in Madison Square

HERALD & GREELEY SQUARES:
Macy's Herald Square

TIMES SQUARE:
Times Square subway station and lobby of the Marriott Marquis Hotel (Broadway and 46th Street)

REGULATIONS: Smoking is prohibited in Herald and Greeley Squares, Madison Square, and on the Times Square pedestrian plaza

MAP & FURTHER INFORMATION AVAILABLE AT: www.madisonsquarepark.org/;

www.heraldsquare.com/; www.nycgovparks.org/parks/M032/;

www.tdf.org/tkts

BY SUBWAY:

MADISON SQUARE:

N, R to Broadway and 23rd Street

6 to 23rd Street and Park Avenue South, walk west 1 block on 23rd Street

HERALD & GREELEY SQUARES:
B, D, F, M, N, Q, R to 34th Street-Herald Square and 6th Avenue

TIMES SQUARE, TKTS BOOTH:
1, 2, 3, 7, N, Q, R, S, A, C, E to Times Square-42nd Street

BY BUS:

MADISON SQUARE:

M1, M2, M3, M4, M5, X63, X64, X68 to 5th Avenue and 26th Street

BxM4, BxM3, BxM11 (all drop-off only; transfer to BxM10 downtown service, am rush hours with MetroCard only) to 5th Avenue and 26th Street

BxM6, BxM7, BxM7A, BxM9, BxM10 (all drop-off only) to 5th Avenue and 23rd Street

X2, X5, X17 to 23rd Street and Madison Avenue

X1, X7, X9, X17 to Broadway and 22nd Street, walk north 1 block

X10, X12, X27, X28, X63, X64, X68 to Madison Avenue and 25th Street

HERALD & GREELEY SQUARES:
M34, X17, X22, X31, M4, Q32 to 34th Street and Broadway

M5, M7, X1, X7, X9 to 6th Avenue and 34th Street

BxM2, QM2, QM2A, QM3 to 6th Avenue and 35th Street

M4, Q32 to 32nd Street and 6th Avenue

TIMES SQUARE & TKTS STEPS:
M42, X30 to 42nd Street and Broadway

M7 to 7th Avenue and 45th Street

M20, M104 to 7th Avenue and 47th Street

M42, X17, X22, X30, X31 to 42nd Street and 7th Avenue

BY PATH:

MADISON SQUARE:

Newark–33rd Street and Hoboken–33rd Street lines to 23rd Street and 6th Avenue, walk east one block on 23rd Street

HERALD & GREELEY SQUARES:
Newark–33rd Street and Hoboken–33rd Street lines to 33rd Street and 6th Avenue

PLAZAS AND CIRCLES

24 COLUMBUS CIRCLE

Columbus Circle is located at the southwest corner of Central Park, at the intersection of 59th Street and Broadway

C olumbus Circle was long one of New York's problem children. Such an opportunity for urban grandeur! Yet such a disaster.

Back in the 1960s the architect John Barrington Bayley proposed surrounding the circle with colonnaded buildings with convex façades—a Bernini colonnade on Broadway. Though an entirely sensible suggestion, modernist architects never took it seriously. They preferred the circle to remain one of the greatest missed opportunities in the city's history.

Then, in the first decade of the 21st century, Columbus Circle became kind of chic. The Time Warner Center, designed by David Childs of Skidmore, Owings & Merrill, opened in 2003. It replaced the New York Coliseum, which, when Robert Moses built it in 1954, was the city's main convention center. It was a banal beached whale of a building, its vast blank façades making a border vacuum (to use Jane Jacobs's phrase) of the whole west side of the circle.

The nearly invisible window wall in the Time Warner Center, with its satisfying view, looking east, of Columbus Circle and 59th Street, was created by glass technologist James Carpenter, a MacArthur Fellowship recipient in 2004.

The center of Columbus Circle, once a no-man's-land, was redesigned by the Olin Partnership in 2002–5 and has become a hit with New Yorkers.

In the 1980s developer Mortimer Zuckerman commissioned Moshe Safdie to design Columbus Center. But critics said the proposed complex was too large and would cast outsize shadows across Central Park. In addition, the Metropolitan Transportation Authority's sale of the site to the highest bidder, overriding the site's zoning, was called into question, and

Christopher Columbus looks south toward the sea. The Columbus Monument, in the form of a rostral column, a gift to the city from its Italian-American community, was dedicated in 1892 on the 400th anniversary of Columbus's arrival in the New World.

The upscale mall in the Time Warner Center, with a down escalator leading directly into a Whole Foods Market.

the Municipal Art Society successfully sued to keep Columbus Center from being built. (The MTA acquired the site when the Triborough Bridge and Tunnel Authority, which operated the New York Coliseum, became part of the MTA in the late 1960s.)

Columbus Center must indeed have been gargantuan, because the Time Warner Center is super-colossal. The twin-towered mixed-use structure—offices, apartments, restaurants, shops, television studios, a hotel, and performance venues for Jazz at Lincoln Center—dominates the circle as no building has ever done, and one need not love the building to agree that David Childs handled a hugely daunting design challenge with considerable skill.

It's the four-story base that matters most in relation to the circle as a public space. Myron Magnet, writing in *City Journal*, likes everything about Time Warner Center except the base: "If only ... The atrium, lined by four stories of shops, didn't resemble a suburban shopping mall that seems more Manhasset than Manhattan!" The Project for Public Spaces calls it "anti-urban ... essentially a shopping mall inside, with little or no hint from the outside that anything is going on." The street-level façades, if more attractive than those of the old Coliseum, are no less blank.

Inside, Time Warner presents us with the latest attempt to build a shopping mall in Manhattan. In suburbia, the enclosed mall makes sense. But in Manhattan, the place above all others in America known for the vitality of its street life? Other Manhattan malls include the Trump Tower atrium on Fifth Avenue at 56th Street and Manhattan Mall, carved out of the old Gimbels department store on

Sixth Avenue at 32nd Street. Time Warner is by far the most elegant of these, with restaurants ranked among the best, and most expensive, in the country.

My favorite thing about the complex is the view from its fourth floor. Looking out on the circle, one sees, on the left, Attilio Piccirilli's and H. Van Buren Magonigle's elaborate Maine Monument (1913) at the entrance to Central Park, and the previously largest building on the circle, the Trump International Hotel & Tower, Philip Johnson and Alan Ritchie's transformation of the old Gulf & Western Building into a glitzy hotel and apartment complex. To the right, 2 Columbus Circle, originally designed by Edward Durell Stone as the home of Huntington Hartford's Gallery of Modern Art, was reclad in 2008 by Portland, Oregon, architect Brad Cloepfil and reopened as the Museum of Arts and Design. Stone's was perhaps the only building that made any attempt to relate to the circle in a meaningful way.

The one and only inarguably great thing in the circle is its centerpiece, the magnificent rostral column topped by a statue of Christopher Columbus. Designed by the obscure Gaetano Russo, the column dates from 1892. The circle's recent redesign to afford easier access to the column is very welcome—though Project for Public Spaces is quite right in saying that much more of Columbus Circle should be pedestrianized. What's not wonderful is how the circle's buildings have consistently failed to take their cues from this marvelous column, and in the process made a mess of the city's finest opportunity for grandeur. —F.M.

RESTROOMS: Public restrooms can be found in the Whole Foods and on the upper floors of the Time Warner Building, 10 Columbus Circle (10 am–9 pm)

BY SUBWAY: A, B, C, D, 1, to 59th Street-Columbus Circle

BY BUS: M1, M5, M7, M10, M20 to Columbus Circle

GRAND ARMY PLAZA, BROOKLYN 25

Grand Army Plaza is situated at the northernmost point of Prospect Park in Brooklyn, at the intersections of Flatbush Avenue and Vanderbilt Avenue, and Eastern Parkway and Prospect Park West

C alvert Vaux and Frederick Law Olmsted laid out the Plaza, as it was at first simply known, in the 1860s as the main entrance to their 585-acre masterpiece, Prospect Park. Though populous neighborhoods would grow all around the park, in the early years this was a sparsely settled part of Brooklyn. The Flatbush Avenue streetcars carried people from the densely populated neighborhoods nearer the waterfront to the Plaza.

Old and new meet at Grand Army Plaza, where the bike lane along Prospect Park West joins the oval traffic circle around the Soldiers' and Sailors' Memorial Arch, and a Richard Meier–designed residential building overlooks the scene.

The great oval space, renamed Grand Army Plaza in 1926, also served as a place for civic gatherings—and as a means of keeping such gatherings out of the park proper. At first the Plaza was pretty barren, with only a statue of Abraham Lincoln (by Henry Kirke Brown, later moved to the Concert Grove in the southeastern part of Prospect Park) and a simple fountain. In 1873 the simple fountain yielded to an extravagant Victorian Gothic fountain with colored jets of water. In 1889, at the behest of Brooklyn's mayor Seth Low, the city sponsored a competition for the design of a triumphal arch to adorn the Plaza. The winner was John Hemenway Duncan, and President Grover Cleveland attended the 1892 dedication of the arch. At the time, the arch bore none of the bronze sculpture that enlivens it and makes it, in the words of the architectural historian Henry Hope Reed, "one of the nation's great works of art" and, among the triumphal arches of modern times, "second only to the Arc de Triomphe in Paris." The sculpture appeared between 1894 and 1901. It consists of the quadriga (a chariot pulled by four horses) atop the arch and the two dense, dramatic groups—Army and Navy—on, respectively, the west and east piers facing the park. These three sculptural groups by Frederick MacMonnies surely rank among the greatest works ever produced by an American sculptor.

In the 1890s, under the great Brooklyn park commissioner Frank Squier, the architecture firm McKim, Mead & White was commissioned to redesign entrances all around the park, including at Grand Army Plaza. That is when the beautiful stone fence, brick pavements, and bronze vases edging the park, the two wonderful gazebo-like streetcar shelters, and two of the high columns holding aloft bronze eagles were built. (The other two such columns came earlier, courtesy of Duncan.) All of these elements are as handsome in design and execution as anything of their kind can be.

How, then, given the presence of such beautiful things, did Grand Army Plaza end up in the Project for Public Spaces' "Hall of Shame"?

What should be, in the words of the Design Trust for Public Space, "one of the world's great urban spaces," instead turned into a pedestrian nightmare, with utterly bewildering arrangements of stoplights that left pedestrians feeling stranded in the midst of relentless streams of oncoming cars. Getting to the arch or to the Bailey Fountain (1932, Egerton Swartwout, architect; Eugene Savage, sculptor) north of the arch for a close inspection seemed to take forever—and few attempted it. It was as if the city had decided to deny the public access. The Project for Public Spaces also notes the high berms that line Plaza Street West and Plaza Street East, forming an oval around the "inner plaza," where the fountain stands. Vaux and Olmsted liked to use berms, like those along the western edge of Prospect Park, as a way of blotting out the sights and sounds of the surrounding city from the park user's experience. The very purpose of a large metropolitan park like Prospect Park is to take its users out of the city and immerse them in nature. Policing such spaces is always problematic (a reality Vaux and Olmsted understood), and many nefarious activities can take place in such parks. William H. Whyte, who profoundly influenced the Project for Public Spaces' point of view, argued, in the case of Bryant Park (p. 234), that cutting off small parks and squares from surrounding streets made them isolated and dangerous. The inner plaza is a fine space, with benches surrounding the recently restored fountain. Yet it feels remote and possibly unsafe. Moreover, New York, a city rich in many things, is not rich in fountains, which are an essential embellishment of civilized cities. Other major city fountains—the Pulitzer Fountain in Manhattan's Grand Army Plaza at 59th Street and Fifth Avenue, the Lowell Fountain in Bryant Park, the Victorian fountain in City Hall Park—occupy, and define, places of high visibility. Brooklyn seems to want to hide its Bailey Fountain.

In 2008 the Design Trust for Public Space, a nonprofit urban design advocacy group founded in 1995, sponsored a competition for "Reinventing Grand Army Plaza." This project grew from Brooklynites' frustration with the plaza, and proposals for ways to make it into a place for people to use and enjoy flooded in from designers around the world. The city responded not by implementing any of the competition plans, but with a series of remedial (and less costly) steps—decreasing the portion of roadbeds used by cars (paint and planters), realigning stoplights, and the like—that have without question made Grand Army Plaza infinitely easier to get around in. Yet, with the exception of the weekend Greenmarket, which takes place in the part of the plaza nearest to the park, and various special events that are held in the plaza, it still fails to measure up as the kind of people magnet it should and could be. We need more. Stay tuned.

There are a number of landmarks and other things of note in the vicinity of the plaza. The Brooklyn Public Library occupies a large, beautiful Art Moderne building (built 1937–41) at the corner of Flatbush Avenue and Eastern Parkway. Go inside for a look at its splendid catalogue room, one of the finest modernist rooms in the city. Just inside Prospect Park, looking out onto the plaza a few feet to the west of Flatbush Avenue, is MacMonnies's bronze statue of James S. T. Stranahan, the Brooklyn businessman and civic leader who oversaw the construction of Prospect Park in the 1860s and 1870s. It is an exceptionally fine statue (standing figures are very difficult) of an outstanding personage in Brooklyn's history. And be sure to look at the bicycle lane along Prospect Park West south of the Plaza. This is the type of lane that transportation commissioner Janette Sadik-Khan implemented in various parts of the city, based on the ideas of the famous Danish city planner Jan Gehl. Cars no longer park at the curb, but a few feet out from the curb. The space between the parked cars and the curb forms a bike lane—which is now actually protected from, rather than threatened by, cars. This being New York, vociferous objections to these lanes arose from some quarters. The objections involved pedestrian safety and aesthetics. My own feeling is that pedestrians are no less unsafe than before, and possibly a little safer; they can see oncoming bikes much more clearly. As for aesthetics, the new lanes look a little less weird with the passing years. —F.M.

HOURS: Greenmarket held year round on Saturdays, 8 am–4 pm

RESTROOMS: Located across from the plaza in the Brooklyn Public Library at the southeast corner of Eastern Parkway and Flatbush Avenue

REGULATIONS: Smoking is prohibited

Dogs are allowed but must be leashed

MAP & FURTHER INFORMATION AVAILABLE AT: www.prospectpark.org

BY SUBWAY: Q to 7th Avenue and Flatbush Avenue, walk south 2 blocks on Flatbush Avenue

2, 3, 4 (nighttime only) to Grand Army Plaza

S (Franklin Avenue Shuttle) to Botanic Garden and Eastern Parkway, walk north half a block, then west 4 blocks on Eastern Parkway

2, 3, 4, 5 to Franklin Avenue and Eastern Parkway, walk west 4 blocks on Eastern Parkway

BY BUS: B41, B69 to Grand Army Plaza and Flatbush Avenue

GANSEVOORT PLAZA

26

Gansevoort Plaza is located on 9th Avenue between Gansevoort Street on the south, and 14th Street on the north, with a smaller triangular plaza just north of 14th Street.

Gansevoort Plaza in the Meatpacking District was not always a plaza. In 2005 the irregular parcel of land where Greenwich Street turns into 9th Avenue and is intersected by Gansevoort Street, Little West 12th Street, West 13th Street, and West 14th Street, was a jumble of competing traffic lanes and a mishmash of pedestrian crossings. It took neighborhood intervention, a study by Project for Public Spaces (PPS), and action by the New York City Department of Transportation to transform this space, as well as one on the north side of 14th Street, into two safe, welcoming pedestrian oases.

The confusing street pattern in what is today the Gansevoort Market Historic District owes its heritage to the evolution of the city's street plan. Here in the northwest corner of historic Greenwich Village, the irregular pattern of streets that characterized the early city bumped up against the Commissioners' Plan of 1811, which called for new streets in Manhattan to be laid out in a grid

This section of Gansevoort Plaza is located north of 14th Street along 9th Avenue. The panoramic view was shot from the upper floors of the Apple store bordering the site.

A ground view of the northern section of Gansevoort Plaza. The cantilevered apartment building appended to a six-story 1905 brick warehouse, located at the corner of Ninth Avenue and 15th Street, is the Porter House by Gregg Pasquarelli of SHoP Architects (2003).

system. The "piazza-like space" where Gansevoort and Little West 12th Streets met Ninth Avenue was the result.

Though the intersection mimics that of European cities, where a number of streets often converge to form a town square, the traffic patterns were never clear. Was this area a pedestrian zone, as it would be in Europe, or a vehicular one? That's what the 2005 study by the Project for Public Space, an organization that works with city officials and community groups to produce quality public areas, tried to help sort out.

The issue pitted community residents against the owners of some of the neighborhood's fashionable restaurants and clubs. Because the Meatpacking District has a rollicking nightlife, cars, limousines, and taxis were competing with pedestrians at intersections and in spaces where there was no clear indication of which group had preeminence.

The results of the city's and PPS's efforts are visible today: granite blocks and bollards demarcate the pedestrian and vehicular areas south of 14th Street. On the north side of 14th Street, planters delineate the triangular parcel of land wedged between Hudson Street and 9th Avenue that once was the site of a tangle of traffic lanes, but now is filled with tables and chairs for visitors.

The southern section of Gansevoort Plaza is paved with cobblestones. In summer 2011 a portion of it was briefly occupied by a pop-up Tommy Hilfiger store.

The traffic patterns have been set; open space, defined. The Meatpacking District has a town square, of sorts. Or, at the very least, outdoor spaces where pedestrians can sit and watch the action. A story of history, community, and reconciliation. —R.L.

MORE INFORMATION ABOUT RECENT REDEVELOPMENT AVAILABLE AT: www.pps.org/projects/gansevoortplaza/

BY SUBWAY: L to 8th Avenue and 14th Street, walk south 1 block on 8th Avenue, turn right on 13th Street, walk 1 block and bear left on Gansevoort Street

A, C, E to 14th Street and 8th Avenue, walk south 3 blocks on 8th Avenue, continue as above

1, 2, 3 to 14th Street and 7th Avenue, walk west 2 blocks on 13th Street, through Jackson Square, bear left on Gansevoort Street

BY BUS: M11 to Greenwich Street and Horatio Street, walk north 1 block on Greenwich Street

M14 to Hudson Street and Horatio Street, walk north 1 block on Hudson Street, turn left on Gansevoort Street

M20 to 8th Ave and 14th Street, walk south 1 block on 8th Avenue, turn right on 13th Street, bear left on Gansevoort Street

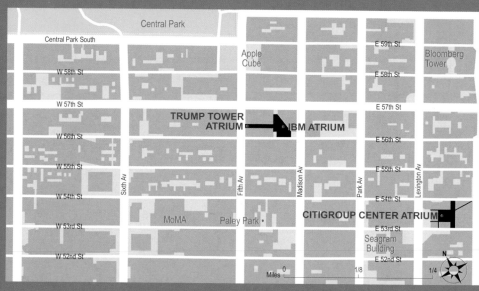

MIDTOWN ATRIUMS

Map by John H

ATRIUMS

MIDTOWN ATRIUMS

27

Citigroup Center is located at 153 East 53rd Street (at Lexington Avenue); entrances on Lexington Avenue between 53rd and 54th Streets, on the corner of 54th Street and 3rd Avenue, and mid-block

Trump Tower is located at 725 Fifth Avenue, at the corner of 56th Street

The former IBM Building is located at 590 Madison Avenue, between 56th & 57th Streets

Citigroup Center Atrium

The late 1970s and 1980s witnessed a wave of "atrium skyscrapers" in midtown Manhattan. The comprehensive revision of New York City's zoning code in 1961 encouraged skyscraper developers to provide outdoor plazas on their building lots. In no time, plazas proliferated in midtown. The mother of them all, at Ludwig Mies van der Rohe's Seagram Building (1958) on Park Avenue between 52nd and 53rd Streets, actually predated—and partly inspired—the new zoning. With "incentive zoning" came the atrium. Developers traded with the city: amenities for height and bulk. If the Seagram Building was the trailblazer of the outdoor plaza, Citicorp (now Citigroup) Center, opened in

Outdoor plaza:
Mies van der
Rohe's Seagram
Building (1958).

An urban amenity—midday music at Citigroup Center.

1977, pioneered the skyscraper atrium. An atrium is an indoor space, typically expansive and high ceilinged, that provides many of the same conveniences and amenities found on the streets outside—from stores and restaurants to, well, plazas. What makes an atrium significantly different from a plaza is that it may occupy multiple floors (though not all atriums do), and it is climate controlled, so that in cold or inclement weather it remains perfectly usable. What, then, distinguishes an atrium from a shopping mall, the reader may ask. Two things, for starters. In the typical atrium, the space devoted to sitting and reading and conversation and coffee drinking and people watching—the basic plaza functions—occupies a far greater percentage of the total space than in a suburban mall. Second, in a midtown atrium, one does not enter from and exit into a parking lot with a view of an expressway, but from and onto the bustling, chaotic streets of midtown.

Citicorp Center, designed by Hugh Stubbins & Associates, held great significance for New Yorkers in 1977. The city was still reeling from its near-bankruptcy, and all social indicators pointed downward. The commercial real estate market crashed in mid-decade, and Citicorp represented the first major project in some years. The eye-catching, sun-reflecting, silvery aluminum shaft, 914 feet high, its top sheared at a 45-degree angle, became an instant "icon." Functionally, the building fascinated. In order to build the tower, Citicorp had to buy the old St. Peter's Lutheran Church. As part of the deal, Citicorp agreed to build a new St. Peter's on the site, and render it a distinct structure. Hence the elevation, on gigantic stilts, of the tower over the new church and over a large, sunken plaza. That outdoor plaza serves mainly as a conduit to and from the subway. The real plaza is inside. The six-level skylit atrium includes two levels of retail around the building perimeter. The central court is a large space with movable chairs and tables. When the space first opened, critics and public alike met it with generous praise. As Ada Louise Huxtable noted in the New York Times, the developer went well beyond what the zoning specified in creating a public amenity. The urbanist William H. Whyte praised the Citicorp atrium as one of the city's most successful public spaces—just as he had praised the plaza of the Seagram Building. Indeed, for the New Yorker of circa 1980, the Citicorp space buzzed with excitement. A large, multilevel Conran store served as retail anchor among many smaller, quirkier merchants. Several restaurants (including the outstanding Auberge Suisse) lured fine diners, and Citicorp programmed the space with everything from Dick Hyman piano recitals to a fabulous toy train display at Christmas. The atrium even offered well-maintained public restrooms. Eventually, Conran's left and Barnes & Noble moved in. The restaurants went through their predictable life cycles. Many other amenity-packed developments competed with Citicorp, and in time the excitement wore off, though it remained a high-quality public space. When, however, a post-9/11 security alert suggested a plot to drive a car bomb into Citicorp Center, the once-welcoming atrium, though it never closed (many feared it would), became a little forbidding. Much of the "privately owned public space" in New York shares that forbidding aspect. It's quite intentional! Citicorp bucked that trend for more than two decades. Lately, though, this atrium seems to be showing new signs of life.

HOURS: Arcade, open-air concourse, open 24 hours

Covered pedestrian space and through-block arcade, 7 am–11 pm

RESTROOMS: Located near the northeast (women's) and southeast (men's) corners of the covered pedestrian space

REGULATIONS: Smoking is prohibited

See regulations under former IBM Building Atrium below for rules of conduct

MAP & FURTHER INFORMATION AVAILABLE AT:
www.nyc.gov/html/dcp/html/priv/153e53.shtml

BY SUBWAY: E, M to Lexington Avenue and 53rd Street

N, Q, R to Lexington Avenue and 59th Street, walk south 6 blocks

6 to 51st Street and Lexington Avenue, walk north 2 blocks

BY BUS: M1, M2 to Madison Avenue and 53rd Street, walk east 2 blocks

M3, M4, Q32 to Madison Avenue and 52nd Street, walk east 2 blocks and north 1 block

M101, M102, M103, X63, X64, X68, QM2, QM5, QM6, QM10, QM12,

QM24 to 3rd Avenue and 55th Street, walk south 1 block

BM1, BM2, BM3, BM4, BM5, M31, M57, QM3, QM15, QM16, QM 18, QM21, X17, X22,
X31, X68 to 57th Street and 3rd Avenue, walk south 3 blocks

QM1, QM4 to 3rd Avenue and 56th Street, walk south 2 blocks

X2, X5 to Lexington Avenue and 52nd Street, walk north 1 block

M15 to 2nd Avenue and 54th Street, walk west 1 block

Trump Tower Atrium

Trump Tower opened on Fifth Avenue and 56th Street in 1983. Designed by Swanke Hayden Connell Architects, the flagship mixed-use (residential, office, retail) building of media-celebrity developer Donald Trump added another multilevel atrium to midtown. Today, many people find this atrium, with its counters selling Donald Trump–themed merchandise, to be garish and tacky. In the beginning, however, it appeared Trump really did want to impart "class." The atrium contains plenty of seating, opportunities for food

Trump Tower is glossy from top to bottom.

and drink, and well-maintained public restrooms. It's also very much a vertical shopping mall—as some commentators noted, much like a bit of Hong Kong dropped into midtown Manhattan. The pinkish-hued marble walls and chrome accents are as different as can be from the sleek, silvery palette of the Citicorp atrium. The Trump atrium's best feature is its waterwall. Such walls—arguably the city's most successful one is nearby in Paley Park (1967), on 53rd Street just east of Fifth Avenue (p. 240)—provide soothing white noise and remind us of how important the auditory dimension is in urban design. Some of the public seating is close enough to the water feature that one may be misted by an occasional refreshing spray. In its early years, the atrium included an outpost of the movie producer Dino di Laurentiis's ambitious DDL Foodshow (a kind of Eataly before its time), a first-ever American branch of the Munich department store Ludwig Beck (designed by Pritzker Prize–winning architect Hans Hollein), and a first-ever American branch of the Paris department store Galeries Lafayette. All of these failed to last. Galeries Lafayette yielded to Niketown!

HOURS: 8 am–10 pm daily

RESTROOMS: Located on the concourse level and second floor, as well as in the bars and restaurants in the atrium

REGULATIONS: Smoking is prohibited

See regulations under former IBM Building Atrium below for rules-of-conduct

MAP & FURTHER INFORMATION AVAILABLE AT: www.trumpatrium.com or www.nyc.gov/html/dcp/html/priv/7255th.shtml

BY SUBWAY: 4, 5, 6 to Lexington Avenue and 59th Street, walk south 3 blocks on Lexington and west 3 blocks on 56th Street

F to 57th Street and 6th Avenue, walk east 1 block and south 1 block

N, Q, R to 57th St and 7th Avenue, walk east 2 blocks and south 1 block

B, D, E to 7th Avenue and 53rd Street, walk east 2 blocks and north 3 blocks

E, M to 5th Avenue and 53rd Street, walk north 3 blocks

1 to 50th Street and Broadway, walk east 2.5 blocks and north 6 blocks

BY BUS: X63, X12, X14, X30, X64, X42 to 57th Street and 5th Avenue, walk south one block

M1, M2, M3, M4 to Madison Avenue and 58th Street, walk south 2 blocks and west 1 block

M31, M57, X10, X17, X27, X28, X31, Q32 to Madison Avenue and 57th Street, walk south 1 block and west 1 block

BxM3 (drop-off only), BxM4 (drop-off only), M5 to 5th Avenue and 55th Street, walk north 1 block

BxM6, BxM7, BxM8, BxM9, BxM10, BxM11 (all drop-off only) to 5th Avenue and 58th Street, walk south 2 blocks

Former IBM Building Atrium

From the Trump atrium, one can pass through Niketown right into the atrium of the former IBM Building on the southwest corner of Madison Avenue and 57th Street. Here the experience is altogether different. The landscape architects Zion & Breen designed the lofty atrium to be as much like an outdoor plaza as possible, with the thinnest of vitreous membranes separating it from the street. Stands of bamboo grow, birds fly around. Art shows, often by well-known artists, enliven the space. A branch of the Italian Obikà Mozzarella Bar offers high-quality eats. At one time, a basement space accessed from the atrium housed the excellent IBM Gallery of Science & Art, and later the always-interesting Dahesh Museum. Now it houses Bonhams auction house— not quite the same sort of amenity for the people.

The least successful of the midtown atriums is just across 56th Street. The former AT&T Building (now Sony Tower) by Philip Johnson and John Burgee garnered considerable press attention when it opened in 1984. The vast arch at its base, the granite sheathing, and especially the "Chippendale highboy" top seemed to mark the definitive break with the orthodox Modernist architecture of the preceding decades. Ultimately, the rather ungainly building had little influence, not least for the poor quality of its public space. Its sidewalk arcade along Madison always felt dark and damp, and had ludicrously heavy metal chairs and tables that, while technically movable, required the strength of a Ukrainian weightlifter. After the gov-

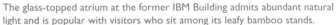

The glass-topped atrium at the former IBM Building admits abundant natural light and is popular with visitors who sit among its leafy bamboo stands.

ernment breakup of AT&T, the remnants of the company retreated to their New Jersey campus and gave up the Chippendale building to Sony, who won permission to enclose the sidewalk arcade and make it a Sony products showroom. Some amenity. The building's midblock, through-block atrium, while providing seating and programming, nonetheless also never felt right.

No one guessed it at the time, given Citicorp's huge early lead, but today the best and freshest-seeming of the atriums belongs to the former IBM Building. —F.M.

HOURS: Covered pedestrian space and seating area: 8 am–10 pm, sometimes closed for private events

RESTROOMS: Located on the lobby's lower level

REGULATIONS: Smoking is prohibited.

No sleeping or smoking, drinking of alcoholic beverages, shopping carts, sitting on atrium floors or heated vents, radio playing, gambling, or disorderly conduct

For an excellent discussion of visitor regulations at privately owned public spaces, see urbanomnibus.net/2012/rules-of-conduct

MAP & FURTHER INFORMATION AVAILABLE AT:
www.nyc.gov/html/dcp/html/priv/590mad.shtml

BY SUBWAY: 4, 5, 6 to Lexington Avenue and 59th Street, walk south 3 blocks on Lexington and west 2 blocks on 57th Street

N, Q, R to Lexington Avenue and 59th Street, walk south 3 blocks on Lexington Avenue and west 2 blocks on 57th Street

BY BUS: M1, M2, X2, X5, X22 to Madison Avenue and 56th Street

M31, M57 to 57th Street and 5th Avenue, walk east 1 block on 57th Street

URBAN GARDEN ROOM   28

The Bank of America Tower is located at One Bryant Park, on the northwest corner of 42nd Street and 6th Avenue; the Urban Garden Room is on the ground level with a dedicated entrance midblock between 42nd and 43rd Streets on 6th Avenue

The Urban Garden Room, on the ground level of the Bank of America Tower, is an inviting Midtown way station. This public space, which is separate from the building's lobby, is cloistered, quiet, and well designed.

It's also easy to miss. The main entrance is discreetly placed midblock between 42nd and 43rd Street on 6th Avenue. Yet it would be a mistake to bypass this nicely proportioned, light-filled space. It's the perfect place to while away time between business appointments, to feel the sun's rays on a winter's day, or to lunch with colleagues. This public retreat is within blocks of Times Square, but totally removed from it in spirit.

It's also a whimsical space. Four large green sculptural forms dominate its interior. They aren't quite topiaries and they aren't quite sculptures. Visitors "haven't seen anything like this before," a guard on duty said.

The largest of the forms, in the shape of an archway, reaches nearly to the ceiling, which is more than 40 feet high. The three other forms—the smallest about 7 feet high—are either rounded or more straight-edged. All of the forms are about a foot deep and appear furry and shaggy. They rise up from a bed of white stones in the stone pavement.

Visitors feel compelled to study these green shapes as they would a magician's trick to figure out how they are constructed. The ivy, ferns, mosses and lichens, and other low-light plants are, in fact, set within a galvanized steel frame with a watering system. Soil fills in the steel form and is covered in porous fabric.

These leafy, growing forms give the elegant Urban Garden Room its character, providing a blast of color in an otherwise glass room. The green frames act as walls without being walls, subdividing the space and injecting horticultural humor into the business district. They offer privacy from the people sitting at neighboring tables, while the floor-to-ceiling glass windows provide a panoramic view of the passing pedestrian parade outside.

It's clear that the planners learned lessons from Bryant Park, which is diagonally across the street. The urban room is a social space. As at Bryant Park, one can rearrange the seating to accommodate one's needs. There are plenty of portable chairs and lots of small tables for chess players, Web surfers, and groups of people talking and eating together. The space is well tended—a guard is always present—and, not surprisingly, there's a host of rules—the typical no-nos of public space on a major corporation's premises—no smoking, audible music, pets, littering, alcoholic beverages, and so on.

The room, which opened in September 2009, was designed as part of the 52-story Bank of America Tower by Cook + Fox Architects. It was commissioned by the building's owner, the Durst Organization, and completed in 2008. The living forms were designed by Margie Ruddick of the architectural firm Wallace Roberts & Todd of Philadelphia. She credits her mother, sculptor Dorothy Ruddick, who studied with Josef Albers at Black Mountain College in Asheville, North Carolina, and designed fabrics for Knoll, with suggesting the distinctive twists within the forms. That these sculptural forms are part of a building with a LEED Platinum rating for its environmentally sustainable operations makes sense; they're green forms in a green building.

The Urban Garden Room is open to the public seven days a week, but the greenery requires plenty of maintenance. There are weekend days when

The largest of the living sculptures in the Urban Garden Room, which opened in 2009 in the Bank of America Tower.

the space is "down," so that the living sculptures can get the care and feeding they need. The rest of the time these living sculptures take care of us. —R.L.

HOURS: 8 am 8 pm

RESTROOMS: Located in Bryant Park on 42nd Street between 5th and 6th Avenues, about half a block from the Bank of America Tower

REGULATIONS: Smoking is prohibited

Audible music, pets, and alcoholic beverages are prohibited

No littering, running, skateboarding, or rollerblading

No inappropriate attire or disruptive behavior

BY SUBWAY: B, D, F, M to 6th Avenue and 42nd Street-Bryant Park

7 to 5th Avenue and 42nd Street, walk west 1 block west on 42nd Street

1, 2, 3, N, Q, R to 7th Avenue and Times Square-42nd Street, walk east 1 block on 42nd Street

BY BUS: M5, M7, X9 to 6th Avenue and 42nd Street

QM10, QM12 to 6th Avenue and 43rd Street

M42, X17, X22, X30, X31 to 42nd Street and 6th Avenue

X1, X7 to 6th Avenue and 41st Street, walk north 1 block

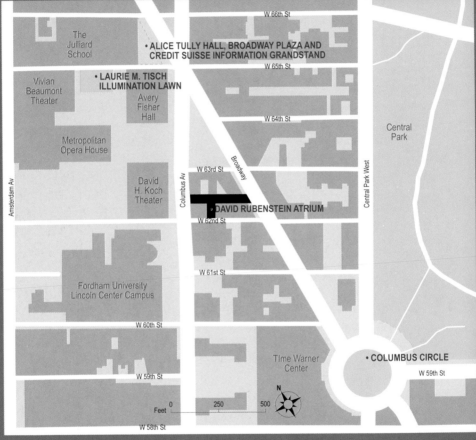

The Julliard School

• ALICE TULLY HALL, BROADWAY PLAZA AND CREDIT SUISSE INFORMATION GRANDSTAND

W 66th St

W 65th St

• LAURIE M. TISCH ILLUMINATION LAWN

Vivian Beaumont Theater

Avery Fisher Hall

W 64th St

Central Park

Metropolitan Opera House

Amsterdam Av

David H. Koch Theater

Broadway

Columbus Av

W 63rd St

DAVID RUBENSTEIN ATRIUM

W 62nd St

Central Park West

W 61st St

Fordham University Lincoln Center Campus

W 60th St

W 59th St

Time Warner Center

• COLUMBUS CIRCLE

W 59th St

N

Feet   0   250   500

W 58th St

COLUMBUS CIRCLE AND LINCOLN CENTER AREA

Map by John Hill

CULTURAL INSTITUTIONS

LINCOLN CENTER FOR THE PERFORMING ARTS

29

The complex is located on the Upper West Side from 62nd to 66th Streets, between Columbus Avenue/Broadway and Amsterdam Avenue

The open spaces of the Lincoln Center campus are more fun since architectural firm Diller Scofidio + Renfro was given the assignment of bringing new life to the aging public areas of the performing arts complex. In 2006 they began transforming, altering, tweaking, and sprucing up many of the best-known spaces and buildings in ways that make one want to hang out there, whether attending a performance or not.

The most playful area is the Laurie M. Tisch Illumination Lawn, a tilted, grassy green roof on top of Lincoln, the center's newish upscale restaurant. The elevated lawn's twisted geometry—a hyperbolic paraboloid—is visually distinct from the straight-edged Lincoln Center buildings and allows spectators to be above its plaza while remaining part of the action. This tilted grass plane, completed in collaboration with FXFowle Architects in an area where there was once a walkway across 65th Street that cast dark shadows on the street below, is a green swath for lovers, toddlers, sunbathers, tourists, and, of course, the Lincoln Center audience.

Each group tends to find its own territory. Tourists climb to the top to take in the view toward the Juilliard School, Alice Tully Hall, and Broadway (visible since the 65th Street pedestrian bridge was removed). Children run barefoot through the grass. Repeat visitors look down on the reflecting pool with its Henry Moore sculpture (Modernist fans rue the changes to the now truncated reflecting pool and its reconfigured surrounding plaza, originally designed by modernist Dan Kiley in collaboration with architect Eero Saarinen in the mid-1960s). At the very top, near performance time, as patrons sprint toward the various theaters, it can feel a little bit like standing on the balcony at Grand Central Terminal watching commuters run across the concourse to catch a train.

One of the surprising aspects of the lawn's design is its steep angle. (There are grab bars near the bottom of the lawn for support while descending. Maybe that's why the lawn is "weather dependent," which means that it is

A springtime view of the Vivian Beaumont Theatre, to the left, and, straight ahead, the reflecting pool with its Henry Moore sculpture, the Laurie M. Tisch Illumination Lawn, and the Juilliard School across 65th Street in the background.

closed in inclement weather.) Another surprise is that the 10,000-square-foot surface has no shrubs. No matter. Shrubs might just get in the way of people watching.

The cleverly redesigned fountain in the main plaza is another great place to watch the crowds. The jets of water shoot upward in a choreographed sequence of highs and lows and in different textures, from frothy to stream-lined, reaching a visual climax that is superbly lit. The Los Angeles–based firm WET, which has designed water extravaganzas everywhere, including Las Vegas, helped create this water show. The base of the fountain, formerly above waist level, has been lowered and widened so that visitors can now recline or sit on it more easily.

Lincoln Center's plaza itself has been rejiggered to offer a more invit-ing face onto Columbus Avenue. (The taxi ramp that once ran parallel to Columbus Avenue has been banished below ground so that there is no longer a roadway separating pedestrians from the main plaza.) Flashing LED screens embedded into the risers of the seven shallow steps of the 170-foot-wide Grand Stair leading to the plaza announce productions.

Although sort of a gimmick, it's an alluring one that pulls the eye to the signs. Black and white stone paving has replaced the plaza's original Italian travertine; it may be a bit harsh, but it will probably wear better than the travertine, which tended to react poorly to the freezing and thawing cycles of New York's winters.

Cross 65th Street to enjoy the wonderfully redesigned spaces, interior and exterior, at the Juilliard School and Alice Tully Hall. The building, designed by Pietro Belluschi (1968), once had a blank white exterior wall facing Broadway. Diller Scofidio + Renfro (best known for designing New York's imaginative and popular elevated park, the High Line (see p. 156), in collaboration with FXFowle Architects, have stripped away a portion of the stone façade to create a glass front with a soaring corner angle, resembling the prow of a futuristic ship. The box office is now visible from the street, as is the attractive restaurant American Table Café and Bar by Marcus Samuelsson (see p. 266).

Most alluring are the steep flights of concrete steps that flank a grandstand in front of Alice Tully Hall. Though close to the street, the grandstand itself is sufficiently angled to block most street noise. Run-on concrete benches, which begin at the northern end of the steps, are below sidewalk level—close to Broadway and yet hidden from it. It's a

The Laurie M. Tisch Illumination Lawn overlooking the Hearst Plaza reflecting pool, adds visual dynamism to the Lincoln Center campus.

The concrete grandstand in front of Alice Tully Hall, with the West 65th Street sidewalk to the right.

sleight of hand that works beautifully for an exterior public space so near traffic lanes.

More good-looking steep steps lead up to the lobby of the Juilliard School on 65th Street inside the Irene Diamond Building. The steps flank eleven rows of luscious wood-lined benches that permit sitters to watch the Juilliard students coming and going, as well as the audience arriving at the Peter Jay Sharp Theater.

The David Rubenstein Atrium at Lincoln Center, on Broadway between 62nd and 63rd Streets, designed by Tod Williams Billie Tsien Architects, and one block east of the Lincoln Center campus, is a reconceived atrium. This public space, originally the Harmony Atrium, opened in 1979, was part of the city program that gave incentives to developers if they provided accessible public space. Over five hundred privately owned public spaces (POPS) were created, some less well designed than others, some less accessible than others, but all still under scrutiny since Occupy Wall Street brought this strange amalgam of public-private ownership to the public's attention (see Zuccotti Park, p. 250).

Now the atrium has a new personality and great new design touches: thick-slabbed green marble benches, a drippy fountain, and a large-scale textural wall by Dutch artist Claudy Jongstra. With its high ceiling and two giant plant walls, the attractive area serves multiple purposes: to meet up for a tour of Lincoln Center, buy tickets, watch a free performance, buy a snack, use the public restrooms, use WiFi, or just hang out.

This inviting open space, like other transformed areas at Lincoln Center, acknowledges that the show can be at street level, as well as on the stage, and that watching the public is as enjoyable as watching performers. —R.L.

Laurie M. Tisch Illumination Plaza is accessible from 65th Street between Amsterdam and Columbus Avenues at street level or via Hearst Plaza at Lincoln Center

A virtual tour is available at: www.lincolnristorante.com/

HOURS: Access is strictly monitored; the lawn is closed in case of inclement weather

Alice Tully Hall is located at 10 Lincoln Center Plaza (Broadway at 65th Street)

The open-air concrete grandstand is protected from direct exposure to the elements by an overhang projecting from Alice Tully Hall.

One of the two green wall installations by the New York and France–
based firm Plant Wall Design, on the east side of the David Rubenstein
Atrium, designed by the architectural firm Tod Williams Billie Tsien. Admire
the living plant wall, catch a bite to eat, purchase tickets for a Lincoln
Center performance, use the restrooms, or just enjoy the space, one
of the more than 500 privately owned public spaces in New York.

BOX OFFICE HOURS: Monday – Saturday: 10 am–6 pm;

SUNDAY: noon–6 pm and for 30 minutes past the start of any performance

RESTROOMS: Lobby of Alice Tully Hall: open only on performance days

GARAGE LEVEL: open daily

The Julliard School, Irene Diamond Building, is located at Broadway and 66th Street

The David Rubenstein Atrium is located on Broadway between 62nd and 63rd Streets

HOURS: Weekdays: 8 am–10 pm

Weekends: 9 am–10 pm

Public restrooms and free WiFi are available

ADDITIONAL INFORMATION AVAILABLE AT: new.lincolncenter.org/live/

ACCESSIBILITY INFORMATION:

new.lincolncenter.org/live/index.php/accessibility-information-map

BY SUBWAY: 1 to Broadway and 66th Street-Lincoln Center

BY BUS: M66 to 65th Street and Columbus Avenue

M5 to Broadway and 66th Street

M104 to Broadway and 66th Street; Broadway and 63rd Street

M7 to 66th Street and Columbus Avenue

M11 to 66th Street and Columbus Ave; 63rd Street and Columbus Avenue

GREEN ROOFS

30

BROOKLYN GRANGE, QUEENS

Brooklyn Grange is located at 37-18 Northern Boulevard, Long Island City, Queens

There are lots of reasons for the proliferation of green roofs on New York City buildings, and it is a safe bet that many more will be installed in the future. That they are good for the environment has become increasingly clear: plants and soil catch and absorb rainwater, so there is less runoff into the city's sewer system, and less heat is reflected off the roofs. The benefits for the buildings are insulation from heat in the summer and cold in the winter. When vegetables are grown on the rooftops they provide a source of local food—often the one affordable food option in a neighborhood—and cater to an increasing interest in urban agriculture.

But green roofs with highly engineered systems allowing for the propagation of rooftop vegetation have not always been the goal. In the 1930s, when Rockefeller Center was under construction, rooftop gardens were planted on two low-scale buildings flanking the Channel Gardens—the British Empire Building and Maison Française. They weren't meant to be walked on, much less used for growing vegetables; the flowers, shrubs, and trees were a bonus for office workers to look down on. In other words, an amenity.

Another green roof, one of the largest in midtown, is hiding in plain sight. And it's surely not a vegetable garden. Bryant Park, behind the New York Public Library (see p. 234) is actually a grassy landscaped area above the New York Public Library's subterranean book stacks. In other words, a roof that doesn't look like a roof. Office workers are attracted in droves to its well-tended lawn.

A green roof on top of the Bronx County Courthouse along the Grand Concourse was only the second green roof on a municipal building in the United States. Completed in 2006, the government officials' goals were to save air-conditioning and heating costs and reduce air pollution. In the case of the ABC Carpet Outlet building, on the Bronx River across from Concrete Plant Park (see p. 123), a local workforce was trained to install the 10,000-square-foot green roof, with project support from the Bronx Overall Economic Development Corporation, in partnership with the Bronx Borough President's Office.

For others, green roofs offer the possibility of doing good and creating a competitive advantage. Acumen Capital Partners, a real estate investment

The view from the one-acre farm on the roof of a former industrial building in Long Island City, Queens, takes in the Manhattan skyline to the west and the low-scale neighborhood buildings below. *Courtesy of Anastasia Cole Plakias, brooklyngrangefarm.com*

company, was converting the Standard Motor Products building (1919) on Northern Boulevard for office use when Ben Flanner, founder and head farmer of Brooklyn Grange, approached them. They reached a deal.

The for-profit Brooklyn Grange runs a one-acre commercial organic farm on top of the former industrial building in Long Island City (the organization's origins were in Brooklyn, which explains its name, but the largest roof they found to farm was in Long Island City, Queens). They have a long-term lease, a community focus, and a reputation as pioneers in the new field of rooftop farming.

The group sells its vegetables to businesses and restaurants, and also sells produce in the "farm" building's lobby on Wednesday afternoons and in occasional markets in Williamsburg and Greenpoint. They offer tours of the rooftop farm, provide corporate retreats to foster bonding while farming, and have a staff deeply committed to urban farming, from beekeeping to composting.

Keep looking up. Brooklyn Grange has expanded and now has a twenty-year lease for a second one-acre farm on the roof of Building 3 at the Brooklyn Navy Yard. New York City rooftops are the new frontier. —R.L.

HOURS: Visitation days and market schedule vary by season; see Web site for current information and for information on workshops and events

MAP & FURTHER INFORMATION AVAILABLE AT: www.brooklyngrangefarm.com

BY SUBWAY: E, M, R to 36th Street and Northern Boulevard, walk east 2.5 blocks on Northern Boulevard

PARKS

WASHINGTON SQUARE PARK

31

The park is located between University Place, Waverly Place, West 4th Street, and MacDougal Street

Washington Square Park in Greenwich Village has been a prominent gathering site for New Yorkers for, well, seemingly forever. Long before protesters camped out in Zuccotti Park (p. 250), Washington Square was a meeting place for the widest assortment of New Yorkers, a veritable people's park. Michael Kimmelman, architecture critic for the *New York Times*, has called the space a "spectacle." Not surprisingly, attempts to alter its landscape have been met with protests. The park isn't large—only 9.75 acres—but it packs a punch.

Since 1798, when the city began using the space as a burial ground for the poor—a potter's field—and to bury victims of the yellow-fever epidemic of 1822, the area has had purpose. Located at a sufficient remove from the city proper, for a time it was also a place for public hangings. From 1828 to 1851 it served as a military parade ground and only after that was transformed

Chess in Washington Square Park is a tradition, whether the players compete in the park's southwest corner, where the benches and tables are reserved for them, or in a more impromptu setting on a park bench.

There is no such thing as an unusual juxtaposition in Washington Square Park. A hipster plays piano for an older fan while another listener balances on the rim of the fountain's basin.

into a park. It has been managed by the New York City Department of Parks, now the NYC Department of Parks and Recreation, since 1870, when the department was formed.

Just north of the park, on Washington Square North, stands the "Row," a line of Greek Revival townhouses built in the 1830s that retain the look and feel of old New York. Novelist Henry James, whose grandmother lived at 18 Washington Square North, was a frequent visitor as a young child and recognized the area's qualities in *Washington Square* (1881): "I know not whether it is owing to the tendernesses of early associations, but this part of New York appears to many persons the most delectable."

The park's fountain and basin has been a defining feature of its landscape, as well as a reflection of changing design sensibilities over time. Different proposals have been put forth to eliminate it, change its character, or move it. The original fountain and basin were built in 1852 and positioned equidistant between Washington Square East and Washington Square West. In 2004, when the Parks Department announced a major redesign of the park, which had become run-down from overuse, they recommended moving the fountain 23 feet east so that it would align with Washington Square Arch and Fifth Avenue. The Village's many grass-roots community groups, and the Project for Public Space, a nonprofit watchdog organization promoting quality open spaces, argued against it. To paraphrase former City Council member Carol Greitzer, "Why does the fountain need to be lined up!"

This was just one of the Parks Department's many proposals, which also included chopping down more than 10 trees to make way for the realignment, placing a 4-foot iron fence around the park's perimeter, removing the asphalt mounds constructed as part of adventure playgrounds, revamping the popular chess area in the southwest corner of the park and relocating the dog runs.

The $16-million-plus park redesign, under Parks Department landscape architect George Vellonakis proceeded, beginning in December 2007. And, yes, the fountain was moved. The funky mounds of asphalt, part of the 1970 community-based redesign, were removed. The traditional area for chess players in the southwest corner was rejuvenated. Small dogs were given their own area opposite NYU's Bobst Library; bigger dogs had another section. Vellonakis points out that his redesign provided more green space. Also more formality; the paths were straightened out and the aligned fountain is now visible from Fifth Avenue.

The present redesign is, in fact, fairly tepid compared to the changes that Robert Moses, as commissioner of parks, advocated in a series of plans between 1935 and 1958. During that period, cars still drove through the square on single-lane, narrow roads; buses picked up passengers at an outdoor terminal in the park, west of the fountain, where there was a turnaround so the buses could change direction and head back up Fifth Avenue, then a two-way street.

In his sweeping plan of 1958, Moses proposed putting a wider, depressed, north–south roadway through the park to connect Fifth Avenue on the north with the new Title I housing to the south of the park. The widened road, twenty-four feet on each side and separated by a narrow mall, would continue south to connect with West Broadway, which was to be renamed Fifth Avenue South. The new housing to the south would thus be assured of a vaunted Fifth Avenue address. (In fact, the highway would have passed right through the spot where the realigned fountain now stands.)

Moses went up against Greenwich Village groups, including neighborhood activist Shirley Hayes and her Washington Square Park Committee, and urban planner Jane Jacobs, a brilliant grass-roots organizer. They enlisted luminaries like Eleanor Roosevelt, who had lived at 29 Washington Square West for several years, and urban critic Lewis Mumford. Jacobs, who had brought her sons to the park to play, brought them back to protest. (Decades later at an outdoor memorial service for his mother in Washington Square Park, Ned Jacobs recalled the "Save the Square" placards at the demonstrations.)

The grass-roots groups, which generated plenty of press coverage, prevailed in a rare Moses defeat. The park not only didn't get a new highway but its advocates won a key goal: to close the park to traffic altogether. The last car went through in 1958; the bus turnaround was shut down in 1963. As Emily Kies Folpe says in her excellent book, *It Happened on Washington Square*, "For the first time since the Parks Department took over the park in 1870, Washington Square was traffic-free." (One might even argue that this was the beginning of the shift in priorities that one can see today in the New York City Department of Transportation's closure of some traffic lanes, dedicating them to pedestrians or turning them into bike lanes.)

When the park became whole—its parts reunited without traffic—its future as a place to gather became more assured. It remains a breeding ground for radical thinkers, folk singers, dog lovers, and young parents and children, among others. (On a personal note: Thank you to the activists: I am a second-generation park visitor who was brought there as an infant in the 1950s when my grandmother resided at One Fifth Avenue. I brought my own son to the park in the late 70s and early 80s, not an easy time for the city or the square.)

The park's most visible monument is Washington Square Arch, whose upper band is now beautifully illuminated with soft yellow and white lights. The first arch, built in 1889 to commemorate the 100th anniversary of George Washington's inauguration, was made from plaster and wood, and sited approximately 100 feet north of the present arch. Its immediate popularity led to the design of a more permanent one, this time from more durable white Tuckahoe marble. Completed in 1892 and dedicated in 1895, it, like the first, was designed by Stanford White, the acclaimed, and infamous, architect of the firm McKim, Mead & White. White needed only to look to Europe for inspiration: the Arc de Triomphe in Paris, which itself was modeled on the ancient Arch of Titus in Rome.

Today the perimeter of the park and the surrounding blocks are dominated by New York University's buildings. The park's open space, a haven for students, serves as a shortcut between buildings, a place to hang out between classes or meet up with a date. The square has become a de facto symbol of NYU, the largest private university in the United States, with over 50,000 students, and a marketing device to attract students to the casual lifestyle of the school and the city.

It is no surprise, then, that NYU's ambitious, expansionist building plans are closely watched by community groups. The school's wish list for new facilities plays out in a very public process. In June 2012, the City Planning Commission voted to allow NYU to proceed with its revised plans, pending final approval by the City Council, to build four new buildings on the

Vista from the Tisch Fountain north to Washington Square Arch and Fifth Avenue.

superblocks south of Washington Square Park, where the Washington Square Village and Silver Towers apartment complexes stand (the Title I plot). The land, owned by the university, covers 12 city blocks, but its detractors claimed that it was not large enough to support 2,500,000 square feet of new structures. When NYU compromised with a pared-down proposal, commission member Irwin Cantor said of the revised provisions, which had been accepted by the City Planning Commission, "We hope that we have made everyone unhappy to some extent." On July 17, 2012, two City Council committees approved another pared-down version, reducing the original proposal by more than a fifth, to 1.9 million square feet, and added community amenities, such as building and maintaining public spaces on Bleecker Street and LaGuardia Place. On July 25, 2012, the full City Council approved the plan, amid very vocal opposition, by a vote of 44-1; construction will begin in 2014.

As the Village becomes denser and NYU continues to build, regardless of the amount of new square footage, Washington Square Park will retain its significance and visibility. Any attempt to mess with it will ignite a family squabble in which the whole city is the family. (As an example, the Parks Department received criticism for naming the formerly no-name fountain the Tisch Fountain after it received a $2.5 million donation for the work from the Tisch Foundation.)

If only all of the city's parks could be loved so vigorously! If only all of the city's parks could have as many vigilant users and stakeholders! The impact could be more funding and oversight for the ugly duckling parks as well as the crown jewels like Washington Square Park. But it's a sure bet that the centrality of Washington Square Park will keep it front and center in the public's imagination and in the open-space wars, and that's a very good thing for this historic city park. —R.L.

RESTROOMS: Located on Washington Square South between Sullivan and Thompson Streets

REGULATIONS: Dogs are permitted in areas of the park subject to posted restrictions

Smoking is prohibited

MAP & FURTHER INFORMATION AVAILABLE AT:
www.nycgovparks.org/parks/washingtonsquarepark

BY SUBWAY: 6 to Astor Place, walk west 4 blocks on 8th Street, walk south 2 blocks on University Place

A, C, E, B, D, F, M to 6th Avenue and West 4th Street-Washington Square, walk east 1 block on Washington Place

1 to 7th Avenue and Christopher Street-Sheridan Square, walk east 3 blocks on Washington Place

BY BUS: M3, M8 to 8th Street and 5th Avenue, walk south 1 block

M1, M2, M5 to 8th Street and University Place, walk south 1 block

32 UNION SQUARE

Union Square is located from East 14th to East 17th Streets between University Place and Park Avenue South; short streets on either side of the park—Union Square West and Union Square East—link Broadway and Park Avenue South on the north side of the square to Broadway and Fourth Avenue on the south side, and to University Place.

At 14th Street, Broadway and Fourth Avenue don't cross (as Broadway and Fifth Avenue do at 23rd Street), but rather do a kind of dance—a tango, it reminds me of—forming the first "union" of major north–south thoroughfares, and suggesting this as the place for a public square, something elite 19th-century New Yorkers clamored for.

And so in the 1830s, the city planted and fenced in Union Square. Around it rose townhouses, and the neighborhood became a fashionable faubourg.

The Union Square Greenmarket is the best known of the city's open-air markets; regional farmers sell produce, flowers, and other products four days a week to more than 250,000 customers.

Precious little remains to remind us of that long-ago time, for Union Square, even by the lightning-fast standards of New York, did not stand still. Over the next two decades, as the well-to-do continued their uptown migration, high-end commerce invaded Union Square, with such stores as Tiffany's and Brentano's Literary Emporium, restaurants such as Delmonico's and Lüchow's, and theaters. Society ritually congregated, as we know from Edith Wharton's *The Age of Innocence* (set in the 1870s), at the Academy of Music on the northeast corner of 14th Street and Irving Place.

But then Delmonico's moved to 26th Street. Tiffany's went to 37th Street. The Metropolitan Opera House (at 39th Street) put the Academy of Music out of business. In their place loft buildings began to rise around Union Square—a classic New York pattern. As the rich moved uptown, they developed the land on which they had formerly lived with lofts or tenements. It's where Old Money's money came from.

After 1900 the labor movement grew vigorously. Like everything else in New York, the unions found it advantageous to bunch together in one

Pathway along the western edge of Union Square Park. The trucks and tents of the Greenmarket vendors can be glimpsed on the left.

part of the city. (It may be hard to believe, but it's pure coincidence that the unions clustered around "Union" Square.) New Yorkers of a certain age remember the old Union Square of the unions, when the now-trendy Coffee Shop (Union Square West and 16th Street) was actually a coffee shop where tough men discussed union business over breakfast. Their daughters' wedding receptions took place upstairs, at the Marc Ballroom, named for the grandson of the founder of the Provision Salesmen and Distributors Union. (Did any union guy ever think that that ballroom would one day be rented by Sony Entertainment, Goldman Sachs, or *Wired* magazine?)

Not coincidentally, Tammany Hall built its headquarters on the east side of the square in 1928 (in the building at Union Square East and 17th Street that now houses the New York Film Academy). The amorphous north end of the square, where the Greenmarket sets up, was once the scene of political rallies, as well as of Hyde Park Corner–like oratory. Again not coincidentally, the union-era square became a discount shopping mecca. S. Klein on the Square was the Macy's of discounters—before Century 21, before Target. (Klein's was where Zeckendorf Towers now is, at Union Square East and 14th Street.) This was the Union Square into which Andy Warhol inserted himself when he established his "Factory" in the old, exotic Decker Piano Building on Union Square West. (Warhol moved his Factory around, but this was the one where Valerie Solanas shot him in 1968.)

Union Square changed yet again. Tawdriness set in. Drug dealers appeared. It's hard to imagine now, but not long ago Union Square was a backwater. There were no fine restaurants. Even Lüchow's decided to move, to Times Square, where it soon died. The Greenmarket helped change everything. I refrain from saying categorically that it did change everything. At first, the notion of going to Union Square to buy your fine produce had a radical tinge to it. In 1978 John McPhee wrote a classic *New Yorker* essay, "Giving Good Weight," about the city's Greenmarkets. It's now a classic period piece. He said that at Union Square, vendors "took along iron pipes for protection." Whew!

Everything *did* change in the 1980s. The city shook off its fiscal torpor, and Wall Street roared as most people couldn't remember it roaring before. The decade saw the Midtown office market hypertrophy, with the result that the loft buildings and office buildings of "Midtown South" benefited. At the same time, the Villages both West and East went into real estate over-

Playing chess and hanging out on the steps at the park's southern edge.

drive as well. Union Square was peculiarly well positioned to benefit from the growth coming at it from both ends, had the right kinds of buildings, and was a transit hub. That's why I say Greenmarket or not, Union Square would have boomed.

But the flavor would have been very different. The Greenmarket is the first thing that comes to mind when people think of Union Square. Barry Benepe (father of recent parks commissioner Adrian Benepe) and the Council on the Environment of New York City established the Greenmarket in 1976. The idea was for independent farmers from the nearby region to truck in their produce (and other foods) several days a week, and from stalls vend their locally grown, super-fresh goods to hungry urbanites. Benepe—a native New Yorker, an architect, and a founder of Transportation Alternatives, which advocates for bicyclists, pedestrians, and public transportation users—felt that the Greenmarket program (there are more than forty Greenmarkets scattered about the city, with the largest in Union Square) would benefit—indeed save—local farmers who, in the 1970s, felt under siege in a world dominated by big agribusiness, as well as city residents, for whom there had not been such ready access to locally grown, minimally handled, and impeccably fresh produce since the 19th century. The Greenmarkets may appear to be a product of the food-obsessed 21st century—until we realize that the greenmarket helped make the food-obsessed 21st century. Today, countless New York restaurants, as well as home cooks, rely on Greenmarket goods. Fabled restaurateur Danny Meyer (Union Square Café, Gramercy Tavern, Maialino, Shake Shack) says that he strategically located his restaurants as close to the Union Square Greenmarket as he could. And chef Mario Batali met his wife at the stall of Coach Farm, a Columbia County cheese maker that has been at the Greenmarket since its beginning.

In addition to the Greenmarket, Union Square boasts a bronze George Washington on horseback, one of the finest equestrian statues in the country, the handiwork of Henry Kirke Brown and John Quincy Adams Ward, dedicated in 1856. It stands in the southern part of the square, looking across 14th Street, at or near a place Washington traversed as he rode down from the Bronx to reclaim New York from the British on November 25, 1783. The sculptor Brown also gave us the standing bronze of Lincoln in the northern part of the park, along the lateral pathway on the line of East 16th Street. The Lincoln dates from 1870. Lincoln, too, passed through Union Square: on April 25, 1865, the sixteenth president's funeral cortège moved north on Broadway from City Hall to a prayer service at Union Square. From the square the cortège proceeded to the Hudson River Railroad depot on West 34th Street. The paths of Washington and Lincoln,

The redesigned and revitalized northern end of the park.

the former entering the city, the latter leaving it, 83 years apart, crossed in Union Square. It is hallowed ground.

It took a while, but the city finally spruced up the 3.5-acre square in the 1980s and 1990s. More recently, Transportation Commissioner Janette Sadik-Khan extended her pedestrian mall and bike-path program, in which green-painted, planter-lined surfaces reclaim roadbed from motorists, to Broadway and 14th Street along the square, effectively increasing its size and making it safer and easier to enter and exit than ever before. The amorphous and confusing square has emerged as one of the city's principal hubs of energy. Statues and produce aside, it's not what anyone would call beautiful. Almost every building surrounding the square houses national chain stores. Nor is it always pleasant: on days when the Greenmarket is not open, the northern end is depressingly barren. At the southern end, youth congregates. Occupy protesters coexist with raucous skateboarding teens. (The sound of skateboards on city pavements grates in a way few other urban noises do, jackhammers not excepted.) Nevertheless, Union Square feels like the heart of the city. —F.M.

HOURS: 6 am–midnight daily

RESTROOMS: Located in the Pavilion at the northern end of the park, open all year

REGULATIONS: Dogs are allowed, see park signs for specific information

Smoking is prohibited

Free Wi-Fi

MAP & FURTHER INFORMATION AVAILABLE AT: www.unionsquarenyc.org

BY SUBWAY: N, R, Q, 4, 5, 6, L to 14th Street-Union Square

BY BUS: M1, M2, M3 to Union Square East and 15th Street

M4 to 14th Street and University Place

X1, X7, X9, X10, X12, X17, X27, X28 to Broadway and 13th Street

M101, M102, M103 to 3rd Avenue and 17th Street, walk west 2 blocks

M5 to 5th Avenue and 17th Street, walk east 1 block

33 BRYANT PARK

Bryant Park is located from 40th to 42nd Streets between 5th and 6th Avenues, behind the main branch of the New York Public Library

Bryant Park, like many small parks and squares in America's older cities, began as a potter's field in the early 19th century. In 1842 the city built its vast Croton Distributing Reservoir along the east side of the field, which was rechristened Reservoir Square. At that time, this area was still well north of the centers of population in New York City. The reservoir, however, with its high walkways that afforded spectacular views, was a popular destination for Sunday outings. In 1853, the city held its first "world's fair," the Exhibition of the Industry of All Nations, or Crystal Palace Exhibition, at Reservoir Square. In 1884, Reservoir Square became Bryant Park, in honor of the recently deceased William Cullen Bryant, who as America's most popular poet and as editor of the *New York Evening Post* had campaigned tirelessly for the creation of Central Park. In the 1890s, the city razed the reservoir to replace it with the New York Public Library. That magnificent building, designed by Carrère & Hastings, opened in 1911. Bryant Park at that time had a naturalistic layout, with looping walkways and irregularly shaped lawns, except at its east end, where the park met the wraparound terrace of the New York Public Library. That beautiful, balustraded terrace remains largely intact. Of particular note are the "comfort stations" on the north and south

One of the strategies to rejuvenate Bryant Park was to provide year-round programming. The temporary ice-skating rink during the winter months is an example.

sides. Carrère & Hastings based their design of these comfort stations on the monumental statue bases by Ange-Jacques Gabriel on the Place de la Concorde in Paris. In time, with the general decline of Bryant Park, these structures deteriorated and ceased to offer their intended amenity. In 1992, as part of the spectacular overhaul of the park (see below), the architects Kupiec & Koutsomitis renovated the structures, returning the northern one to use as a restroom facility and converting the southern one into a park storage facility. Of the northern one, we may safely say that in all of America there is no more beautiful freestanding restroom structure. The great monument to William Cullen Bryant, a seated figure in bronze by Herbert Adams, with architecture by Carrère & Hastings, occupies the place of honor in the center of the terrace. The statue of Bryant rests on an elaborate pedestal under a semidome behind a grand arch and an entablature supported by Roman Doric columns. On either side sit urns, and balustrades stretch to north and south. No more majestic setting for a statue exists in New York.

As grand as the library made the east end of Bryant Park, the west end suffered for many years from the presence of the Sixth Avenue elevated railway. The el roared overhead from 1878 to 1938, casting a shadow and intermittently showering the park with metallic shrieks and screeches. At the northern edge of Brooklyn Bridge Park (p. 97), trains rumble overhead on the Manhattan Bridge. The noise brings an abrupt halt to conversation down below, but the height of the bridge's trackbed (much higher than standard elevated tracks) and the openness of the waterfront setting mitigate the intrusion. At Bryant Park, the el was a major and persistent bother.

In 1932, just a few years before the el came down, the Architects' Emergency Committee, founded to help unemployed architects, sponsored a competition to redesign Bryant Park. The winner was architect Lusby Simpson (1895–1954), who had worked for the great classical architect John Russell Pope. Aided by landscape architect Gilmore D. Clarke and Parks Department staffers Harry J. Freer and Clarence Dale Badgeley, Simpson gave us no less than America's finest classically designed park, surpassing Washington, D.C.'s Meridian Hill Park and Chicago's Grant Park. Simpson moved the Josephine Shaw Lowell Fountain (Charles Adams Platt, architect), which had stood well inside the park since 1912, to its present site just in from Sixth Avenue, extended the library's raised terrace around three sides of the park, and put a large rectangular lawn in the center.

Much of the Simpson design remains intact, but beginning in 1980 the privately operated Bryant Park Restoration Corporation (BPRC), set up through the largesse of the Rockefeller Brothers Fund, began the process of reclaiming Bryant Park from years of deterioration and disuse, and from a well-earned reputation for unlawful activities, particularly drug dealing. In 1974 the New York City Landmarks Preservation Commission designated Bryant Park a landmark, ensuring that any renovation would preserve the essentials of Lusby Simpson's plan. In 1988 the BPRC presented a renovation plan by the landscape architecture firm Hanna/Olin. Robert Hanna (1934–2003) and Laurie Olin (b. 1938) formed their company in Philadelphia in 1976. They worked in Seattle for the influential landscape architect Richard Haag before both becoming professors at the University of Pennsylvania. The partnership they formed there soon went on to become one of the most successful and influential landscape architecture firms of the 1990s. Hanna and Olin parted ways in 1996. Hanna/Olin and the later Olin Partnership have made a huge mark on New York—Bryant Park, the Battery Park City Esplanade (p. 49), Wagner Park (p. 52), and Columbus Circle (p. 194) bear the unmistakable imprint of one or the other of these firms.

At Bryant Park, in addition to Hanna/Olin, a nondesigner served as tutelary spirit. That was William Hollingsworth Whyte, known as "Holly." Whyte was born in West Chester, Pennsylvania, in 1917, and died in New York in 1999. He worked for many years as an editor at *Fortune* magazine, and in 1956 wrote the bestselling book *The Organization Man.* He developed a passion for cities and an intense desire to understand how New York worked—or did not. He devoted *Fortune* resources to pioneering urban studies, including the series of articles collected into the seminal book *The Exploding Metropolis* (1958). For that book, he recruited Jane Jacobs to write an essay called "Downtown Is for People," and he later arranged for her to expand that essay into her first book, *The Death and Life of Great American Cities,* in 1961. In the 1970s and 1980s Whyte made close-grained observational studies of how people use city streets and open spaces. They became the basis for his remarkable film *The Social Life of Small Urban Spaces* (1980), made in conjunction with the Municipal Art Society of New York, and his book *City: Rediscovering the Center* (1988). Whyte sought to figure out why some places attracted people and others repelled them. In the 1980 film,

The Bryant Park Restoration Corporation works hard each year to create a perfect green lawn. Add movable chairs and some sunshine, and the crowds gather.

Bryant Park served as an example of a repellent space. How could that be, given the beauty of its design?

Whyte believed that the park was too aloof from neighboring streets. As Paul Goldberger of the *New York Times* put it in 1992, the park, as rebuilt in the 1930s, "was reconstructed on a podium, set several steps above the street, and cut off from the city by a series of plinths, balustrades, high hedges and granite walls. The park could not be seen clearly from the street, and people inside could not see back out to the sidewalk, a set of conditions ideal for drug dealers but of little comfort to anyone else." The essentials of Simpson's plan, Whyte felt, should stay, but a few key changes were necessary. Thus, the BPRC built new entrances, widened existing entrances, introduced a host of new amenities (spotlessly maintained restrooms, food kiosks, a carousel, an ice-skating rink, al fresco movie screenings), and instituted exceptionally vigilant management and security. But three of the changes are of special note. One is the replacement of hedges along the north and south sides with two 300-foot-long, 12-foot-deep perennial gardens designed by the renowned Lynden B. Miller. The idea was to set the park off from its surroundings without obscuring the lines of sight into and out of it. A key Whytean principle is that an open space should be of, and not merely in, the city. Cut such a space off too much from surrounding streets and it ceases to be a part of the self-regulating processes of city life, becoming too readily suited to vice and crime. The second is the introduction of Parisian-style movable chairs into the park. We associate movable chairs with the Tuileries and Luxembourg Gardens in Paris, but the immediate inspiration for Bryant Park was only ten blocks uptown, at Zion & Breen's tiny Paley Park on 53rd Street just east of Fifth Avenue. Whyte made Paley Park one of the stars of *The Social Life of Small Urban Spaces*. By now the name William H. Whyte is likelier to make people think "movable chairs" than anything else. Whyte championed the Parisian and Paleyan notion that park users should be able to move their seating—into or out of the sun, into or out of groups of people, away from undesirable characters, into dyads, and so forth—instead of its being fixed like standard park benches. The success of the movable seating at Paley Park and Bryant Park made this feature, for a number of years, de rigueur in open-space design in New York, and has waned only with the rise of Landscape Urbanism. Finally, some significant new structures were added to the park, designs of the architectural firm Hardy Holzman Pfeiffer Associates. These include the food kiosks at the western end of the park. A bit more conspicuous is the 18-foot-high Hugh Hardy–designed restaurant pavilion, which opened to the south of the Bryant Memorial in 1995; it is in fact a much scaled-down version of an earlier proposal and, making extensive use of vine-covered trellises (an enlarged version of one of the two kiosk designs at the western end of the park), with large windows overlooking the park and an open roof deck, strikes a note halfway between formal and casual. To the north of the Bryant Memorial Hardy placed more casual tented bar and dining areas.

Bryant Park is today unquestionably the most popular place in Midtown for office workers to eat lunch in nice weather. On a beautiful day, the jammed park takes on an almost party-like atmosphere. Extensive programming keeps the park in constant use all day long and all year round. It attracts locals and tourists in equal numbers, one of the marks of a successful public place. Indeed, Bryant Park's turnaround symbolized, arguably more than any other single thing, the turnaround of New York as a whole. The park's lessons continue to reverberate throughout the country. —F.M.

HOURS: November–February, Sunday–Thursday: 7 am–10 pm

Friday, Saturday: 7 am–midnight

March: 7 am–7 pm (8 pm after daylight savings)

April: 7 am–10 pm

May–September: 7 am–11 pm

October: 7 am–9 pm

Restrooms: 42nd Street at the Library (east) end of the park

Regulations: Dogs must be leashed, picked up after, and kept off of the lawns

Smoking is prohibited

Free WiFi

AN AUDIO TOUR AVAILABLE AT ITUNES OR AT:

www.bryantpark.org/plan-your-visit/audio_tour.html

MAP & FURTHER INFORMATION AVAILABLE AT: www.bryantpark.org

BY SUBWAY: B, D, F, M to 6th Avenue and 42nd Street-Bryant Park

7 to 42nd Street and 5th Avenue

S to Grand Central-42nd Street, walk west 1 block on 42nd Street

4, 5, 6 to Lexington Avenue and Grand Central-42nd Street, walk west 2.5 blocks on 42nd Street

N, R, Q to Broadway and Times Square-42nd Street, walk east 1 block on 41st or 40th Street

1, 2, 3 to 7th Avenue and Times Square-42nd Street, walk east 2 blocks on 41st or 42nd Street

BY BUS: M5, M7 to 6th Avenue and 42nd Street; 6th Avenue and 40th Street

M20, M104 to 7th Avenue and 41st Street, walk east 2 blocks on 41st Street

X1, X7, X9, X10, X12, X14, X17, X27, X28, X68 to 5th Avenue and 41st Street

M42 to 42nd Street and 5th Avenue; 42nd Street and 6th Avenue

M1, M2, M3, M4, Q32, to 5th Avenue and 41st Street

QM10, QM12 to 6th Avenue and 43rd Street

34 PALEY PARK

Paley Park is located at 3 East 53rd Street between Fifth and Madison Avenues (closer to Fifth) on the north side of the street

Paley Park, on 53rd Street just east of Fifth Avenue, in the midst of one of the most congested and frenetic parts of midtown Manhattan, proved that the tiniest park, designed right and put in the right place, could have an impact as great as that of a park twenty or a hundred times its size. At less than an acre (4,200 square feet, or 0.96 of an acre), Paley Park is small indeed. What makes this tiny park, which opened in 1967, so great? It occupies a single building lot, cradled between two buildings, which, with the rear of a building on 54th Street, tightly define the space, turning it into what architects like to call an "urban room." Landscape architects Zion & Breen placed a 20-foot-high waterwall across the back of the park. In this compact space, the sound of the water (1,800 gallons a minute) effectively blocks out the city noises that, at the intersection of 53rd Street and Fifth Avenue, are pretty intense. Ivy covers the side walls (Robert Zion said these were the park's "lawns"), there are several well-spaced, shady locust trees,

Small and perfect, with the soothing sounds of a waterfall.

and there are a few potted plants. These plantings are crucial to the park's success, but do note that they are not overwhelming in number. The park (or parklet) is also set off from its surroundings by being ever so slightly raised: the park's pavement is four steps above the 53rd Street sidewalk. This is just enough to set the park off, but not enough to make it seem at all cumbersome to access the park. A discreet food stand offers park users sandwiches and coffee—because who does not like to nibble or sip when relaxing in a park? Yet such stands were rare in public-space design at the time Paley Park came along. (Not today: Think of Shake Shack in Madison Square!) And then the finishing touch: movable chairs and tables. How silly it seems that such a simple thing is often the difference between an extremely successful public space (as here) and one that is completely dead. Park users want the freedom to move their chairs into groups, to move them for privacy (perhaps away from that leering man), to move them into and out of the sun (so important!), and at Paley Park they can. Famed urbanist William H. Whyte's minute observation of how people actually use Paley Park led him to champion many of its elements in other public-space design projects, notably in his role as a consultant in the 1990s redesign of Bryant Park on Sixth Avenue between 40th and 42nd Streets (p. 234). Whyte, indeed, made Paley Park a star of his seminal 1980 film *The Social Life of Small Urban Spaces*.

Paley Park ranks with the former IBM Building atrium (also by Zion & Breen; p. 210) as one of the two best examples of Modernist landscape design in New York. By Modernist we mean that there is little here that is imitative of traditional styles—no ornamental hardscape flourishes, little "artistry" in the use of plantings. The elements are simple, the lines clean. Yet we also often identify Modernist landscapes with a reversal of the traditional figure-ground relationship found in historic urbanism. The traditional architect articulates urban open space as a room, with well-defined borders, a void among solids. In much Modernist architecture, the reverse occurs: buildings are solids dropped into defining voids (for example, the "towers in a park" superblock). Here, however, Modernist elements serve a traditional purpose: this is the purest example of a public room in Manhattan.

The site on which Paley Park was built was occupied from 1929 to 1965 by one of New York's most legendary nightspots, the Stork Club. Owned by Sherman Billingsley, for more than three decades the Stork Club was home to "café society," which included a mix of socialites and media celebrities. Frank Sinatra, Marilyn Monroe, and various Kennedys were regulars. When it closed, William S. Paley, the media executive who founded the Columbia Broadcasting System (CBS), created Paley Park through his eponymous foundation. To this day, Paley Park is privately owned, but open to the public. The Project for Public Spaces, a highly respected watchdog and advocacy group concerned with the design of public spaces, has placed Paley Park—all 0.96 acres of it—on its list of the World's Best Parks. They are absolutely right. —F.M.

HOURS: 8 am–7:30 pm, closed in January

Refreshment stand: 8 am–5 pm, closed Saturdays and Sundays

RESTROOMS: None

REGULATIONS: Paley Park is a privately owned public space (not a city park) and smoking is permitted

Pets are prohibited

MAP & FURTHER INFORMATION AVAILABLE AT: The management office can be reached at 212.355.4171. There is no Web site.

BY SUBWAY: F to 6th Avenue and 47th–50th Street-Rockefeller Center

E, M to 5th Avenue and 53rd Street

6 to Lexington Avenue and 51st Street, walk north 2 blocks on Lexington Avenue and west 3 blocks on 53rd Street

BY BUS: M3 to 5th Avenue and 53rd Street

35 CONSERVATORY GARDEN, CENTRAL PARK

The Conservatory Garden is located on the east side of Central Park between 104th and 106th Streets, with entrances at the Vanderbilt Gate (5th Avenue and 105th Street) and the 106th Street gate inside the park

So much has been written about Central Park, not least by this writer, that, given this book's limited space, we decided not to retell its well-known story, not in its totality, anyway. Rather, our focus is on one of the 20th-century changes made to the park by a man whom, for better or worse, we must credit as one of the park's authors, along with Frederick Law Olmsted, Calvert Vaux, and Jacob Wrey Mould.

Robert Moses came to work for New York City in 1934. He had earlier distinguished himself for his parks and parkways on Long Island. For a city mired in the Depression and advanced physical decay, getting Moses was a coup. As Robert Caro told us in *The Power Broker* (1974), the city jumped through hoops to secure Moses's services.

Walter Schott's delightful sculpture of frolicking maidens is the centerpiece of the French-influenced north section of the Conservatory Garden.

Moses's initial mandate was to fix the city's parks. Caro is very good in describing the parks' rotten condition in 1934. Even in the affluent 1920s, the Tammany-run city government neglected the parks, which were in deplorable shape when the Depression hit. We think we've seen dying parks—Central Park in the 1970s was a pitiable mess. But it had fewer thriving plants in 1934 than it did in 1980, when the Central Park Conservancy began its extraordinary rehabilitation of the park.

No one denies that much of what Moses added to Central Park over the years did great damage to it. Yet so many of the amenities that people use most heavily in the park, even if they're contrary to Olmsted's and Vaux's intentions, came by way of Moses—the perimeter playgrounds, the Great Lawn, Wollman Rink, Lasker Rink and Pool, a hugely upgraded zoo (upgraded again in the 1980s), and much more.

Moses's most felicitous intervention by far was the Conservatory Garden, entered at Fifth Avenue and 104th Street through the Vanderbilt Gate, a magnificent iron gate, made by Bergotte & Bauviller of Paris, that once adorned the Fifth Avenue mansion of Cornelius Vanderbilt II and that his daughter Gertrude Vanderbilt Whitney donated to the city in 1939.

The Conservatory Garden borrows its name from the greenhouse that once occupied the site. Moses dismantled the greenhouse in 1934. (It is sad

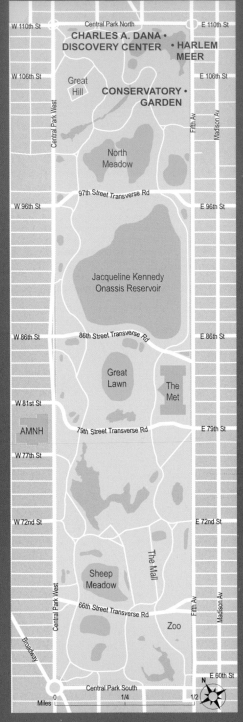

CENTRAL PARK

Map by John Hill

that Manhattan is today without a greenhouse.) The Conservatory Garden opened in 1937. We credit its design to the ubiquitous Gilmore D. Clarke and his landscape architect wife, the delightfully named M. Betty Sprout (1906–1962).

Central Park on the whole follows English precedents, drawing on the work of John Claudius Loudon and Joseph Paxton, among others; indeed, it was chiefly designed by an Englishman, Calvert Vaux. The Conservatory Garden, in contrast, brings French and Italian traditions into Central Park. We should perhaps call it "Conservatory Gardens," for in fact it is three quite separate gardens.

The center garden is Italian in inspiration. The Italian is a classical tradition, without the contrived naturalism of the English tradition though more relaxed than what we think of as the French formal garden. For many people, Italian gardens (about which Edith Wharton wrote so well) are the most delectable of all gardens. Here, crabapple allées border a large, central, yew-hedged lawn. The lawn culminates at its western end in a simple classical fountain and semicircular pergola. When the crabapple trees bloom pink

All the water features in Central Park are man-made, including the Harlem Meer in the northernmost section of the park, not far from the Conservatory Garden.

and white in April and May, the scene makes your heart leap. The garden here is of the same genus as the Osborne Garden in the Brooklyn Botanic Garden, by Harold ap Rhys Caparn, and Rector Park, by Innocenti & Webel, in Battery Park City (p. 48).

The garden to the south is English. In spring it blooms with cornelian cherry trees, crabapples, daffodils, forsythia, hyacinth, magnolias, pansies, quince, summer snowflakes, tulips, virginia bluebells, and witchhazel. Bessie Potter Vonnoh's fountain is an original feature of the garden. Surrounded by a reflecting pool filled with water lilies, it honors writer Frances Hodgson Burnett and depicts characters from her classic children's tale *The Secret Garden* (1911). Burnett's friends, who paid for the fountain, found this to be the perfect "secret garden" setting for it.

The north garden is French. Spring bursts into bloom with thousands of tulips. They surround, in circular parterres, one of the city's most delightful public sculptures. The Three Dancing Maidens Fountain, which once graced the Yonkers estate of Samuel Untermyer, dates to before 1910, and made its way to Central Park in 1947. Walter Schott, the sculptor of the deliriously dancing maidens (who put one in mind of Matisse's *Dance*), was once ranked as Germany's most prestigious sculptor, the favorite of Kaiser Wilhelm II.

The Central Park Conservancy and the outstanding public gardener Lynden B. Miller refurbished the Conservatory Garden in the 1980s. Ms. Miller did not merely design the plantings but took charge of the whole project, from fund-raising to devising a long-term maintenance plan. We owe as much to her as to Mr. and Mrs. Clarke for this wonderful retreat, which had nothing to do with Olmsted and Vaux. —F.M.

HOURS: 8 am–dusk

RESTROOMS: Located in the Conservatory Garden (wheelchair access)

REGULATIONS: Smoking is prohibited

Wheelchair access at 106th Street gate

Quiet Zone, headphones required for radios

No running, rollerblading, biking or sports

MAP & FURTHER INFORMATION AVAILABLE AT: www.centralparknyc.org

BY SUBWAY: 6 to Lexington Avenue and 103rd Street, walk west 3 blocks on 103rd Street and north 2 blocks on 5th Avenue, enter through the Vanderbilt Gate

6 to Lexington Avenue and 110th St (Harlem Meer), walk south to 103rd Street

BY BUS: M1, M2, M3, M4, M106 to 5th Avenue and 104th Street, walk north 1 block along 5th Avenue and enter the garden through the Vanderbilt Gate

M1, M2, M3, M4 to Central Park North and 5th Avenue (Harlem Meer), enter the park at Frawley Circle and walk south along the Meer to 103rd Street

The rambling paths through the Liz Christy Garden are a welcome departure from the city's rigid rectilinearity.

LIZ CHRISTY GARDEN

36

The garden is located on the northeast corner of the Bowery and Houston Street, with entrances on Houston Street and the Bowery

Hidden in plain sight on busy Houston Street between Chrystie Street and the Bowery, the Liz Christy Garden appears to be a modest neighborhood garden, fenced off from the hum of the Lower East Side and quietly tended by devoted volunteers. But this humble appearance belies its place in New York's landscape history. Founded in 1973 by a group of local volunteers fed up with the decay of the Lower East Side, it was the first community garden in New York City.

In the 17th century, this corner of the Bowery and Houston Street was part of the farm of Peter Stuyvesant, the last Dutch governor of New Amsterdam, but by the 1970s it had become a vacant, garbage-filled lot. In the early 1970s local artist and gardening enthusiast Liz Christy and a group of radical urban gardeners who called themselves the Green Guerillas began

The garden's layout takes full advantage of its narrow footprint along East Houston Street and boasts an impressive variety of plant species.

conducting a series of floral assaults on the neglected areas of the Lower East Side. They planted window boxes, dug tree pits, and lobbed seed bombs (balloons or Christmas ornaments filled with seed and fertilizer) over the chain-link fences of abandoned lots in the hope of injecting some natural beauty into the urban landscape. The lot on the corner of the Bowery and Houston Street, rented for $1 a month from the city's Department of Housing Preservation and Development, became their showpiece, and the Bowery Houston Community Farm and Garden, as it was then called, was born. From this lot, the Green Guerillas ran workshops, tutorials, and plant giveaways to engage the community and inspire other groups to start their own gardens. In 1986 the garden was renamed Liz Christy's Bowery-Houston Garden in honor of its founder, who died in 1985.

Today the garden is an oasis of greenery in a bustling neighborhood. The iron fence surrounding it can barely contain the riotous flora, and the garden's trees spill over to shade the sidewalk outside. A narrow plot, the garden hugs the façades of the buildings that surround it on two sides. From the Bowery entrance, though, it appears quite long. Winding paths make the most of its narrow footprint, ending in charming cul-de-sacs furnished with benches, a perfect setting for contemplation or intimate conversation. At the garden's inception, the Green Guerillas experimented to find out which plants could thrive in an urban setting. Today gardeners grow an impressive variety of plants, including wildflowers, vegetables, berries, herbs, and flowering perennials. The garden is also home to a grape arbor, weeping birches, fruit trees, and a dawn redwood. A small pond is populated by koi and red-eared slider turtles, and a resident cat named George conducts regular patrols.

What makes the Liz Christy Garden a true local gem is its universal appeal. Whether you come simply to sit silently, drinking in the freshness of the place, or to catch sight of *Campsis radicans* and *Armeria martim*, the garden is pleasing. For the herbally ignorant and black-thumbed among us, it is an inviting leafy retreat, but to the horticulturist it is a treasure trove of species rarely seen in city gardens.

The passion that inspired the community garden movement in New York is sustained by volunteers today. Even in the dead of winter, they are out, tending their patches and educating passers-by about the garden. Though the garden appears to have burst forth naturally out of the cracks in the concrete of the Lower East Side, Mother Nature has had many a helping hand in reconquering this patch of Gotham. The garden's success and beauty are a testament to the diligence and dedication of these volunteer gardeners as well as the support of the community at large.

Envisioned, built, and maintained by volunteers and buoyed by visitor donations, the Liz Christy Garden is a tribute to the power of community action. In 1976 it won the Mollie Parnis Dress Up Your Neighborhood award, the first of many awards and commendations that would spread the message of the community garden movement to neighborhoods throughout the city. Today there are more than 750 community-sponsored open-space projects, from vegetable allotments to parks. The Liz Christy Garden is not only the historic birthplace of the community garden movement in New York City but also a fantastic example of its success. —E.C.

HOURS: Saturdays: noon–4 pm (all year)

Sundays: noon–4 pm (May–September)

Tuesdays and Thursdays: 6 pm–dusk (May–September)

All hours weather permitting

RESTROOMS: None

REGULATIONS: Dogs must be kept on paths

Picking or cutting plants or flowers and walking in beds or gardens are prohibited

Smoking is prohibited

FURTHER INFORMATION AVAILABLE AT: www.lizchristygarden.us

BY SUBWAY: F to 2nd Avenue, take the Houston Street exit; the garden is on the left

BY BUS: M21 to East Houston Street and 2nd Avenue

M103 to the Bowery and East Houston Street

37 ZUCCOTTI PARK

Zuccotti Park is located between Trinity Place and Broadway at Liberty Street, next to and south of One Liberty Plaza at 165 Broadway

Zuccotti Park used to be called Liberty Plaza. It provided a zoning bonus for One Liberty Plaza across Liberty Street, the hulking, 2.2-million-square-foot black steel skyscraper loved by real estate agents and corporate space planners. Tower and plaza date from 1973. At that time, the *New York Times*'s architecture critic Ada Louise Huxtable eloquently celebrated the new series of plazas extending from the east along Liberty Street: Chase Manhattan Plaza, the plaza of 140 Broadway, and Liberty Plaza. These embodiments of the new zoning, which encouraged plazas, opened up the streetscapes of this part of lower Manhattan just enough to create stunning vistas of old and new,

BELOW AND FACING PAGE When the Occupy Wall Street protesters chose Zuccotti Park as their headquarters, they inadvertently got lucky. Unlike city parks, which have an official closing time, Zuccotti Park, a privately owned public space, is open 24 hours a day.

of grand old masonry structures reflected in the smoky glass sides of the new towers, whose reflected light also bathed the older buildings in an ethereal glow. This, said Huxtable, was what New York was all about, artful, dramatic minglings of old and new, enhancing each other. Liberty Street, she said, "compares in effect and elegance with any celebrated Renaissance plaza or Baroque vista."

The attacks of September 11, 2001, devastated Liberty Plaza. Completely rebuilt, to a design by Cooper, Robertson & Partners, the plaza reopened in 2006. It bore a sculpture, *Joie de Vivre*, by Mark di Suvero. It also bore a new name, Zuccotti Park, after John Zuccotti, chairman of Brookfield Properties, the large real estate company that owns One Liberty Plaza.

In 1916 New York enacted its first zoning code, which in part was a response to the proliferation of sheer-walled skyscrapers: henceforth, the city required tall buildings to be stepped back at prescribed intervals to allow sunlight to reach the sidewalks. This accounts for the distinctive

stepped silhouettes of so many New York skyscrapers. In 1961 the city amended the zoning code to encourage public open spaces. Buildings could once again rise sheer, as long as they left enough of the site open at ground level. The earliest plazas, such as those of the Seagram Building (1958) on Park Avenue between 52nd and 53rd Streets, and One Chase Manhattan Plaza (1960), actually predated—and strongly influenced—the new zoning rules. After 1961, plazas proliferated throughout Manhattan, in residential neighborhoods such as the Upper East Side and Murray Hill, as well as in the business districts. Most plazas, alas, are dull and uninviting. The Liberty Street plazas, though, ranked among the most successful implementations of the new zoning.

The new zoning created a strange animal: privately owned public space. In other words, under the zoning rules, the private builder owns the plaza and is responsible for its upkeep, but because the builder acquired a "bonus"— usually extra square footage—in exchange for the plaza, it is obliged to keep the plaza forever open to the public, just as though it were a city park. In practice, it's a bit knotty. In 2000 Jerold S. Kayden undertook an exhaustive study of New York's more than 500 plazas for the Municipal Art Society of New York. His book *Privately Owned Public Space: The New York Experience* revealed that many of these spaces flout the law and are for all intents and purposes private spaces. But in 2000, the Liberty Street plazas did not count among the culprits. Even 9/11 did little to diminish the public's access to them.

Then came the summer of 2011, and the Occupy Wall Street move-ment. Thousands of mostly youthful protesters camped out in Zuccotti Park, creating a tent city that served as home base and headquarters as the Occupiers marched through the streets of the Financial District and else-where to voice their righteous anger over a financial system that privatized gains and socialized losses. Down to Zuccotti Park came movie stars and academic hotshots to make speeches. Down came celebrity chefs to pro-vide food. The Occupiers made music and, sometimes, scuffled with police. The whole thing, which lasted several months, was mostly orderly—in fact, became a tourist destination. But the police, forced to divert resources to the area, disliked the situation. And Brookfield Properties, owner of Zuccotti Park, really disliked it.

As for who makes the rules that govern use of such privately owned public spaces, the city defers to the owner with only the proviso that any rules be "reasonable." As Jerold Kayden pointed out in 2011, Brookfield's rules—which prohibited activities like skateboarding—never envisioned anything like the Occupy encampment. Brookfield, after the fact, redrew its guidelines. (The Occupy protesters broke up following police crackdowns and the onset of cold weather.)

However, the most lasting legacy of Occupy involves not Zuccotti Park but nearby Chase Manhattan Plaza. Once the pride of the mighty Chase Manhattan Bank, it contains a sunken garden by Isamu Noguchi and a sculpture, *Four Trees*, by Jean Dubuffet, and was, every inch of it, a public place. But JPMorgan Chase (the current owner) feared an Occupy onslaught and fenced off the large plaza. No longer may tourists dawdle there or office walkers make a shortcut across it at lunch hour. What 9/11 failed to do, tear of protesters in the wake of the financial meltdown that began in 2008 succeeded in doing: closing Chase Manhattan Plaza. For good? No one knows. The barriers, at this writing, still look provisional. Can the city step in? No. This is not a bonus space. JPMorgan Chase bears no legal responsibility to open it to the public.

One only wishes they knew the P.R. gold they would mine by admitting their mistake and reopening it. But the banks, living in their bubble, seem beyond P.R. So much for Renaissance plazas and Baroque vistas. —F.M.

HOURS: 24 hours

REGULATIONS: Per the posted sign: Camping, erecting tents or other structures, lying on the ground or benches, impeding walkways, the use of tarps or sleeping bags, bicycling, skateboarding, rollerblading are all prohibited. No storage of personal property on grounds, benches, sitting areas or walkways, no removal of objects from trash receptacles.

RESTROOMS: No permanent restrooms

MAP & FURTHER INFORMATION ABOUT ADJACENT ONE LIBERTY PLAZA: www.brookfieldofficeproperties.com/us/new-york/one-liberty-plaza

BY SUBWAY: R to Church Street and Cortlandt Street, walk south 2 blocks on Church Street

A, C, J, Z, 2, 3, 4, 5 to Fulton Street and Broadway walk south 3 blocks on Broadway

BY PATH: Newark–WTC or Hoboken–WTC lines to World Trade Center, walk south 3 blocks on Church Street

BY BUS: X10, X11, X12 to Broadway and Liberty Street

M5, X1, X3, X8, X10, X12, X15, X17, X17A, X17C to Church Street and Liberty Street

ABOVE AND FACING PAGE The 16-acre site under construction.

38 NATIONAL SEPTEMBER 11 MEMORIAL

The entrance to the memorial is at the northeast corner of Greenwich and Albany Streets in lower Manhattan

The Port Authority of New York and New Jersey built the World Trade Center complex mainly in the late 1960s and early 1970s. The center's original six buildings occupied a "superblock" (meaning that the city demapped streets on the site) bounded by Church Street on the east, Vesey Street on the north, West Street on the west, and Liberty Street on the south. Of the "Twin Towers," One World Trade Center ("Tower One") stood on West Street between Liberty and Vesey, and Two World Trade Center ("Tower Two") stood on Liberty between West and Church. (Seven World Trade Center, across Vesey Street from the superblock, rose

only in 1987.) Six World Trade Center, at the southeast corner of West and Vesey, connected via aerial bridge over West Street to the Winter Garden of Battery Park City (p. 33).

How did the Port Authority, a supragovernmental "public authority" with the sole responsibility of managing port and transportation infrastructure and operations shared by New York and New Jersey, end up as the developer of a megacomplex of business buildings in lower Manhattan? Once, another pair of twin towers stood on part of the site, along Church Street. These were the Hudson Terminal Buildings, built by the Hudson & Manhattan Railroad over a subterranean railroad station. The first railroad to tunnel under the Hudson River, the Hudson & Manhattan carried New Jersey commuters to and from their Manhattan jobs. When the railroad faced bankruptcy in the 1960s, the Port Authority stepped in to save it, seeing it, rightly, as a necessary piece of the regional transportation network. In saving the railroad, the Port

Authority assumed proprietorship of the Hudson Terminal Buildings and underground station.

The Port Authority granted the Trade Center commission to a Seattle-based, Japanese American architect, Minoru Yamasaki, as well as to New York's Emery Roth & Sons. Yamasaki made his name with buildings he designed in Saudi Arabia that skillfully integrate Islamic motifs into otherwise thoroughly modern structures. Critics applauded the choice of Yamasaki to design the complex. The completed work, however, drew little but critical opprobrium. Distorting scale, arid public spaces, and the wanton destruction of a lively old commercial neighborhood counted among the charges against the World Trade Center. In addition, the center came on the market at the worst possible time. Manhattan in the mid-1970s, mired in fiscal woe, needed not a square foot, let alone many millions of square feet, of new office space. Only by siphoning government agencies from other lower Manhattan buildings could the Trade Center fill any of its space at all.

But make no mistake: the events of September 11, 2001, shattered and scarred even the Trade Center's loudest critics. On New York's day of greatest infamy, Islamic militants affiliated with the al-Qaeda terrorist organization flew two jumbo jetliners into the Twin Towers. In spectacular fashion, on live television, the towers imploded, leaving nearly three thousand dead and covering lower Manhattan in grisly gray dust for months.

Immediately, calls went out for plans to rebuild the World Trade Center. Circumstances, largely involving conflicts in coordinating the needs of the several stakeholders in the project (including the city and state, the Port Authority, private developer Larry Silverstein, and victims' families), thwarted progress. Also of immediate concern was an appropriate memorial for the site. Such an emotionally searing event required the most careful attention.

Some critics—this writer among them—suggested waiting even longer for a memorial. The most devastating event in American history, the Civil War, found its best memorials thirty years later. But the process pushed on, and a highly publicized competition in 2004 yielded the memorial that we see today, designed by architect Michael Arad and landscape architect Peter Walker.

The memorial occupies the site of the Twin Towers, in accord with Daniel Libeskind's master plan for the rebuilding site. New building sites, including those of One and Four World Trade Center (rising at the time of writing), surround the memorial space. On the very large footprint of each tower, Arad placed a 192-foot-square hole with 30-foot-deep walls, water falling down their sides. At the bottom, the water flows into another, smaller, central hole. It is on one level an attractive, minimalist water feature, like the waterwall at Paley Park (p. 240), absorbing the city noises around it. But Arad tried very

One of the two reflecting pools of the National September 11 Memorial, which was dedicated and opened to the public on the 10th anniversary of the 9/11 attacks.

hard to evoke the concept of a void, which he did by having the water literally disappear into the second hole. The 2,983 names of those who perished on 9/11 (here and at the Pentagon and in a Pennsylvania field) and also in the bombing of the World Trade Center in 1993 appear in bronze etchings surrounding both pools. At night the names, illuminated from behind, glow.

Peter Walker's landscaping around the memorial pools is simple, dignified, and restrained, using a modernist vocabulary. There are grass strips, oak trees (which, when they grow out, promise a fairly dense thicket), and simple benches. The concept is a great one: to sustain the somber mood of the memorial pools and at the same time form usable public space. For this is (or will be) a public space. Eventually, people will sit here to take a load off their feet after a shopping expedition at Century 21, office workers will eat sandwiches and chat, parents will play with their children, people will read their newspapers and e-readers. We must not expect from this space either the William H. Whyte amenities or the Landscape Urbanist wild grasses. That said, a good deal of the site's history, including salvage from the Twin Towers and other parts of the complex, will be displayed in a museum, designed by the international architecture firm Aedas, below the plaza. The wedge-shaped building pointing between the two memorial pools is the museum's entry pavilion, designed by the Norwegian firm Snøhetta. Right now, people can view the memorial only by acquiring a ticket in advance. At some future date, however, it will be a free and open public space, taking its place in the life of lower Manhattan. Until that time, it cannot and should not be judged. The surrounding buildings will also greatly affect the memorial. Right now, the surroundings amount to a construction site.

Is there another memorial in the city that has struck the balance between reverence and memory, on the one hand, and succeeded as a usable, affable public space, on the other? I would say that Edward S. Hewitt and William Lawrence Bottomley's Wireless Operators Memorial, dedicated in 1915 in Battery Park (p. 33), though what it commemorates resonates little with New Yorkers today, is a contender. Here a semicircle of park benches faces an attractive fountain and a simple but strong cenotaph bearing the names, beginning with that of Jack Phillips of the *Titanic*, of wireless telegraphers who perished with their ships. We don't want skateboarding teens around the 9/11 memorial, but mothers and their babies, and lunchtime office workers, may be just the companionship the deceased would most welcome. —F.M.

FOR UP-TO-DATE HOURS OF OPERATION, GO TO:
www.911memorial.org/hours-operation

RESTROOMS: No public restrooms at the memorial site or in the nearby hotels; public restrooms in Wagner Park, in nearby Battery Park City, and Federal Hall on Wall Street, open Monday–Friday, 9 am–5 pm

REGULATIONS: Visitors passes are required for entry, see: www.911memorial.org

No baggage larger than 8"x 17" x 19" is permitted on site, no bag storage facility

FOR A FULL LIST OF RULES AND REGULATIONS, SEE:
www.911memorial.org/visitor-rules-and-regulations

MAP & FURTHER INFORMATION AVAILABLE AT: www.911memorial.org

BY SUBWAY: A, C, J, M, Z, 2, 3, 4, 5 to Fulton Street, take Fulton Street exit, walk west to Church Street, south 5 blocks to Thames Street, turn right on Thames, and continue west 1 block to the entrance

2, 3 to Park Place, exit on Church Street, walk south 8 blocks and turn right on Thames Street, continue west 1 block to entrance

E to World Trade Center, take Church Street exit, walk south 7 blocks, turn right on Thames Street, and continue west 1 block to entrance

R to Rector Street, exit on Trinity Place, walk north 2 blocks, turn left on Thames Street, and continue west 1 block to entrance

R to Cortlandt Street, exit on Church Street, walk south 3 blocks, turn right on Thames Street, and continue west 1 block to entrance

1 to Rector Street, exit on Greenwich Street, walk north 2 blocks, and turn left on Albany Street

One World Trade Center became the tallest building in New York City when its final steel columns were put in place on April 30, 2012.

BY BUS: M5 (south) to Broadway and Thames Street, walk west 2 blocks on Thames Street

M5 (north) to Trinity Place and Rector Street, walk north 1 block and turn left on Thames Street

M20 (south) to South End Avenue and Albany Street, walk south .5 block, turn left on Albany Street, and continue 3 blocks (crossing West Street)

M22 (south) to Vesey Street and North End Avenue, walk south through the World Financial Center to Albany Street (about 3 blocks), turn left on Albany Street, and continue across West Street

BY PATH: Newark–WTC or Hoboken–WTC lines to World Trade Center

ABOVE At Pier 6 in Brooklyn Bridge Park (see p. 97)

RIGHT In the Citigroup Center Atrium (see p. 205)

BELOW By Columbus Circle (see p. 194)

Eating and Drinking

A Sampling of Places to Eat and Drink Where the Space Is Right

ABOVE By the Bell Ringers' Monument, officially the James Gordon Bennett Memorial, in Herald Square (see p. 183)

ABOVE In the middle of Times Square (see p. 183)

LEFT By the living green forms in the Urban Garden Room, Bank of America Tower (see p. 211)

Don't leave home without your brown bag because there are innumerable public and private spaces, both indoors and out, to sit and eat informally. Of course, food and drink can also be purchased at ubiquitous kiosks, food carts, and cafés.

Inland: Informal Spaces

BOHEMIAN HALL & BEER GARDEN

29-19 24th Avenue, Astoria, Queens

www.bohemianhall.com

Its name says it all: this beer garden was opened in 1910 by Czech and Slovak immigrants. Today it is the last remaining original beer garden in the city; it continues to be run by a fraternal organization devoted to Czech and Slovak culture, as seen in the photo (facing page) of children performing a traditional Slovak folk dance. The large outdoor space, protected by the garden's high walls, has numerous shade trees and plenty of picnic

BELOW AND FACING PAGE Bohemian Hall & Beer Garden

tables on a sandy surface. Hundreds of people, mostly young professionals, congregate here to enjoy beer and sausage. The Astoria landmark is a short walk from the nearby N or Q line, Astoria Boulevard stop, and there is bike parking outside.

BRYANT PARK

Located between 40th and 42nd Streets and 5th and 6th Avenues, behind the New York Public Library (see p. 234)

www.bryantpark.org

Sit on the lawn or on one of the many movable chairs, and dine alfresco.

DAVID RUBENSTEIN ATRIUM, LINCOLN CENTER FOR THE PERFORMING ARTS

Broadway between West 62nd and 63rd Streets (see p. 215)

www.lincolncenter.org/Atrium

Chef Tom Colicchio's 'wichcraft café is casual and enticing. Or bring your own food. Lots of free tables.

FORMER IBM BUILDING ATRIUM

590 Madison Avenue, at 57th Street (see p. 210)

A great place to take a breather and sit at one of the small tables among the bamboo stands. Coffee and snacks can be purchased at the atrium kiosk.

MADISON SQUARE PARK

(see p. 183)

Shake Shack

Southeast corner of Madison Square Park, near Madison Avenue and East 23rd Street

www.shakeshack.com

The line to order shakes, burgers, hot dogs, fries, and frozen custard has not disappeared since this Danny Meyer establishment opened in 2004. Eat at the tables in the sandy lot and pretend you're at the beach before going back to work.

Shake Shack, Madison Square park

Park Avenue Plaza Arcade

PARK AVENUE PLAZA ARCADE

55 East 52nd Street, between Park and Madison Avenues

With the soothing sounds of a waterwall and live piano music, this through-block arcade provides seating and a most pleasant respite from the hustle and bustle of Midtown.

RIVERBANK STATE PARK

(see p. 88)

Caridad Restaurant

3533 Broadway, just south of 145th Street

www.caridad145.com

After a vigorous workout at Riverbank State Park (see p. 88), treat yourself to some great Latin food in this neighborhood establishment: sopa de pollo, cubano sandwich, tostones (crispy fried plantains), and a host of traditional rice dishes.

Inland: Restaurants

ALICE TULLY HALL, LINCOLN CENTER FOR THE PERFORMING ARTS

American Table Café and Bar by Marcus Samuelsson

70 Lincoln Center Plaza, in Alice Tully Hall, 1941 Broadway at 65th Street (see p. 217)

212.671.4200

Open and light-filled, convenient space, famous chef, casual fare.

BRYANT PARK

Bryant Park Grill

25 West 40th Street

www.arkrestaurants.com/bryant_park

Depending on the season, Bryant Park Grill features a variety of spaces that take advantage of its great setting right in Bryant Park (see p. 234): in addition to the indoor year-round restaurant, there's an outdoor seating area on the 40th Street side; an outdoor after-work bar; and a great roof space for special events.

COLUMBUS CIRCLE

59th Street and Broadway (see p. 195)

Robert, atop the Museum of Arts and Design

2 Columbus Circle, 9th floor

www.robertnyc.com

The food is excellent, and the views are even better. Sit by the windows of this modern, upscale museum restaurant and take in four different approaches to open space: the broad expanse of Central Park; Columbus Circle directly below, a pedestrian-friendly urban space that was once a no-man's concrete island in a swirl of traffic; the two interconnected glass towers of the Time Warner Center, whose atrium is a mecca for fancy indoor shopping; and the Broadway Malls, the median that divides Broadway north of Columbus Circle, planted with trees and flowers and featuring benches in small open spaces at intersections with the east–west streets.

Time Warner Center

10 Columbus Circle, near the southwest corner of Central Park

www.shopsatcolumbuscircle.com

Lots of upscale restaurants in the complex, but also smaller eateries. There's Whole Foods in the basement—no views, but fast; Chef Tom Keller's renowned Bouchon Bakery, on the third floor, with both an eat-in and a take-out menu, so you can have your choice of spectacular view to accompany the equally spectacular fare; A Voce, a fine Italian restaurant complete with white tablecloths and stunning views; and the Japanese restaurant Masa, one of the most critically acclaimed and expensive restaurants in the city.

ERIE BASIN

(see p. 110)

Fort Defiance Café

365 Van Brunt Street at Dikeman Street, Red Hook, Brooklyn

fortdefiancebrooklyn.com

Named after a fort that was built in Red Hook during the Revolutionary War, this café serves breakfast, lunch, and dinner seven days a week, retro cocktails in the evening, and, on occasion, acclaimed New Orleans–style muffulettas at lunch.

GREEN-WOOD CEMETERY

500 25th Street, Brooklyn (see p. 165)

Lots of choices within walking distance, recommended by Art Presson, Green-Wood's Superintendent of Grounds.

al di là

248 5th Avenue, Brooklyn

www.aldilatrattoria.com

Venetian-inspired food in a friendly establishment run by an American chef and her Italian husband.

Bonnie's Grill

278 5th Avenue, Brooklyn

www.bonniesgrill.com

Regional American cuisine, hot and spicy.

Sidecar

560 5th Avenue, Brooklyn

www.sidecarbrooklyn.com

Inventive drinks and menu.

HIGH LINE

(see p. 156)

www.thehighline.org/about/high-line-food

Chelsea Market

75 9th Avenue (between 15th and 16th Streets)

chelseamarket.com/

The ground-floor passage stretching from 9th to 10th Avenue in the beautifully restored brick building (formerly the Nabisco factory) near the southern terminus of High Line houses a series of food shops and restaurants.

The Porch

On the High Line at West 15th Street

www.thehighline.org/about/high-line-food

40-seat open-air café, with food from family farms focusing on sustainable practices, operated by Friends of the High Line in partnership with The Green Table, a restaurant in Chelsea Market.

Cookshop

156 Tenth Avenue (at 20th Street)

cookshopny.com/

Upscale American with a focus on seasonal availability and a sustainable conscience.

Co.

230 9th Avenue (between 24th and 25th Streets)

www.co-pane.com

The place for artisanal pizza in Chelsea—thin crust, many inventive toppings.

Le Parker Meridien Knave Bar

Le Parker Meridien Knave Bar

118 West 57th Street, between 6th & 7th Avenues

www.parkermeridien.com

This bar is set down plunk in the middle of public space that was usurped by the hotel. Guests who enter off of 57th Street pull their luggage through the space to get to the check-in desk. When the waitress asks for your drink order, tell him or her you don't have to buy anything to occupy public space, and they'll go away.

LINCOLN CENTER FOR THE PERFORMING ARTS

(see p. 215)

Lincoln

142 West 65th Street

www.lincolnristorante.com

Located beneath a dramatic sloping green roof, the Laurie M. Tisch Illumination Lawn, and overlooking the reflecting pool and the Lincoln Center plaza, this spacious, upscale Italian restaurant could not be situated more conveniently for ticketholders—or people watchers.

TRUMP TOWER

725 Fifth Avenue between 56th and 57th Streets (see p. 208)

www.trumpgrill.com

Inside the Lincoln, under the sloping green roof, looking south at the Lincoln Center campus.

Trump Tower

www.trumpcafe.com

www.trumpbar.com

Options around the Trump Atrium include the Trump Grill, which offers lunch, the Trump Café serving breakfast and other food throughout the day, and the Trump Bar, which offers a "You're Fired" cocktail.

By the Water's Edge: Informal Spaces

BATTERY PARK CITY

World Financial Center, Winter Garden

Located on West Street between World Financial Center 2 and 3, between Vesey and Liberty Streets , and across from the World Trade Center site (see p. 46)

www.worldfinancialcenter.com/shopping_and_dining.htm

On warm days it's great to pick something up from one of the many take-away places in the center and eat on the wide terraces facing the Hudson River, but better yet is buying a grilled-before-your-eyes hamburger from the food vendors situated outdoors on the terraces by the tables and chairs.

It is also a treat to dine beneath the palm trees in the Winter Garden. The dependable chains are there—Così, Starbucks, Au Bon Pain, and others—but so is a real New York establishment, P. J. Clarke's, established 1884. For more of a culinary adventure, check out the fleet of food trucks located outside 4 World Financial Center, North End Avenue at Vesey Street (try Rickshaw Dumplings for a quality product). For the truck schedule, go to: www.worldfinancialcenter.com/foodtrucks.

Battery Park City

BROOKLYN BRIDGE PARK

(see p. 97)

Grimaldi's

19 Old Fulton Street, Brooklyn, near Pier 1.

www.grimaldis.com

The pizza at Grimaldi's is as famous as the line to get in.

ERIE BASIN

(see p. 110)

Fairway

480–500 Van Brunt Street, Red Hook, Brooklyn

www.fairwaymarket.com/store-red-hook/

The café in this branch of a renowned New York food market overlooks the Statue of Liberty and offers both indoor and outdoor seating. Shop and eat; open for breakfast, lunch, and dinner.

IKEA

1 Beard Street, Red Hook, Brooklyn

www.ikea.com/us/en/store/brooklyn/restaurant

There are plenty of meal deals with subsidized prices, especially for kids, to encourage the family to shop, and eat, together at the big furniture emporium. Anytime—breakfast to dinner. As at all IKEAs, the signature dish is Swedish meatballs and gravy.

CENTRAL PARK

Harlem Meer Snack Bar

Inside Central Park at 110th Street between 5th and Lenox Avenues

Great for a quick bite when visiting the Charles A. Dana Discovery Center or the nearby Conservatory Garden (see p. 242).

RIVERSIDE PARK SOUTH

(see p. 78)

Pier 1 Café

Pier 1, at West 70th Street

www.piericafe.com

Outdoor dining, open May–October. There is seating both for patrons and for those who just want to take in the view.

WEST HARLEM PIERS PARK

(see p. 92)

Fairway

2328 12th Avenue at 130th Street

www.fairwaymarket.com

This New York City market is renowned for its huge inventory and great prices. Grab a sandwich and eat outdoors across the street in West Harlem Piers Park.

Central Park Boathouse

By the Water's Edge: Restaurants

CENTRAL PARK BOATHOUSE

(see p. 274)

East 72nd Street and Park Drive North

www.thecentralparkboathouse.com

Great setting on the lake's edge; so-so food.

BROOKLYN BRIDGE PARK

(see p. 97)

River Café

1 Water Street, Brooklyn

www.rivercafe.com

This floating restaurant on the East River, now a classic, has been around since the late 1970s, long before the neighborhood was ever referred to as DUMBO. Sited just south of the Brooklyn Bridge, the glass-enclosed restaurant serves New American cuisine and has sweeping views of the East River bridges and Manhattan.

RIVERBANK STATE PARK

(see p. 88)

Tian at the Riverbank

679 Riverside Drive at 145th Street

www.tianattheriverbank.com

Situated right in the park with to-die-for views of the Hudson River and George Washington Bridge, Tian offers Latin/Asian fusion cuisine in a sleek modern setting.

RIVERSIDE PARK

(see p. 81)

West 79th Street Boat Basin Café

West 79th Street at the Hudson River

www.boatbasincafe.com

A fairly mysterious place to find if you're not jogging along the water's edge in Riverside Park. Walk west on 79th Street, cross Riverside Drive, walk under the green highway overpass bridge, and take the staircases on either side of 79th Street down to the restaurant. The reward is a wonderful outdoor café set among the limestone arches of a rotunda and an open-air patio overlooking the marina on the Hudson River. Casual fare in a great space.

WEST HARLEM PIERS PARK

(see p. 92)

Dinosaur Bar-B-Que

700 West 125th Street at 12th Avenue

www.dinosaurbarbque.com

Lots of beers, plenty of ribs, casual party atmosphere, and right across from West Harlem Piers Park.

Boating on the 20-acre man-made Central Park lake.

ABOUT THE CONTRIBUTORS

ELIZABETH CHRISTIAN studied Conservation of Historic Buildings at the University of Bath in the U.K. and has worked in heritage management and historic preservation at sites around the United States, including Green-Wood Cemetery.

TAMARA COOMBS is the former director of programs and tours at the Municipal Art Society, where she initiated and coordinated the first public walking tour of Freshkills Park in 2006. She lived on Staten Island for more than 20 years and wrote about the landfill from a local perspective for the John McAslan + Partners entry in the Fresh Kills: Landfill to Landscape competition.

JOHN HILL, who made the maps, is an architect, an adjunct professor at New York Institute of Technology, and the author of *Guide to Contemporary New York City Architecture* (W.W. Norton, 2011). He blogs at A Daily Dose of Architecture (archidose.blogspot.com/).

ROBIN LYNN conceived and edited *10 Architectural Walks in Manhattan* by Francis Morrone and Matthew Postal (W.W. Norton, 2009), and co-authored *A Walking Tour of Cast Iron Architecture in SoHo* with Margot Gayle (Friends of Cast Iron Architecture, 1983; second edition, New York Metropolitan Chapter of the Victorian Society of America on behalf of Friends of Cast Iron Architecture, 2011). For more than a decade she organized architectural walking tours for the Municipal Art Society. Robin teaches English and New York City history to new New Yorkers at the College of Mount Saint Vincent's Center for Immigrant Concerns and Community Impact at Columbia University.

FRANCIS MORRONE is a writer and historian specializing in the architecture and social history of the 19th and 20th centuries, with particular emphasis on New York. He is the author of ten books, including *The Architectural Guidebook to New York City* (1994) and *An Architectural Guidebook to Brooklyn* (2001). His book *The New York Public Library: The Architecture and Decoration of the Stephen A. Schwarzman Building*, co-written with Henry Hope Reed, was published by W.W. Norton in May 2011 on the occasion of the 100th birthday of the library building. Morrone wrote the column "Abroad in New York," as well as weekly art and architecture criticism, for the *New York*

Sun for some six years and is a regular contributor to several periodicals. He has written more than a thousand articles for publication. He lectures widely and is well known for his walking tours of New York, many of them sponsored by the Municipal Art Society of New York. In April 2011 *Travel & Leisure* magazine named him one of the thirteen best tour guides in the world (one of only two in the U.S.). He estimates he has led 1,800 walking tours in all five boroughs of New York City. He is the recipient of New York University's coveted Excellence in Teaching Award and of the Arthur Ross Award of the Institute of Classical Architecture & Art.

EDWARD A. TORAN studied architecture and art history, and worked as an interior architect for large corporations for more than thirty years. He has conducted research in work-space development, applied arts, and industrial design, and has written and lectured extensively on these topics. Experienced in graphic and exhibition design, he brings a long-standing interest in photography as a communications tool, as well as his skills as a computer programmer, to his varied projects. He was the photographer for *10 Architectural Walks in Manhattan* (W.W. Norton, 2009).

INDEX

[Page numbers in italic refer to captions.]